# ADVANCE ACCLAIM

"With deep sensitivity and humanity, Dr. Tominey illuminates how our everyday conversations shape who we are and what we become. Tominey captures the heart of what kids are implicitly asking and seeking. With impeccable perception and rare insight, she explains how to talk to children about real-world topics, while also providing essential messages to help them develop into confident, caring, and compassionate people. Grounded in emotion science that's conveyed with the same warmth and wisdom she promotes, *Creating Compassionate Kids* is a beacon for 21st-century families."

—**Kathryn Lee, Director of RULER for Families, Yale Center for Emotional Intelligence**

"In *Creating Compassionate Kids,* Dr. Tominey communicates the power of adult-child conversation through compelling and descriptive examples, and an engaging narrative that embeds key insights from developmental science. Family activities, book recommendations, and discussion questions provide wonderful opportunities to extend and apply learning. You'll finish the book feeling inspired and empowered to turn everyday moments into opportunities to support the next generation of compassionate children."

—**Elisabeth O'Bryon, Ph.D., co-founder of Family Engagement Lab**

"Developing compassion begins with understanding, and for young children, understanding emerges in conversation. Written with wisdom and sensitivity, *Creating Compassionate Kids* guides adults into these conversations and their significance to young children. Through conversational examples that are insightfully discussed, Shauna Tominey provides thought-provoking reflections on the growth of compassion and its foundations in developing self-awareness, resilience, and close relationships in childhood. A valuable resource for adults who care for kids."

—**Ross A. Thompson, Ph.D., Distinguished Professor, Department of Psychology, University of California Davis**

"*Creating Compassionate Kids* is a must-read book for anyone working with or raising young people. Infusing research and examples from her personal and professional life as a parent, researcher, and parent educator, Dr. Tominey helps us how to have vulnerable, courageous, and loving conversations that foster compassion in adults and young people alike. Dr. Tominey's writing is approachable and informative, and she equips her reader with actionable and developmentally-appropriate tools for creating compassionate kids."

—**Dena N. Simmons, Ed.D., CHES, Assistant Director, Yale Center for Emotional Intelligence, Associate Research Scientist, Yale Child Study Center**

CREATING
COMPASSIONATE
KIDS

# CREATING COMPASSIONATE KIDS

## Essential Conversations to Have with Young Children

Shauna Tominey

W. W. Norton & Company
Independent Publishers Since 1923
New York • London

**Note to Readers:** Models and/or techniques described in this volume are illustrative or are included for general informational purposes only; neither the publisher nor the author(s) can guarantee the efficacy or appropriateness of any particular recommendation in every circumstance.

For information about permission to reproduce selections from this book, write to Permissions, W. W. Norton & Company, Inc., 500 Fifth Avenue, New York, NY 10110

For information about special discounts for bulk purchases, please contact W. W. Norton Special Sales at specialsales@wwnorton.com or 800-233-4830

Manufacturing by LSC Willard
Production manager: Katelyn MacKenzie

Library of Congress Cataloging-in-Publication Data

Names: Tominey, Shauna, author.
Title: Creating compassionate kids : essential conversations to have with young children / Shauna Tominey.
Description: First edition. | New York : W. W. Norton & Company, [2019] | Series: A Norton professional book | Includes bibliographical references and index.
Identifiers: LCCN 2018016670 | ISBN 9780393711592 (hardcover)
Subjects: LCSH: Parent and child. | Compassion. | Compassion in children. | Caring in children.
Classification: LCC HQ755.85 .T655 2019 | DDC 177/.7—dc23
LC record available at https://lccn.loc.gov/2018016670

W. W. Norton & Company, Inc., 500 Fifth Avenue, New York, N.Y. 10110
www.wwnorton.com

W. W. Norton & Company Ltd., 15 Carlisle Street, London W1D 3BS

1 2 3 4 5 6 7 8 9 0

*To my compassionate kid*

# Contents

# Acknowledgments

When I first started working as an early childhood educator (before I became a parent), I spent a lot of time worrying. I worried that I wouldn't know what to do and that I wouldn't know what to say to a child every time a new situation came up. And so, not knowing what to say, I listened. I listened to the way other adults talked with children, hoping to learn how to have those same conversations myself. I was impressed with how easily words came to other teachers and parents—they always seemed to know the right thing to say to a child. I figured it was only a matter of time before I did too. Once I heard an example of every possible conversation, I would have a script that I could use to have conversations with any child at any time about any topic. Boy, was I wrong.

I quickly learned that just as no two children are alike, no two conversations are alike either. It's impossible to prepare yourself for the moment when a three-year-old steps out on the playground and proudly proclaims that his father's penis is "THIS BIG" like a fisherman holding his hands up to show the size of his prized catch. Nothing can prepare you for the moment when a four-year-old leans in and whispers that when she grows up, she wants to be a "boy . . . or a fish." And there is certainly nothing that prepares you for the moment when your own child wraps her arms around you and says, "I love you" for the first time.

With each new conversation, I started to realize that I wasn't the only one feeling worried. Most of the other adults I met confessed that they were worried too—worried that they didn't know what to do or say to ensure their child had what they needed to thrive. Over time, I came to see that there was no recipe for the perfect conversation with a child. There were many different ways to have a conversation and many ways to help a child thrive. Over the last 20 years, I have had the privilege of listening to conversations between children and adults in many different settings. It is the shared wisdom from all of these children, families, and colleagues that inspired this book.

I am grateful to all of the children and families who have invited me into their lives and who have shared their conversations with me. Each has touched my life in a meaningful way. I am grateful to my many colleagues, including teachers, parenting educators, researchers, and others for showing me many different ways to have a positive impact. I would like to give special thanks to Megan McClelland, my mentor, colleague, and friend at Oregon State University, who continually inspires me to grow in new directions, leading to our first book (*Stop Think Act: Integrating Self-Regulation in the Early Childhood Classroom*) and our self-regulation intervention ("Red Light, Purple Light"), which has taken on a life of its own. Thank you to Susan Rivers for being a model of compassionate mentorship and introducing me to the Yale Center for Emotional Intelligence—an opportunity that has profoundly shaped who I am. Thank you to my dear friends and colleagues, Sharon Shapses, Elisabeth O'Bryon, Dena Simmons, and Melissa Struve Thomas for inspiring me to be my best self and for shaping my inner voice. And, thank you to my colleagues who are part of the Oregon Parenting Education Collaborative—a statewide initiative to make parenting education available and accessible to all Oregon families. I am honored to be a part of this innovative and important work and to have the opportunity to learn from so many individuals dedicated to supporting parents.

I am grateful to my own family for serving as the inspiration for my personal and professional path. I am especially thankful that my daughter is surrounded by a compassionate community, including all four of her grandparents and a caring network of extended family and friends. Thank you to my dad, Bob, for passing on his love of writing. Thank you to my mom, Wanda, for taking care of our family in big and small ways. Thank you to my sister, Stacey, for staying up late to edit my book proposal and for being a model of a compassionate parent and aunt. And thank you to my mother-in-law, Terrie, for being the first to read an entire draft of this book.

I am forever grateful to my husband, Colin, for his never-ending love and support and for taking our daughter on weekend adventures, making it both hard for me to write this book (some adventures were too great to pass up), but also possible. And finally, thank you to my daughter, Winter, for being the light of my life, for sharing many of the conversations in this book with me, and for inspiring me to be a more compassionate parent.

CREATING
COMPASSIONATE
KIDS

# 1

# Creating compassionate kids:
## *The importance of conversations*

IF YOU HAD TO PICK one word to describe the world you want your child to grow up in, what would it be? Safe? Understanding? Resilient? Compassionate? When I have asked this question to rooms full of parents, teachers, principals, superintendents, social service professionals, business leaders, and other community members, these are the words they choose.

No one ever chooses the word literate. No one chooses mathematical. And yet, academic skills like reading and math are what we focus on teaching our children. These are the skills teachers are held accountable for teaching in school. We know and believe that academics are important. We want our children to be good readers. We want our children to understand math, but what about the other skills—those that lead to a world that is safe, understanding, resilient, and compassionate?

The day before my daughter's fifth birthday, our car was broken into. Someone entered our closed garage and broke the back window, stealing a $200 tablet that we had left on the backseat. When I picked up my daughter from school, she said, "Mom, I keep thinking about the car window. I'm scared." I felt scared too, and I told her so. I also felt angry, frustrated, violated, disappointed, and let down.

My daughter asked, "Why would someone do that?" I kept asking myself the same question. Why *would* someone do that? How did someone have to feel to steal another person's property—to violate another person's sense of security? Whoever did it certainly did not increase my confidence that I was raising my daughter in a compassionate world.

When I filed the police report, I described the pry marks I saw around the edges of the window. The police officer who took my call said, "It must have been kids. They didn't know what they were doing. Otherwise, they would have opened the window without breaking it." Kids. I found myself suspiciously eyeing every middle school– and high school–age kid I saw the rest of that day. I didn't like feeling that way—that I couldn't trust the kids around me—that the kids in our community were failing us.

Coincidentally, I gave a talk on mental health to a diverse group of middle and high school students at Yale University the next day. As part of the talk, I asked students to think about how they wanted to feel at school and at home. The feelings they chose included: safe, happy, respected, loved, and "like I matter." I asked how often they were having these feelings, and most shared that they had these feelings 50 percent of the time or less. Many said that they had these feelings less than 25 percent of the time. When I asked them how they actually felt during the day, the feelings they wrote down included: stressed, frustrated, disappointed, anxious, confused, overwhelmed, and isolated. Taking a step back, I realized that these were likely the same feelings the kid who broke into our car was having.

The students sitting in the room with me were feeling stressed by academic demands and peer pressure, frustrated by instances of bullying, disappointed by troubled friendships, anxious about relationships and sex, confused by messages they were hearing in the media, overwhelmed by challenges at home, and isolated because they felt that they had no one to talk with about any of these issues. These kids were surrounded by adults telling them that academics was the key to their success, but they didn't know how to manage all the conflicting feelings they had that were getting in the way of their learning. I realized in that moment that it is not the kids who are failing us; we are the ones failing them.

At the end of my talk, I packed up my supplies and turned to find a line of kids waiting for me. These kids were dying to talk about their feelings with someone—anyone who would listen without judgment. One shared with me that he was drowning under the pressure his parents placed on him to achieve academically. He was so stressed he couldn't think straight and couldn't wait to be old enough to leave home. Another asked how to survive the bullying she was experiencing at school. She felt safe at home, but didn't know what she could do to survive each day until she could get home again. Another student told the opposite story—she felt safe at school, but not at home, and didn't know how or whom to ask for help.

As it turns out, the feelings these kids shared weren't unique to them. Later that year, my colleagues at the Yale Center for Emotional Intelligence surveyed 22,000 high school students from around the United States. When asked how they were feeling, students around the country shared many different feelings. Seventy-five percent of the feelings they named were categorized as "unpleasant feelings," with tired, stressed, and bored coming up the most often. When asked how they wanted to feel, students shared that they wanted to feel energized, excited, and happy (Yale Center for Emotional Intelligence, 2015). Other studies are revealing similar patterns in our youth. In a statewide survey of 8th and 11th graders conducted in 2017 with 28,139 students, the Oregon Health Authority found that significant numbers of youth in each grade (18.7 percent and 22.4 percent, respectively) reported that they had emotional or mental health care needs that were not met over the last year (Oregon Health Authority, 2017). Twenty-five percent of eighth graders and 33.8 percent of 11th graders rated their emotional and mental health as fair or poor.

Helping middle schoolers and high schoolers feel happy isn't exactly what this book is about, but there's a connection between how we feel and how we act. Kids who feel happy, excited, energized, respected, loved, safe, and "like they matter" probably aren't going to break car windows, isolate themselves when times get tough, or fall apart in the face of a challenge. Instead, these kids are more likely than their peers to have the skills they need to build relationships with others, to be more engaged learners and higher achievers, to thrive in the face of hardship, and to have greater compassion.

Before going any further, let's talk for a moment about compassion. **Compassion** means having **empathy**—the ability to think about other people's feelings—but that's not all. Compassion means wanting and actively trying to make other people's lives better, which is what most parents want for and aim to do for their children! Helping children to be more compassionate does not necessarily mean teaching them to put themselves aside and put others first. It has to include teaching them the skills they need to manage their own well-being. After all, it's hard to think about someone else's feelings when you're struggling to manage your own.

## TAKING CHILDREN'S FEELINGS SERIOUSLY DURING EARLY CHILDHOOD

Teaching compassion (and related skills like self-awareness, empathy, and resilience) begins early and comes from feelings of trust. When children are young, they turn to the adults in their lives for everything—they crave attention from their parents and caregivers and thrive when they receive it. When young children trust the adults in their lives, they want to learn from them and they want to be like them (Bowlby, 2008). How many parents would say the same of their teenagers? Maybe a few, but most parents of adolescents agree that they wish their teens would spend *more* time talking with them, *more* time listening to them, and *more* time learning from them. By the time children reach adolescence, many are distancing themselves from their families. It is not unusual for teens to rely increasingly on their friends and the media for information, but let's consider what happens between early childhood and adolescence that leads to this shift.

Part of this shift is typical development. The gradual separation that occurs between adolescents and their parents is an important and necessary step that gives teens an opportunity to practice decision making and problem solving on their own, while helping them learn to build networks of social support, and exercise independence on their way to becoming self-sufficient adults (Rubin et al., 2006). Another part of this shift, however, is a product of the relationship we foster with our children from birth (Moretti & Peled, 2004).

Although seeking independence is a normal and expected process, there are things we may do—without meaning to—that make the separation between ourselves and our children more sudden and abrupt than it needs to be. As children reach their teen years and stress is at an all-time high, it would be nice to know that our children feel comfortable coming to us with their questions, that they will ask us when they need advice, and that they will seek out wisdom from our experiences as they make their way through the world. Throughout childhood, however, there are many ways we might send the message to our children that we are not available to support them in this way. We might instead communicate that we are not open to talking about societal issues, that we do not take their feelings seriously, and that if they are looking for information, they should look somewhere else.

Think about the following conversation:

**Emily** (Trevor's mom): Did you hear that Michelle's parents are getting a divorce?

**Curtis** (Trevor's dad): Really? What happened?

**Emily:** Oh, who knows? They haven't been getting along for a long time. I heard a rumor about an A-F-F-A-I-R.

**Trevor** (age three): What are you talking about? What does A-F-A-F-R spell? What's divorce?

**Emily:** Don't worry about it. We're just talking about grown-up stuff.

During the early childhood years, when children like Trevor are most interested in listening to and learning from us, parents often act to shelter them from stressful or difficult topics. When we realize young children have caught a glimpse of the news or that they have overheard adults talking about money trouble, relationship problems or divorce, work stress, violence, or other serious issues, it is not uncommon to hear adults say: "This is a grown-up conversation," "I'll tell you about it when you're older," or "This is not something you need to worry about now."

At the heart of each of these responses is a good intention—a desire to keep our children safe. We are showing children that we care about them. We are telling children that we want to let them be kids as long as possible. We know our children will have plenty to worry about soon enough, so why start their worrying now? We have the best intentions when we choose to protect our children in this way, but by doing so, we miss a critical opportunity to shape the way children view the world around them and to help them develop skills they need to effectively manage challenges with our guidance (Sheridan, Sjuts, & Coutts, 2013). In addition, we may be teaching children that they can't trust us to tell them the truth about challenging topics, or that we don't trust them with this information.

| *What we mean* | *What children may hear:* |
|---|---|
| I love you so much. | I'm not comfortable talking about this. |
| I want to protect you. | Don't ask me these kinds of questions. |
| I don't want you to worry. | I'm not interested in talking about this. |
| I want you to feel safe. | I don't think you can handle this. |

When we tell young children that certain conversations are for "grown-ups," we are communicating to them that we are not willing to talk with them and not available to answer their questions about these issues. By the time we believe that children are old enough to talk about "grown-up" topics, they may already have found other ways to get this information, especially if we have not laid a supportive foundation for open discussions from the start. When children hear about these same issues from other children on the playground (and eventually the Internet), they discover new ways to find information about the topics they didn't learn about from their parents.

We send these same messages when children ask questions at an embarrassingly loud volume in the grocery store.

"Is that lady having a baby? Her tummy's humongous!"
"What's wrong with his leg?"
"Why is his skin that color?
"Does she have two mommies?"
"Are we rich or poor?"
"Why is that man wearing a dress?"

As we feel ourselves turning red in those moments, our instinct is often to respond with: "Shhhh!" or "It's not polite to talk about things like that." With each of these responses, we send the message that the issue a child brought up needs to be kept private, or is one that we are not willing to talk about openly. If children receive this message often enough, they will begin to believe it. If we instead think about these questions as being part of how children learn, we can answer their questions in a way that teaches them about the world and keeps them coming back to us for advice, guidance, and support.

My own daughter once said to me, "Mom, when I grow up I'm going to marry 'Billy,' but he doesn't like my singing. That means I can't sing for the rest of my life! Can you *imagine?!?!*" She covered her face with her hands in a dramatic gesture. Even with my knowledge that a marriage between these 4-year-olds was unlikely to become a reality, showing her that I took her concern as seriously as she did demonstrated that her feelings mattered to me. After all, parents who take their children's feelings seriously at age 4 are more likely to have children who will turn to them as a source of comfort, support, and information the next time an issue arises, whether they are 4 or 14 (Gottman, 2011).

## THE IMPORTANCE OF CONVERSATIONS IN EARLY CHILDHOOD

Think back to the example presented earlier, about divorce. When Trevor asked his parents, "What's divorce?" what if, instead of telling him not to worry about it, his parents had responded in a different way?

**Trevor:** What's divorce?

**Emily:** Divorce means that two people who are married do not want to be married anymore.

**Trevor:** Why don't they want to be married anymore?

**Curtis:** Well, there are lots of reasons people might get divorced. Maybe they don't love each other anymore. Or maybe they are not getting along, so they are not having a good time being married to each other. Or maybe they want to do different things than one another.

**Trevor:** Are you and mommy going to get a divorce?

**Curtis:** I don't think so. We love each other very much. We get along and like to do all the same things. Mommy and I want to be married to each other for a very, very long time.

With this response, Emily and Curtis show Trevor that it is okay to ask questions about divorce and that he can expect to receive honest and open answers, increasing the likelihood that he will turn to his parents the next time he has a question. They also share a lot of information with Trevor, including what divorce is, reasons why people might get divorced, and reassurance that there is no immediate prospect of divorce in his own family. Trevor's parents also communicate respect for one another and shared family values related to what they believe is important in a relationship (e.g., loving one another, getting along, and liking doing the same things).

Sometimes when children ask questions such as "Are you and mommy going to get a divorce?" we worry that we have upset or even traumatized our child—that our child will believe that divorce is imminent or that our child will be plagued with nightmares of divorce. Introducing a new topic can cause worry and anxiety for some children, but most of the time when children ask questions like these, they are just curious. The way we introduce and discuss a topic with a child makes a big difference. Having a conversation and answering questions in a matter-of-fact way communicates to a child that an issue (divorce, in this case) is part of life in our society. And, in fact, it is! With approximately 50 percent of marriages ending in divorce in the U.S., our children probably already know someone who is divorced within their own family or in the family of a friend.

There are many ways that a conversation about divorce might play out, depending on a child's age and developmental stage, as well as interest in and exposure to the topic. We can talk with children about why divorce is hard for parents, why it is hard for kids, how it might help a family, what to do if they are feeling worried about it, and things that are important to think about when it is time to decide if we want to get married and whom to marry. We can also use these conversations to teach children about our own family values and beliefs, whether those beliefs are that divorce is acceptable in any circumstance if a member of a couple is unhappy, that divorce is acceptable only in certain circumstances, or that divorce is not acceptable in any circumstance. This may seem like a lot for a child of three, four, or five, but conversations like these do not happen all at once. Instead, these conversations emerge over days, weeks, months, and years in many different ways, including through stories and play.

What about younger children—infants and toddlers? How do we teach our youngest children about serious issues like divorce? A child's age, developmental level, personality, and other factors affect the conversations we have and what our children are able to understand. Imagine an infant who spends her day smiling, eating, sleeping, cooing, and crying, or a toddler whose only interest seems to be running through the house naked with a diaper on his head. Although neither of these children is ready for conversations about divorce like the one in the example with Trevor, we can still lay the foundation for these conversations through the behaviors we model. For example, the way a parent smiles at an infant when she babbles and coos or the way a parent comforts a toddler during a tantrum shows a child what a warm and loving relationship looks like (Bowlby, 2008). These types of interactions and conversations have the potential to influence our children's relationships now and in the future—both in shaping how they want and expect to be treated, as well as how they will treat others.

## MILLIONS OF NEURONS, MILLIONS OF WORDS

From birth, the conversations we have with our children matter. Young children's brains develop an astounding one million new neural connections every second (Harvard Center on the Developing Child, 2017). You might think of these connections as parts of a child's amazing potential. Many of these pathways will never be used and die off (that's normal), but the pathways that are used again and again are strengthened and become part of the wiring of a child's brain. At birth, a child's brain is estimated to be about 30 percent of the weight of an adult's brain. By age 2, that number jumps to 70 percent and by age 5, a child's brain is 90 percent of the weight of an adult brain (Berk & Meyers, 2012). During this time and in the years that follow, parents have an opportunity to shape the wiring in a child's brain through the words they use and the conversations they have.

There is a wealth of research that points to how important it is for parents to talk with children during their early years. The number of words children hear is connected with language and vocabulary development, as well as school performance (Hart & Risley, 2003). Early language abilities have also been positively linked to social-emotional skills, including managing emotions and getting along with others (Longobardi, Spataro, Frigerio, & Rescorla, 2016; Rose, Lehrl, Ebert, & Weinert, 2017). What's troubling about all this is that not all young children get the same exposure to words and conversations. A landmark study found significant differences in the number of words young children hear from their parents. From birth to age 3, children in the study were likely to have heard 13 million to 45 million words—a difference of 32 million words between children at the low end of the spectrum and those at the high end (Hart & Risley, 2003). It's not just the number of words that matters—it's the words themselves and the quality of conversation between a child and their parent. In fact, one study found that the back-and-forth that occurs between parents and children during conversations (i.e., the number of conversational turns) may be more important than the number of words children hear for language development (Romeo et al., 2018).

Most parents have conversations with their children in some form or another, but these conversations can look really different. Over the past 20 years, I have had the privilege of hearing thousands of conversations between children and their parents. As an early childhood educator, I watched parents say good-bye to their children every morning as they dropped them off at school, sharing rituals ("Learn lots!"), smoothing over challenges from the night before ("Remember that I love you, even when I'm upset."), and making sure their children were ready for the day ("Do you want me to stay with you while you get settled?"). As a parenting educator, I got to know families in their own homes and heard conversations about the ins and outs of daily life from wake-up and bedtime routines ("Huggy snuggy!") to toilet training ("Are you hiding behind the couch again with your diaper?") to reading books together ("Read this one again, daddy!") and all the challenging moments in between ("Will you *please* just get up off the floor and put your coat on?"). As a researcher, I saw the many different emotions that children and parents experience throughout any given day and the impact of emotions on their conversations ("I know you can't think straight when you're tired, but it's time to put your coat on so we can go home.").

Through all these conversations and across settings (rural and urban), socioeconomic backgrounds, races, cultures, and life experiences, every parent I met had something in common: they all loved their children and wanted the best for them. Most families had conversations with their children about how much they loved them, as well as the hopes and dreams they had for them. Many families also had conversations about family values and having good manners—although specific values differed by family. But then, there were differences in conversations, too. While working with military families, deployment, separation, and war were constant topics in conversations that I heard, but not something I heard other families discuss. While working with families in inner city, urban areas, race and how people look at you and treat you based on the color of your skin was a daily reminder of the systemic discrimination some children faced, but these conversations didn't happen in other families. Some families talked with their children about why there wasn't enough food on the table, whereas others discussed which Ivy League school would be best to attend.

There are many conversations families choose to have with their children, some conversations they choose not to have, some that they don't think to have (but would if they did), and still other conversations that they would like to have if they only knew how. When we choose the conversations we have with our children, we usually choose what we know. We answer the questions our children ask and talk about topics that are most familiar to us.

What if we expanded our conversations to include topics that matter to other families, too? How would it benefit my child to know a little bit more about what other children experience, and how would it benefit others to know more about my child? Perhaps these conversations would help us treat one another a little more compassionately.

At the beginning of this chapter, I posed a question: If you had to pick one word to describe the world you want your child to grow up in, what would it be? You may or may not have picked the same words that I did, but chances are you also want your child to grow up in a world that is safe, understanding, resilient, and compassionate. What if we could shape our future society to be one that is safer, more understanding, resilient, and compassionate through the conversations we have with our children? That's the premise at the heart of this book.

As parents and caregivers, we can use conversations to:

- Model compassion in the way we parent our children to help them feel safe and learn to build trust (Chapter II: You are loved: Modeling compassionate parenting).
- Teach our children to value themselves and the world around them as they develop self-awareness and an understanding of others (Chapter III: You are your own person: Building self-awareness).
- Help our children practice the skills they need to face challenges now and in the future, building their capacity for resilience (Chapter IV: You are part of the world around you: Fostering resilience).
- Encourage our children to reach beyond themselves to actively make the world we live in a better, more compassionate place (Chapter V: You can be a helper: Promoting compassion).

This book provides parents with examples of conversations between parents and children, inspired by real conversations and grounded in research on a range of topics critical in today's society. Each of the chapters that follow provides examples of conversations that lay a foundation for creating compassionate kids. Chapter II focuses on how we use conversations to be compassionate parents and help our children feel safe at home. Everything is new to a young child, and the world can be an amazing and confusing place. When children are born, they have everything to learn and only a few ways to express themselves. Children look to their parents to teach them about each new experience, as well as how to communicate effectively as they grow and mature. Approaching parenting with compassion helps children know that, no matter what else happens in their lives, they have someone they can trust and rely on. This trusting relationship and bond lays a foundation for the conversations that follow.

Chapter III includes conversations that help children feel loved and supported for who they are. Children are defined by many different qualities, from the qualities we can see at birth (their sex, skin color, hair, and physical differences); to the qualities that emerge over time (their temperament and personality; likes and dislikes; cognitive, social, and physical abilities and challenges); to the qualities that are shaped by their families (their beliefs, values, and culture); and to the qualities they come to realize over time, including personal, cultural, gender, and racial identity, as well as sexual orientation. For better or for worse, we don't get to decide the qualities our children have when they enter the world, and it's important for us to remember that neither do they. Each one of our child's qualities is part of who they are. The conversations in this chapter aim to help children develop self-awareness in a way that encourages them to value themselves and others.

Chapter IV focuses on fostering resilience. All children experience challenges of some kind. For some children, challenges are relatively minor (e.g., meeting new people, taking tests, facing peer pressure). For others, challenges are more serious (e.g., chronic poverty, systemic discrimination, bullying). We can't predict all the challenges our children will face now and in the future, but we can help them practice skills to navigate those that do arise and let them know that they can trust us—their parents—as sources of support, no matter what. This chapter provides examples of conversations between parents and children on a number of challenging topics. These conversations model ways that parents can encourage children to practice skills related to resilience, as well as to practice empathy through understanding the challenges of others.

Finally, Chapter V concludes the book with conversations focused on developing empathy and practicing compassion, including conversations on making friends, being a part of the community, recognizing privilege, and finding your own voice. These conversations encourage parents and children to think about the ways they can reach beyond themselves to make their community a more compassionate place.

Each chapter includes ideas for specific conversation topics, along with examples of how these conversations might look with children of different ages and at different stages of development. Following these conversations, chapters include question-and-answer sections that apply strategies discussed to common parenting questions and challenges. Additionally, each chapter concludes with suggestions for family activities, children's book recommendations, and discussion questions that aim to help you and your child extend your conversations beyond this book.

Together, the conversations and activities in this book are intended to provide you with the confidence and strategies you need to shape your child's understanding of the world through a compassionate lens, to support your child's development of self-awareness as well as the resilience skills they need to thrive in our current society, and to shape a more compassionate society for our future.

## II

# You are loved:
## *Modeling compassionate parenting*

IN THE BEGINNING, THERE WERE TEARS.

Your tears.

Your child's tears.

The tears of anyone and everyone not getting enough sleep in the household.

During our children's early days, months, and even years, surviving through the tears from one day to the next can feel like a victory. Finding the balance in eating, comforting, diapering, bonding, and sleeping when a new child enters your family can feel like an insurmountable task for many parents, but one that seems effortless for a lucky few. Whether an infant cries continually or rarely cries at all, the sound of our own child crying can raise our heart rate, anxiety, and stress level (Boukydis & Burgess, 1982; Frodi, Lamb, Leavitt, & Donovan, 1978). Cries make most of us feel uncomfortable and can lead us to jump into action. And that's how it should be. Our child's cries (and their smiles and coos too) serve an important purpose. These are the tools our child has to communicate—the tools they have to hold a conversation.

A cry might say: "I'm hungry," "I have indigestion," "I'm uncomfortable and need to be changed," "I want you to hold me," or "I'm so tired, but I can't sleep." A smile might say: "This feels good," "I love it when you hold me," "I'm full and content," or "I know you and recognize you." Each of these conversations helps us get to know our child. Conversations with young children happen in many different ways, including verbally (e.g., words, babbles, and coos) and nonverbally (e.g., eye contact, facial expressions, and body posture).

Imagine what it would be like as an adult if you were only able to communicate like an infant—moving and tensing your body, using facial expressions, and making unintelligible sounds and cries. Now put yourself in a world that you don't understand. What would you need to survive?

- Someone you could trust completely.
- Someone with your best interests in mind.
- Someone committed to making sure your needs were met.
- Someone dedicated to teaching you how to communicate, how to understand the world, and how to thrive.
- Someone who loves you more than they love themselves.

That someone would be a parent. Parents arguably hold the most import-ant responsibility in the world: caring for, teaching, and guiding children. Throughout this book, when I use the word "parent," I am referring to biolog-ical, adoptive, and foster parents; stepparents; grandparents; siblings; family and nonfamily caregivers; teachers; neighbors; and anyone else playing a role in parenting a child. Even before children can understand words, parents can use conversations to build trust and show children that they will be there to guide them and love them, no matter what. Creating compassionate kids begins with compassionate parenting.

## YOU ARE LOVED

The first conversation in this book may seem pretty basic, but it also may be the most important conversation you can have with your child. Letting your child know they are valued and loved creates trust between you and your child, gives your child a model for their relationships with others, and increases the chance that your child will continue having conversations with you, no matter how challenging those conversations might become.

### Key messages:

- You are loved.
- You are loved for who you are now and for who you will be as you grow and change.

**Gillian** (Alex's mom)**:** I love you.
**Alex** (newborn)**:** (watches his mother without making a sound)

**Gillian:** Yes I do! I love your cute little fingers, your little toes, and your nose.

**Alex:** (continues looking at Gillian)

**Gillian:** You keep getting bigger every day. Sometimes I wish you would stay little like this forever, but I can't wait to see who you grow up to be.

*What's happening in this conversation:* In this conversation, Gillian is using her words and actions to communicate to Alex that she loves him. Even though Alex is pre-verbal and not able to respond with words, he can hear the sound and tone of his mother's voice and see the way she makes eye contact, looks at his face, and holds him in her arms. With infants, this is the perfect conversation to have while feeding your child or during the times they are awake and alert.

Conversations that communicate to children that they are loved can and should occur repeatedly with children of any age. The specific words and the context of this conversation might change over time, however. For example, you probably wouldn't tell a school-age child how much you love their cute little toes, but you might let them know what a great kid they are or how lucky you are to have them in your family. Having this conversation with older children can reassure them that they are still loved, even as they grow and change.

How children respond to this conversation will change over time, too. When infants are very young, they might not provide positive feedback, or any feedback at all. Most infants do not start smiling intentionally until they are between 6 and 12 weeks old (Berk & Meyers, 2012). When children start to smile, the sleepless nights almost seem worth it, and it becomes even easier to have conversations like these in hopes of seeing a smile. As children get older, they may start to respond with babbles and eventually words (*"I love you too, dad"*). Whether or not children are able to provide feedback (some children may do so later than others, and some children may never be able to do so), it is important to realize that the time you spend showing and telling your child that you love them matters.

**Eliza** (age two)**:** Dada! Dadadada! Dadadadada!

**Manu** (Eliza's dad)**:** Just a minute, Lizzy.

**Eliza:** Dada! Daaaaada!

**Manu:** Hold on.

**Eliza:** Dada! No phone, Dada. No phone.

**Manu:** Okay. I'm all done. I'm going to put my phone down so that we can spend time together. Did you find a book for us to read?

**Eliza:** Book!

**Manu:** Oh, that's one of my favorites. (phone buzzes)

**Eliza:** No phone!

**Manu:** No phone. This is our special time. I'm going to turn the phone off and put it over here on the table so that it doesn't distract me.

**Eliza:** Dada book!

**Manu:** Yes, let's read the book now. Do you want to sit on my lap or here next to me?

*What's happening in this conversation:* Parents have many different demands on their time and attention. There are times when parents are not able to give their full attention to their children (e.g., during work hours and while juggling household chores along with caring for one or multiple children). Even when we don't need to divide our attention, it can be tempting to stay connected with the world around us (e.g., email and social media). Setting aside technology or other distractions and letting our child know that they have our full attention when we are able to give it is an important way that we can show and tell children they are loved. Doing so also helps us as parents make the most of the time we have with our children so that we benefit from bonding experiences as well.

**Clarissa** (Adam's mom): I know you want to keep playing at the park, but it's time to go! I'm going to start walking toward the car.

**Adam** (age three): Mommy! No! Don't go! Don't go! (begins to cry)

**Clarissa:** Did you think I was leaving without you? I was just starting to walk to the car so that you would come with me.

**Adam:** Don't go, Mommy! (reaches his arms up toward mom and continues crying)

**Clarissa:** I'm sorry I scared you. I love you and I would never leave you without telling you. We'll come back and play at the park another day.

*What's happening in this conversation:* Without meaning to, Clarissa scared her son when he thought she was leaving the park without him. Although parents never truly intend to leave their children behind when they say things like this, there are times when it seems like walking away from a child might be the best way to encourage them to come along. Even joking about leaving them behind may be very scary to a young child who is still developing their understanding of how the world works. Young children think in concrete terms. They take the words they hear literally and may believe them at face value. Reassuring children that you will consistently be there to love and support them is an important message to say out loud and to show children over and over again with actions in addition to words.

**Emmy** (age four): Don't go, daddy!

**Dave** (Emmy's dad): It's time for me to go to work, but Jasmine will take good care of you while I'm gone.

**Emmy:** I don't want Jasmine. I want you to stay!

**Dave:** I know you do. It's hard to say good-bye. I feel sad when we have to say good-bye, too, but I have to go.

**Emmy:** (cries)

**Dave:** One last big hug. I will be home at five o'clock. I know Jasmine has lots of fun things planned for you today, and I can't wait for you to tell me about them when I get home.

**Emmy:** Don't go!

**Dave:** I love you, Emmy, and I will be home soon. Do you remember what we're going to do when I get home from work today?

**Emmy:** Make dinner for mom?

**Dave:** That's right. We're making her a special dinner together. Don't forget, you have our special picture while I'm gone if you feel lonely.

**Emmy:** Okay. Bye, daddy. (sniffles)

**Dave:** Bye, honey. I love you!

*What's happening in this conversation:* In most families, spending time away from a child is a necessary part of life. It doesn't mean you don't love your child. On the contrary, spending time apart can help your child learn important skills, including getting along with other caregivers and teachers and building trust knowing that your parents will come back. In this conversation, Dave lets Emmy know that it's okay to feel upset about being away from someone you love and shares with her that it is sad for him too. He reassures Emmy that he loves her even when they are apart. He also lets her know where he is going and what she will be doing while he is away. Finally, he tells her when he will return.

Some days when Dave leaves for work, Emmy's tears last for a long time before she calms down. Other days, she waves good-bye and runs off to play. Over time, Emmy will cry less often when her dad leaves, knowing that she will have fun with Jasmine and trusting that her dad will come home as promised. Sneaking out the door when your child is calm and has their back turned may seem like a good way to avoid a confrontation, but it is also a missed opportunity to teach your child that they can trust you to let them know when you will leave and come back and to help them learn skills to cope with separation. Through his words and actions, Dave is teaching his daughter that it's okay to feel upset being away from your parents and to trust that you will see them again.

**Brody** (age three): Who do you love most?

**Gina** (Brody's mom): Do you mean who do I love most between you and your brother?

**Brody:** Uh-huh.

**Gina:** I love both of you so much! I don't love either of you more than the other.

**Brody:** But Benny is bigger.

**Gina:** That's true. Your brother is older so I loved him before I even knew you. But, the funny thing about love is that there's no limit—you can have as much as you want!

**Brody:** But you yell at me. You never yell at Benny.

**Gina:** I probably shouldn't yell, but sometimes I get upset, just like you do. When I stepped on your fire truck earlier, it really hurt my foot and I got mad. There are some things Benny remembers to do—like putting his things away—that you don't always do. He's also had more practice than you because he's older. Even when you do things I don't like, I still love you.

**Brody:** I love you, mama.

*What's happening in this conversation:* In this conversation, Gina listens to Brody's question about who she loves most in the family. She takes Brody's feelings seriously and responds accordingly, letting him know that she loves him just as much as she loves his brother, Benny. She also communicates that both of her children are unique individuals who are different from one another.

**Shihan** (Naveed's dad): Is something wrong?

**Naveed** (age five): You don't love me anymore.

**Shihan:** Is that why you were acting sad—because you think I don't love you?

**Naveed:** Uh-huh. You don't.

**Shihan:** I'm glad you told me, but I do love you. I love you very much. Even though we have your brother now, that doesn't mean we don't love you.

**Naveed:** But you only hold him and not me.

**Shihan:** Come here. Come sit with me. It's true. Because your brother is so little, we need to hold him a lot, but that doesn't mean we can't hold you, too. Since you're getting bigger, you don't need to be held as much, but that doesn't mean daddy and I don't love to hold you.

**Naveed:** (hugs his dad)

**Shihan:** Having a new brother means some things will change in our family, and that's okay. Some things will change just because you're growing up, and that would happen even if we didn't have your brother.

**Naveed:** Like what?

**Shihan:** You're getting older and you're going to be able to do more things by yourself, like brushing your teeth, getting dressed, and putting your shoes on.

**Naveed:** I can do that by myself.

**Shihan:** Yes! And your little brother can't yet. And you're going to start kindergarten soon.

**Naveed:** All by myself. Not with brother.

**Shihan:** Yes, by yourself, but with friends and teachers. You know what won't change, though?

**Naveed:** What?

**Shihan:** How much daddy and I love you. How about if you and I have special time each weekend doing something that we like to do together—just the two of us?

**Naveed:** No brother?

**Shihan:** No, brother can stay with dad. Just you and I.

**Naveed:** Yeah!

*What's happening in this conversation:* Even months (or years) after a family change, children may have feelings arise that need support. In this conversation, Shihan lets his son, Naveed, know that he is loved even though their family has experienced changes and that these changes are a normal part of their family's growth and development. He also thinks about what he can do to help ensure that Naveed feels loved and receives the attention he needs.

✳ ✳ ✳

These are only a few examples of the ways that parents can let their children know that they are loved. Together, conversations like these are at the heart of building a trusting relationship with children, also called a **secure attachment** (Bowlby, 2008). Children with secure attachments tend to have higher self-esteem, stronger critical thinking skills, and better academic outcomes than children who don't (Bernier, Beauchamp, Carlson, & Lalonde, 2015; Groh et al., 2014; Murphy & Laible, 2013). They also are likely to have stronger social skills than their peers, including greater empathy and compassion.

Setting up a pattern that shows children you are there for them is especially critical during a child's early months because infants are entirely dependent on the adults in their lives to meet their needs. Sometimes we might worry that picking up an infant too much might spoil them or teach them the wrong lessons (e.g., crying is the way to get what you want), but research shows this isn't true. Being responsive in this way actually leads children to cry less often and calm down more quickly. Knowing that their parent will be there for them when they call (or cry) gives children a "secure base." You might think of a "secure base" like setting up home base in a game of tag. Home base is the spot where anyone can go and be safe no matter what else is happening around them. When children see their parents as their home base, they feel safe venturing out, trying new things, and exploring because they know they have their home base to return to.

It's important to know that children can develop a secure attachment relationship with their parents and caregivers, whether or not they are biologically related or were brought into a family in another way, such as through adoption or foster care (Joseph, O'Connor, Briskman, Maughan, & Scott, 2014). It may take more time, however, to build a secure attachment with an older child who has not had a trusting relationship in the past than if you are building that bond with a child from birth. Through a secure attachment, parents show children how to have relationships with others. When children have a trusting relationship with their parents and caregivers, they are also more likely to want to spend time with them, to want to be like them, and to want to learn from them.

## YOUR FEELINGS HELP YOUR PARENTS KNOW WHAT YOU NEED

Part of building a trusting relationship with your child is showing them that you're doing your best to meet their needs (even when you don't feel like you know what you're doing). Knowing what a child needs can be challenging, especially for a young child who has only a few ways to express those needs. One way that children express their needs is by showing their feelings. If you could choose your child's feelings, you would probably choose for them to spend their days feeling happy, loved, safe, and other pleasant feelings like these. When children feel upbeat or are in a good mood, they show their feelings in a way that makes them easy to get along with and fun to be around. In these moments, family life can feel like a breeze. When children feel upset or have unpleasant feelings like sadness, disappointment, frustration, anger, or fear, it's another story. Unpleasant feelings often come out in the form of crying, temper tantrums, and challenging behaviors. Although most children have many pleasant feelings, they have many unpleasant feelings too. Each of these feelings serves a purpose. All a child's feelings (pleasant and unpleasant) give us important information. These feelings let us know when a child needs something. By paying attention to a child's feelings, we show them that their feelings matter to us and that they can count on us to do our best to figure out their needs.

### Key messages for children:

- All feelings are okay.
- Everyone has feelings.
- Your feelings help your parents know what you need.

**Natalie** (Jamie's mom): Hmm . . . I wonder what it is you are asking me for right now.

**Jamie** (newborn): (cries)

**Natalie:** I already checked your diaper and you just ate so that's not it. Do you want me to hold you and rock you?

**Jamie:** (cries)

**Natalie:** We'll keep trying this for a while and see if it helps.

**Jamie:** (cries)

**Natalie:** Okay, let me try another position to find the one you like the best. That didn't work. I'm still figuring out what you need when you cry like this. I'll keep trying. I hope you know I love you and I'm doing my best.

*What's happening in this conversation:* In this conversation, Natalie tells her son that she recognizes he is trying to tell her something, even though she doesn't know what it is. Natalie lets Jamie know that she loves him and is doing her best to figure out what he needs, even though it's challenging. Every parent has times when they feel at a loss with their child. This is normal. No parent knows what their child needs all the time, or how to manage every situation that arises. Knowing the "right" response in every situation is less important than consistently showing your child that you are doing your best to be there for them. Eventually, Natalie will get better at recognizing Jamie's different cries and she will be able to meet his needs more quickly. As Jamie gets older, he won't remember every interaction that he had with his mom. What he will remember is the pattern he saw—that his mom always did her best to understand his feelings and needs.

**Garrett** (Josh's dad)**:** I have a new food for you to try today.

**Josh** (age four)**:** (changes facial expression from neutral to a slight frown)

**Garrett:** The frown on your face tells me that you're not sure if you're going to like it. Do you want to smell it first? (holds a spoon under Josh's nose)

**Josh:** (facial expression changes from slight frown to slight smile)

**Garrett:** Are you ready to taste it? I see a little smile. It looks like you like what you smelled. Here it comes. (raises spoon to Josh's mouth)

**Josh:** (smile broadens slightly and hand waves)

**Garrett:** I think this was a big hit!

*What's happening in this conversation:* Garrett's son, Josh, is nonverbal. He was identified from a young age as having developmental delays that affect his ability to communicate verbally. Garrett uses words to describe the changes he notices in Josh's facial expressions and body language to put words to Josh's feelings. He uses these cues not only to help Josh recognize his own emotions, but also as a guide for how he responds to his son.

**Dani** (age nine months): (crying)

**Marvin** (Dani's dad): Uh-oh. It looks like you're getting upset about something. I see your lip starting to shake.

**Dani:** (continues crying)

**Marvin:** Okay, let me pick you up. I wonder if you are feeling sad. When I'm sad, my face looks just like that.

**Dani:** (cries more intensely)

**Marvin:** Now you're sounding like you might be angry. Your body is really tense. Let's take a little walk together. Maybe this is what you need right now.

**Dani:** (crying softens and stops)

**Marvin:** Is that what you wanted? A little attention and some cuddles? That helps me feel better sometimes when I'm upset, too.

*What's happening in this conversation:* As an infant, Dani has only a few ways to express his feelings, including using his body (e.g., tensing and relaxing; turning his head toward or away from something; moving, kicking, or flailing his arms and legs), making facial expressions (e.g., smiles, frowns, cries, coos); and using his voice (e.g., loud, soft, crying, yelling). When he feels uncomfortable, he lets his dad know it in the way that he knows how.

As Dani experiences several different emotions, Marvin describes what he sees and hears in Dani's body, face, and voice. Marvin puts words to Dani's feelings, which will help Dani learn the vocabulary that he needs to eventually shift from expressing his feelings through his body to expressing his feelings with words. Having conversations like this one lets Dani know that having and expressing different feelings is okay in his family. Marvin also helps Dani regulate his emotions. This is especially important for adults to do when children are young. When an infant expresses sadness through crying, a parent can regulate their sadness by rocking and singing to them and helping them feel content. When a toddler feels shaken and scared after a fall, a parent might pick them up and say soothing words to help ease their pain. When a preschooler is feeling energetic and excited at bedtime, a parent might use a quiet voice, turn down the lights, and read a book to help calm them down. In these ways and countless others, parents regulate children's emotions every day. As children get older, parents can continue to help children regulate their emotions while also teaching children the skills they need to regulate emotions on their own.

**Madeline** (age two)**:** Car cart! Car cart!

**Leila** (Madeline's nanny)**:** I hope they have car carts at the store today. Let's take a look and see if we can find one. It looks like they are all being used, so we'll have to get a regular grocery cart.

**Madeline:** I want car one! (starts to cry)

**Leila:** I know you do. You were really looking forward to the car cart.

**Madeline:** (cries)

**Leila:** I bet you're feeling disappointed.

**Madeline:** Pointed?

**Leila:** Disappointed. That means sad that something didn't go your way. Can you say 'disappointed'?

**Madeline:** Pointed. I want car.

**Leila:** I know you do and you were feeling disappointed that they didn't have one.

**Madeline:** (cries)

**Leila:** It's okay to cry when you feel disappointed, but when you're ready we can think of something else we can do to make shopping fun today. Maybe we could play I Spy. Have you ever played I Spy?

**Madeline:** I Spy? Little eye!

*What's happening in this conversation:* When there was no car-shaped cart at the grocery store, Madeline expressed her disappointment through her tears. Her nanny, Leila, helped her learn a new word to express the feeling she was having: disappointed. When children are able to name their feelings, they can better communicate how they feel and what they need to others. Leila used this opportunity to build Madeline's emotion vocabulary. By continuing to use the word "disappointed" in different contexts, Leila can help ensure that Madeline learns to use the word on her own. Not only did Leila teach Madeline a new word, she let her know that it was okay to feel this way. When children are very young, like Madeline, parents often take the lead in teaching children the vocabulary they will need to talk about their own emotions. As children get older, parents can use questions to encourage children to name their feelings themselves.

**Shanita** (Ariel's mom)**:** How was your day at preschool?

**Ariel** (age three)**:** Good.

**Shanita:** What did you do today?

**Ariel:** Nothing.

**Shanita:** Was there anything that happened that made you feel excited?

**Ariel:** We had music and we got to dance!

**Shanita:** You love dancing. What about sad? Did anything make you feel sad?

**Ariel:** This. (holds up finger with a Band-Aid)

**Shanita:** Oh no. Did you get hurt?

**Ariel:** I hurt my finger on the slide.

**Shanita:** Ouch. All right, what about calm? Was there anything that happened that made you feel calm?

**Ariel:** We sang a new song, but I don't remember it.

**Shanita:** That's okay. Maybe you can sing it to me later when you learn it a little better. Do you want to ask me about the feelings I had during my day now?

**Ariel:** Yes! Happy!

**Shanita:** Hmm . . . happy . . . I remember something that made me feel happy. Getting a big hug from my daughter when I picked her up from school was definitely a happy moment.

*What's happening in this conversation:* Shanita asks her daughter, Ariel, about the different feelings she had during her day in preschool. This conversation served as a way to learn more about what Ariel's day looked like and showed Ariel that her mom is interested in all her feelings. Parents who regularly talk about emotions are more likely to have children who talk about their emotions as well, making it easier for them to communicate how they feel and to manage their emotions (Lambie & Lindberg, 2016; Seçer & Karabulut, 2016; Warren & Stifter, 2008).

## YOUR PARENTS USE WORDS TO TEACH YOU AND GUIDE YOU

As we learn to use our children's emotion cues to figure out what they need, we also play an important role in helping children learn how to express themselves by showing them how to use words and how to have conversations. Parents can use words and conversations to:

- Describe what they see as they teach children about the world around them.
- Encourage children to pay attention to their own and others' emotions.

- Ask children questions that encourage critical thinking.
- Help children problem-solve when they make a mistake.
- Teach children about what to do as they navigate new and challenging situations.

Whether a child is nonverbal, pre-verbal, or never stops talking, parents can use words to teach and guide them. One of the ways parents do this is by sharing their inner voice with their child. Speaking your inner voice out loud teaches a child about how you think and helps shape your child's inner voice.

- *"Let me look at the shopping list. We need green apples and yellow bananas. I think they are over here behind the red tomatoes. Let's go see what we can find."*
- *"Look at this outfit. It has green and yellow stripes and one, two, three, four, five buttons down the front. You open the hole and push the button through just like this."*
- *"I see your lips starting to frown. Uh-oh. It looks like you might be feeling upset."*
- *"You have red curly hair. Davey has brown hair, and his hair is straight. Polly has brown hair, and her hair is even curlier than yours."*
- *"Time to put my boots on. I looked outside and saw lots of clouds. It might rain, so I better be prepared. First my right boot. Now my left boot."*

Imagine your preschooler searching for his or her own boots saying, *"Uh-oh rain. I better get my boots so I don't have wet feet!"* instead of melting down over wanting to wear different shoes or not wanting to wear shoes at all.

When you speak your inner voice out loud, it might feel like you are "over-explaining" everything. Sharing your thoughts in this way can make older children and other adults crazy, but it's good for young children to hear your thoughts—really! Not only are you bonding, you are helping your child learn vocabulary, teaching them how to use words to communicate, and you are paving the path for critical thinking. Explaining your thought process to your child also helps you make sure that the words you say and the choices you make have a reason and a purpose behind them. Being intentional about your actions and words can help you be the role model you want to be for your child.

## Key messages for children:

- Your parents use words to teach you and guide you.
- When your parents tell you to do or not to do something, there is a reason for it.

**Jared** (Tyesha's dad): That's my cell phone. I'm going to take it away from you because it's not a toy and can break if you suck on it.

**Tyesha** (age eight months): Aaah! Aaah! (reaches for cell phone)

**Jared:** I know you want it, but it's not a toy. Electronics don't go in our mouths. How about your rattle instead?

**Tyesha:** Aaah! Aaah! (pushes rattle away and reaches for cell phone again)

**Jared:** (puts phone behind his back) The phone is gone. All gone. You can choose one of these toys to play with instead. Your rattle and your elephant were made for your teeth! Which one do you want?

**Tyesha:** (reaches for elephant and puts it in her mouth)

*What's happening in this conversation:* In this conversation, Jared uses words to let Tyesha know that his cell phone is not a toy. He gives her other options by showing her toys that she can put in her mouth instead of his phone. Moments like this arise again and again with young children. Once children become mobile (e.g., scooting, crawling, climbing, walking), parents have to continually monitor their children's actions, behaviors, and eventually, their words. Much of this monitoring focuses on keeping children safe by guiding them away from things that they should not do. Parents often use words in this process, saying things like:

"Don't put that in your mouth."
"Don't touch the electrical outlet."
"Don't crawl near the top of the stairs."
"Don't climb on the table."

That's a lot of don'ts. Saying "don't," "no," or "stop" is often the easiest or quickest response when we see our child headed for something they shouldn't, but it's not always what's best for our child. Each of these moments is an important opportunity for parents to teach children what *to* do, rather than just focusing on what *not* to do. Parents can use words to explain what behavior should change and why (e.g., *"Don't touch the stove. The stove is hot! You can get burned and that hurts. Ouch!"*), as well as to explain to children what they can or should do instead (e.g., *"Here's a pot that you can stir on the floor while I'm cooking. See—you can use a spoon and stir just like me. This bowl is not hot."*). Even if you don't think your child can understand your words yet, say them anyway. This is part of teaching children vocabulary and the critical thinking skills they need to understand why we should do some things and why we shouldn't do others. Eventually, most children's brains mature to the point that your words will start to make sense. Children who hear words repeatedly will begin to say those same words to themselves when they are in those situations (*"Stove hot! No touch! Play pot. No hot."*). Hearing these words and replaying them in their own minds will help children make better choices on their own when they are able to do so.

**Patrick** (Rowan's dad): Here we are at the library. We've never been to storytime before, but I think you will really like it. Let's go inside. Do you want me to carry you, or do you want to walk?

**Rowan** (18 months): Walk! Walk!

**Patrick:** You want to walk.

**Rowan:** Walk!

**Patrick:** The children's section is upstairs. Let's walk up the steps. One, two, three.

**Rowan:** One. One. One.

**Patrick:** One, two, three.

**Rowan:** One. Two. One. Two. One. Two.

**Patrick:** Here we are. This is the children's section. Look at all the fun books around!

**Rowan:** Book! Book!

**Patrick:** They even have a coloring table. I see other kids sitting on the rug over there. Let's go join them for the story first, and then we can come back and color.

**Rowan:** Dada up! Dada up!

**Patrick:** You want me to hold you now? Are you feeling nervous?

**Rowan:** Up Dada!

**Patrick:** Up you go. We'll go together. You can sit in my lap if you want. See how all the other kids are getting ready? They look pretty excited!

*What's happening in this conversation:* Even without realizing it, parents teach their children about the world in the way they respond to new places, people, and situations. Children may watch their parents' facial expressions and body language or listen to their words and tone of voice to gather clues about how they should react. This is called social referencing (Heath, 2012). Social referencing can appear in children as young as six months old. In this conversation, Patrick describes to Rowan what he sees as they visit library storytime for the first time. He uses his words to put his son at ease while also modeling with his facial expressions, body language, and tone of voice that this is a place where he feels comfortable and hopes his son feels comfortable, too.

**Rashelle** (age two): (picks up a handful of dog food and puts it in the dog bowl) Cali food. Cali food.

**Wanda** (Rashelle's grandma): Cali already had her dinner so she doesn't need any more. Dog food isn't a toy to play with. It's Cali's food to eat, so we shouldn't touch it unless it's time to feed her.

**Rashelle:** Cali eat! Cali eat food.

**Wanda:** Not right now. Put that food back in the bin and wash your hands. (leads Rashelle back to the dog food bin and helps her wash her hands)

**Rashelle:** Cali more food! (wanders back to dog food bin after washing hands, takes another handful of dog food and puts it in the dog bowl)

**Wanda:** Did you get in the dog food again? It's not time for Cali's dinner. You can help me feed her in the morning. Cali is full. No more food now. You need to wash your hands again.

**Rashelle:** Wash wash. Cali more food. (heads back toward dog food bin after washing hands)

**Wanda:** There is something about that dog food that is really interesting, isn't there? You know what? I have an idea. I have some dried beans. Beans are kind of like dog food. I'm going to put some in a big bowl, and you can use a spoon to scoop the beans.

**Rashelle:** Scoop. Scoop. Scoop. Scoop. (sits down and scoops and pours beans contentedly between containers)

**Wanda:** Ah ha! I figured it out. It looks like you wanted to scoop and pour something. You can play with this instead of the dog food for now, but only when grandma's here so I can make sure you don't put these beans in your mouth.

*What's happening in this conversation:* Although Wanda does not want her granddaughter to play with dog food, she realizes that Rashelle saw her scooping their dog's food every morning and evening and wanted to try it herself. Importantly, Wanda uses words to explain to her granddaughter why she shouldn't engage in one behavior and shows her something else she can do instead. Even after Wanda led Rashelle away from the dog food, she continued to return to it, which is pretty typical for toddlers. This isn't an intentional act of defiance by Rashelle—it's part of her learning process.

As we discussed in Chapter I, young children's brains are developing at an incredible rate. This rapid growth helps children keep up with all that they see, hear, and experience around them. Remember that everything is new to a young child! Children are continually taking in new information, and their brains are doing their best to keep up by building connections and forming new pathways. The patterns that you set up as part of your relationship with your child become part of the wiring in their brain. When children have positive, loving, trusting relationships with the adults in their lives, pathways supporting positive interactions develop, and this becomes part of who they are, how they act, and what they expect from other relationships.

Strengthening pathways in the brain is one of the reasons repetition is so important for children's learning. Think about how children learn new words, for example. A child hears you say a word and then when they are developmentally ready, they try to say that word themselves. You repeat the word many times in many different contexts. Your child copies you, repeats the word over and over, integrates it into their own vocabulary, and new pathways are established! Young children love to hear the same song over and over, read the same book again and again, and hear the same story night after night. This can be annoying to adults, who tend to like novelty, but repetition is how children learn best.

The need for repetition can also help us understand how children learn new actions and behaviors, just like Rashelle in the last conversation. As children become mobile and interact with the world on their own, they often try the same things over and over again. Repeating the same things helps children learn about cause and effect, and seeing your response helps them learn what to do and what not to do.

*"Will this toy make noise if I push the button again? It did! How about now? It did! Let me try one more time. It did again!"*

*"When I pushed the switch up, the light turned on! Down. Off. Up. On. Down. Off. Up. On. Down. Off. Up. On."*

*"Mom said 'No' when I tried to touch the stove. Will she say 'No' this time? Yes. How about now? Yes. How about now? Yes. And now?"*

Children are not necessarily thinking these words, but in a sense, this is what is happening. They are learning by looking for patterns and consistency, and they are watching you for your response. When you see your child do something repeatedly (especially something you have asked your child not to do), it may seem as though your child is not listening and not learning. It might even feel as if your child is intentionally misbehaving because you have asked them not to do something, but they keep doing it. Chances are, however, your child is not trying to make you upset on purpose. Your child is just learning.

So what can a parent do?

Have and keep having conversations!

**Yoshi** (Theresa's mom)**:** Are you ready to go to the park?

**Theresa** (age three)**:** Yes!

**Yoshi:** Okay, what do we still need to do to get ready?

**Theresa:** Shoes! Put my shoes on.

**Yoshi:** I'll put my shoes on, too. Anything else?

**Theresa:** All done.

**Yoshi:** What about a hat?

**Theresa:** Why?

**Yoshi:** Why do you need a hat?

**Theresa:** Why?

**Yoshi:** To protect your face from the sun.

**Theresa:** Why?

**Yoshi:** So you don't get a sunburn.

**Theresa:** Why?

**Yoshi:** A sunburn damages your skin and it hurts!

**Theresa:** Why?

**Yoshi:** Are you just saying "why" to everything I say?

**Theresa:** Why? (giggles)

**Yoshi:** All right, let's go, you goofball. Get your coat!

**Theresa:** Why?

**Yoshi:** Actually, I don't have a good reason for that. I just said it out of habit. You'll probably be warm enough without it.

**Theresa:** Why?

**Yoshi:** Now you're going to get tickles!

**Theresa:** Why? (laughing)

*What's happening in this conversation:* In this conversation, Yoshi answers Theresa's "Why?" questions even though she already answered these same questions the day before. Theresa turned asking, "Why?" into a game, but it was a game that had a purpose. For Theresa, hearing her mother's responses helped her understand the reasons behind what she was being asked to do. For Yoshi, taking the time to explain why she was asking her daughter to do something helped her to be more intentional in her parenting choices. Explaining to children why we are asking them to do something shows them how we think about the world. It also helps us think through the choices we make when parenting.

When we ask children to do something, we often have a reason for it:

Time to brush your teeth!
Why?
Brushing your teeth keeps them clean so that you won't get cavities.

Or

Please stop making that sound.
Why?
Because it's really loud and hurting my ears.

If we can justify to our child why we are asking them to do something (or not to do something), what we ask is more likely to make sense to them, too—if not now, then in the future. Sometimes, however, we might not have a good reason for what we ask a child to do:

Don't take that puzzle out right now. Put it back.
Why?
Because . . . actually, I don't have a good reason. I was going to get a book for us to read, but if you want to work on a puzzle now, that's okay.

When we catch ourselves impulsively telling our child to do something, thinking about the reason behind what we are asking can help us make sure we are asking children something that makes sense from our perspective and from theirs. This also helps our children learn that we have their best interests in mind and that they can trust that our words are well thought out.

## YOU CAN EXPRESS YOUR FEELINGS IN DIFFERENT WAYS

In the same way parents use conversations to teach children about the world around them, parents can use conversations to help children learn to express and manage their feelings. When young children have unpleasant feelings, they often express those feelings in unpleasant ways. They might act out, show aggression, struggle with paying attention or learning, make bad choices, and make life challenging for those around them, including their families! When children have unpleasant feelings, we often do things to try to change those feelings. We might say things like:

"It's okay."
"Calm down."
"Cheer up."
"Don't cry."
"There's nothing to be upset about."

These statements are a few of the ways we tell a child, *"I want you to feel happy instead of how you're feeling."* The problem is, these statements can also tell a child that it's not okay to feel upset. In general, we don't like it when our children are upset, and we want to help them stop feeling upset as quickly as possible. Even though unpleasant feelings are normal (adults have these feelings too), parents are less likely to talk with their child about them than pleasant feelings, and this can send the message that unpleasant feelings are not as good as pleasant feelings. One of the reasons parents avoid talking about these feelings might be that they don't always know how. When a child has a meltdown or a temper tantrum, we just want it to stop. Another reason is that unpleasant and intense emotions can trigger our own unpleasant feelings and might lead us to feel upset, uncomfortable, embarrassed, or even angry.

As discussed in an earlier conversation ("Your feelings help your parents know what you need."), our children's feelings serve a purpose. They help us know what our children need. When children are young, the responsibility for figuring out what they need falls on their parents' shoulders. It's helpful for an infant to cry and scream when they are hurt or upset, but as our children get older, we probably don't want them to express their feelings in this way anymore. We look forward to temper tantrums ending and hope children reach a time when they can say, "I'm feeling sad. Can I have a hug?" or "This is really frustrating! I want to try again, but I need to calm down first." How many adults do you know who can express their feelings this well? Probably not as many as you'd like.

As our children's brains mature and their vocabulary grows, they can play a more active role in choosing how they express their feelings if they are taught how to do so and if they have practice. Moving away from expressing feelings through instincts and impulses to using words is a major shift. Teaching children how to express their emotions in new ways takes time, practice, and lots and lots and lots of repetition. Children will never stop feeling sad, lonely, frustrated, angry, or scared at times, but we can use conversations to teach them how to show and communicate these feelings effectively.

### Key messages for children:

- You can express your feelings in different ways.
- There are things you can think, say, and do to impact your feelings.

**Li** (age four): I don't want a shot.

**Ralph** (Li's dad): I don't like getting shots either. Are you feeling a little nervous about it?

**Li:** Uh-huh.

**Ralph:** Do you remember what getting a shot is like?

**Li:** I remember it hurts a lot! A lot a lot a lot a lot!

**Ralph:** Actually it doesn't hurt THAT much. Do you want me to tell you a story about what getting a shot is like?

**Li:** Okay.

**Ralph:** Well, we'll have your doctor's appointment just like we talked about and at the end, Dr. Wong will ask you which arm you want your shot in. Do you know which one you are going to pick?

**Li:** This one.

**Ralph:** Okay. Do you know if that's your left or right arm?

**Li:** Left!

**Ralph:** That is your left arm! The doctor will get out a little alcohol swab and clean off the spot where you'll get your shot just like this. It might feel a little cold. Then she will get the vaccine ready and count one-two-three.

**Li:** That's when it hurts! Ow! Ow! Ow!

**Ralph:** Well, maybe a little bit. Kind of like a little pinch, but that feeling won't last long—it's really quick.

**Li:** How quick?

**Ralph:** Just a few seconds and then it's over. Do you remember why we get shots?

**Li:** So we don't get sick?

**Ralph:** Well, you'll still get sick, but you won't get certain diseases that can be very dangerous.

**Li:** Oh yeah.

**Ralph:** Is there anything else you want to know about getting a shot?

**Li:** Can I have a sticker?

**Ralph:** Definitely! Dr. Wong always has stickers for you!

*What's happening in this conversation:* When Li tells her dad that she doesn't want to get a shot, he talks with her about what the experience will be like so that she can feel prepared for what is going to happen. This might not make her feel less nervous (many adults feel nervous about shots, even when they know what's coming), but if she had been feeling worried or even terrified, it might bring that fear down a level.

**Nolan** (age two): Noooooo! (crying) No! No! No!

**Aaliyah** (Nolan's mom): Nolan, your shoes are in the middle of the floor where your grandmother could trip on them. Before you go play, you need to put your shoes in the basket by the door.

**Nolan:** (continues crying and starts kicking his feet)

**Aaliyah:** I can see you are really upset. Let's try taking a few deep breaths to calm down.

**Nolan:** (continues crying and gets even louder, kicking harder) NOOOOOOOOO!

**Aaliyah:** Okay. I see you're not ready to calm down yet. It's okay to be angry. I'll sit here and wait until you're ready to talk about it.

*What's happening in this conversation:* When Nolan gets extremely upset over having to put his shoes away (something he does every day without any issue), Aaliyah realizes he must be overly tired. When he starts crying, kicking, and screaming, she attempts to help him calm down by suggesting that he take deep breaths. When she sees that this won't work, she steps back and gives Nolan space to express his anger. When he's ready to calm down, she tries again.

**Aaliyah:** Boy, you were really upset.

**Nolan:** (sniffs)

**Aaliyah:** Did something happen that was upsetting today, or are you feeling tired?

**Nolan:** Not tired.

**Aaliyah:** Hmm . . . I wonder if that's it. Usually you don't mind putting your shoes away. Are you ready to put them away now?

**Nolan:** (stands up and puts his shoes away and then returns to hug his mom)

When children experience an intense emotion like Nolan did, it is important for them to have an opportunity to express that feeling in a safe way. While a child is experiencing an intense emotion, their ability to make good decisions is on hold. They may not be able to think clearly, they may not be listening well, they may not respond in a way they feel good about, and it's not a great time for them to learn. If a child's in the middle of a tantrum, it may not seem helpful to say calmly: "Let me give you some ideas to choose from to help you calm down. Maybe you could take a deep breath or count to five slowly." The child is likely to continue to tantrum, scream, and cry. This doesn't mean that it's hopeless to stop your child from having a meltdown. It just means that the middle of a tantrum isn't the best time to teach your child how to deal with their feelings, but you can coach them during these moments anyway. Talking about intense feelings like frustration and anger needs to happen during stressful moments, and outside of these moments too. Parents can help coach children through tough moments (e.g., *"Remember to breathe." "It's okay to be angry, but it's not okay to hit your brother so I'm going to move your body away from him."*) and then follow up again outside of emotionally charged moments so that children can pay attention and practice these skills when they can actually focus on them.

**Michael** (Charlotte's dad): When I feel angry, my shoulders get really tight. Sometimes I start squeezing my fists like this, and my eyebrows pull together like this. Let me look in the mirror and see how I look. Can you make a face like this?

**Charlotte** (age three): Like this?

**Michael:** Yes. Like that. What does your face look like when you get angry?

**Charlotte:** Watch me! Angry face!

**Michael:** I see your eyebrows pulling together just like mine. What else do you see?

**Charlotte:** Big frown!

**Michael:** Does anything else happen in your body when you feel that way?

**Charlotte:** (starts stomping feet)

**Michael:** Sometimes you stomp your feet. What about your voice? What does your voice sound like when you get angry? Can you say, "I'm angry" in an angry voice?

**Charlotte:** I'M ANGRY!

**Michael:** Oh, that was a really mad voice. When I feel that way, that's how I know when I need to take a few breaths to help myself stay calm.

**Charlotte:** (takes a deep breath)

**Michael:** (takes a deep breath) Just like that. When you're angry, is it okay to hit someone?

**Charlotte:** No!

**Michael:** What about kick someone?

**Charlotte:** No!

**Michael:** What could we do instead?

**Charlotte:** Tell you or mom?

**Michael:** Sure. You can use your words to tell us how you're feeling, just like we practiced and say, I'm angry!

**Charlotte:** I'm angry! Angry! ANGRY!

*What's happening in this conversation:* Michael encourages his daughter, Charlotte, to consider how her body feels when she is angry. Together, they look at their facial expressions in the mirror and act out body language. He also talks with her about ways to express anger that are not appropriate (e.g., hitting), as well as ideas for ways to show anger effectively (e.g., using words to say, "I'm angry!"). By having conversations like these outside of emotionally charged moments, Michael can help his daughter think about the changes that happen in her body when she is angry, which can help her learn to recognize those feelings herself. The next time Charlotte starts

One day, Casey's preschool teacher called his mom to let her know he had been swearing in class. When he came home that afternoon, his mom reminded him that the words he had used at school were bad words and not okay for him to say. She also chastised his dad, Russell, for swearing in front of Casey while driving. She knew bad words slipped out easily when he felt frustrated on the road.

The next day, Casey was riding with his dad in the car. Another driver swerved suddenly in front of them, causing Russell to hit the brakes. Russell swore loudly.

Casey piped up, "Dad, you're not supposed to say those bad words! Next time you get mad, do what mom does and wave one finger instead!"

Like all children, Casey was learning how to express his emotions from his parents. He was learning that there are different ways to express emotions. Some ways are okay at school, but some are not. Some ways are okay for adults, but not for children.

- How do you show your feelings when you're angry, frustrated, sad, disappointed, or stressed?

- How would you like your child to show their emotions when they feel that way?

- What can you do to teach your child your family's rules for how to express different feelings?

to get frustrated or angry about something and uses her body to express herself (e.g., kicking or screaming), Michael can remind her that it's okay to feel this way and encourage her to use words to describe her feelings instead. It's important to realize that just because a child is able to role-play taking deep breaths and staying calm does not mean they will be able to do this when they are in emotionally challenging moments, but practice will help them use these skills more and more often.

**Morgan** (age six): My stomach hurts.

**Chad** (Morgan's grandpa): Uh-oh. When did it start hurting?

**Morgan:** Just now when I started putting my shoes on. I don't think I can go to school.

**Chad:** If you're sick or think you are going to throw up, you definitely shouldn't go to school, but I wonder if you might be feeling nervous or worried about something. Is there anything happening at school today?

**Morgan:** We have a spelling test.

**Chad:** I didn't know about that. Did your teacher send home a list of words to practice?

**Morgan:** There's a list in my backpack, but I forgot.

**Chad:** Oh. I see. Do you think you're feeling worried about your spelling test since you didn't practice?

**Morgan:** Yeah.

**Chad:** Do you think there's anything we could do right now to help?

**Morgan:** I don't know.

**Chad:** We only have a few minutes, but maybe we could take a look at the list together. Next week, we could make a plan to practice a little every day before the next spelling test.

**Morgan:** Okay. My stomach is feeling a little better now.

**Chad:** I'm glad to hear that. I bet you were probably feeling anxious.

*What's happening in this conversation:* Morgan shares with his grandpa that his stomach hurts. Although children do get stomachaches and regular illnesses that might indicate physical issues, children's emotions can affect them physically as well. Some children experience a stomachache feeling when they are worried, nervous, or anxious about something. Sometimes it is easier to talk about what we feel physically in our bodies than it is to identify our feelings. Chad helped Morgan ease his worried feelings, which also resulted in his stomachache going away.

**Jake** (age five): I'm afraid of my room. I don't want to go to bed.

**Ian** (Jake's dad): Why are you afraid?

**Jake:** Because monsters come in my room when it gets dark.

**Ian:** That would be a scary thing. I would be afraid of that, too. It's a good thing that monsters are not real.

**Jake:** Yes they are! I saw one. A really, really big one.

**Ian:** It's okay to pretend about monsters, but they are definitely not real. Would it help you feel better if we check under your bed and in your closet just to make sure there are no monsters?

**Jake:** Yes!

**Ian:** Okay, let's do it together so we can both see that there are no monsters.
**Jake:** Thanks, dad.
**Ian:** You're welcome. Does that help you feel better?
**Jake:** A little.
**Ian:** Is there anything else that would help?
**Jake:** Can you turn on my nightlight?
**Ian:** Sure.

*What's happening in this conversation:* Jake tells his father that he's afraid of the monsters that come in his room after dark. Even though Ian knows there are no monsters, he validates his son's feelings by letting him know that he would be afraid of monsters, too (if they were real). He also takes a moment to reassure Jake that they aren't real by checking under his bed and in his closet. The line between what is real and what is make-believe may be confusing for young children. There are times when they may pretend to be afraid of something, but other times when they have legitimate fears. Taking those fears seriously (whether they are in response to real or imagined things) can help your child feel supported and can be used as an opportunity to help them brainstorm strategies to cope with that feeling now and in the future.

**Seth** (Oliver's dad)**:** You were really frustrated when you couldn't open that container by yourself this morning. I didn't like it that you threw the container on the floor. Now it's broken.
**Oliver** (age five)**:** Sorry, daddy.
**Seth:** Thank you for saying sorry. Now that you're calm, I think it's important that we talk about what you can do next time you feel that way. It's okay to feel frustrated, but it's not okay to throw things like that. What do you think you could do next time instead?
**Oliver:** Ask for help.
**Seth:** Yes. You could definitely ask for help. I'm always happy to help you. And it's okay to say, "I'm frustrated! I need help!" Can you say that?
**Oliver:** I'm frustrated!
**Seth:** What else could you do?
**Oliver:** I don't know.
**Seth:** If you really want to do it by yourself, you could also stop and think

about another way to do it. The container was kind of slippery, maybe you could have used a towel to dry it off and then open it.

**Oliver:** I tried a towel, but it didn't work!

**Seth:** Oh, I see. Well, there might be other ways, too. Do you think you can stop yourself next time and make a different choice?

**Oliver:** Yes, dad.

**Seth:** Do you want to practice?

**Oliver:** Okay.

**Seth:** Here—here's a container. I'm going to pretend I can't open it. (making struggling noises) I can't do it! This is so frustrating! Okay, I'm going to take a deep breath and try again. (takes a deep breath) I still can't do it! Can you help me open this?

**Oliver:** Okay. (struggling noises) Hey! I got it! All by myself! I got it!

**Seth:** You did! Thank you! Now you pretend that you can't open it and I can be the helper.

**Oliver:** Okay! (takes the container and makes struggling noises)

*What's happening in this conversation:* After Oliver experienced a meltdown earlier in the day when he couldn't open a container on his own, he threw and broke the container. His dad, Seth, revisited the incident with Oliver later in the day once Oliver had a chance to calm down. He let Oliver know that he did not like how he had expressed his frustration earlier and helped him brainstorm other ways that he could have responded instead. Seth also modeled what to do and gave Oliver the chance to role-play with him.

**Cristiana** (Goran's mom): The character in that book got really angry. What did she do when she was angry?

**Goran** (age four): She screamed and yelled.

**Cristiana:** That's right. What else did she do?

**Goran:** She threw blocks and pushed her baby brother.

**Cristiana:** She sure did. Do you think throwing things and pushing is okay?

**Goran:** No way!

**Cristiana:** Do you ever do those things when you get angry?

**Goran:** Sometimes.

**Cristiana:** Yeah. Sometimes you yell when you get angry. Sometimes I yell too, but I'm trying to learn not to. What else can we do when we get angry?

**Goran:** Tell someone.

**Cristiana:** Yep. You can definitely tell someone and say, "I'm mad!" or "I'm angry!" That's a good way to let someone know you're angry. What else? Are there other ways to show you're angry?

**Goran:** I don't know.

**Cristiana:** Do you think it would be okay to stomp your feet if you needed to?

**Goran:** Yes. I can stomp my feet fast like this!

**Cristiana:** Sure! That would be okay. If you were angry, you could stomp your feet as long as you weren't hurting someone else. What about squeezing a pillow so tightly.

**Goran:** Like this?

**Cristiana:** Just like that. Let's both squeeze our pillows and pretend we're angry. I'm angry!

**Goran:** I'm angry! Watch this. Squeezy squeezy squeeze!

**Cristiana:** Squeezing helps me feel a little bit better, too. It's okay to be angry. Everyone gets angry sometimes.

*What's happening in this conversation:* In this conversation, Cristiana and her son talk about the fact that it's okay to feel angry and that there are different ways to express that feeling. Rather than encouraging her son not to feel angry or to think about how to calm down right away, Cristiana lets him know that there are ways to express anger that are okay in their family. Children experience many different feelings each day, and each of these feelings can serve as a valuable learning experience. When your child has an unpleasant emotion, rather than trying to shift their feelings too quickly, make sure they have adequate time and space to express those feeling. Help your child learn appropriate ways to express their feelings at home and let them know that it is okay to do so, but that you are also there to help them shift away from that feeling when they are ready.

**Robin** (Juan's mom): This was a really fun morning. I had a really good time going on a walk together.

**Juan** (age four): Me too.

**Robin:** It seems like we've been having a lot of hard mornings lately—lots of tears and trouble getting out of the house. Today wasn't like that. We both stayed calm, and it was really nice.

**Juan:** I like it when you're nice.

**Robin:** You like it when I'm nice? (laughing) I like it when you're nice, too! What do you think was different about this morning from yesterday?

**Juan:** You didn't make me rush. I hate rushing.

**Robin:** You definitely don't like to be rushed. Did you know that you woke up extra early today?

**Juan:** No.

**Robin:** You did! Usually you wake up around 7:00, but today, you woke up at 6:40, which means we had 20 extra minutes.

**Juan:** That's a lot of minutes!

**Robin:** It is a lot. Maybe we need to think about going to bed a little earlier so that we can take our time more often in the morning.

**Juan:** But I don't want to go to bed early!

**Robin:** Not early, just a little bit earlier so that we can enjoy our time together in the morning more. Maybe we'll give it a try.

*What's happening in this conversation:* Problem solving together about emotions can help draw children's attention to the causes of their emotions—both pleasant emotions and unpleasant emotions. Involving children in conversations like the one between Robin and Juan can encourage critical thinking and help you and your child identify things that you can do more often to have the feelings that you like to have together. Conversations like these can also help you identify things that lead to unpleasant feelings for your child so that you can avoid those things in the future when possible, or help your child anticipate and prepare for them.

## EVERYONE IS A LEARNER

As children explore their feelings and the world around them, parents impact *what* children learn as well as *how* children learn. When children are young, they often believe that they can do anything—and we believe they can too! When children struggle to do something, this can be frustrating. For some children, frustration leads them to try harder. For others, frustration leads to giving up. Parents can help children turn challenging moments into learning opportunities by fostering a growth mindset. Having a growth mindset encourages children to approach new experiences with the perspective that everyone is a learner, and everyone has the potential to grow and improve (Dweck, 2015). This is in contrast to having a fixed mindset—the belief that either you have it or you don't. Children and adults who adopt a growth mindset recognize that learning takes time, effort, perseverance, and patience. Children with a growth mindset tend to outperform those who believe that their intelligence or abilities are natural or innate (Dweck, 2015). There are many ways that parents can use conversations to promote a growth mindset and encourage their child to see that being a learner is part of who they are.

### Key messages for children:

- Everyone is a learner.
- Learning is an important part of growing up.
- Learning something new takes time and practice.
- It is okay to ask for help when you need it.

**Eddie** (Heidi's dad): I can't believe it! You're sitting up by yourself!
**Heidi** (six months): (smiles and babbles)
**Eddie:** You did it! Let me get the camera so I can take a picture for grandma. You have been trying so long, and you're finally strong enough! Now you'll probably do it all the time, but it was a tough thing to learn!

*What's happening in this conversation:* In this conversation, Eddie is celebrating his daughter sitting up for the first time by herself. Even though Heidi is pre-verbal, Eddie uses language to communicate with her that the new skill she learned took time and practice. Using language like this from an early age can help children think about each new skill they learn as a process of development and growth. Even if Heidi can't understand Eddie's words now, she will someday. Using this parenting approach now will also help Eddie practice the language he needs to continue promoting a growth mindset for his daughter.

**Ivan** (Joey's dad): Do you want me to help you put your shoes on?
**Joey** (age two): Me do it!
**Ivan:** Okay.

**Joey:** (struggles)

**Ivan:** Do you want some help?

**Joey:** No!

**Ivan:** Okay. I'll sit over here and wait. If you want my help, let me know.

**Joey:** No help. (continues to struggle)

**Ivan:** Sometimes putting your shoes on can be really tricky. Those shoes are kind of tight on your feet so they might not go on very easily. Do you want to try your other shoes instead?

**Joey:** (picks up other shoes and puts them on) Me do it!

**Ivan:** Look at that! Even though it was hard, you kept trying and you did it!

*What's happening in this conversation:* As children progress from infancy to toddlerhood, they take pride in being able to do things for themselves and by themselves. It can be hard for an adult to sit back and watch, however, when a child wants to do something and then struggles. A child might not have the dexterity or skills to do something yet, and end up feeling frustrated. In this conversation, Ivan recognized that Joey wanted to put his shoes on by himself. Ivan offered help, suggesting that Joey might be able to put on other shoes more easily. He also praised Joey for continuing to try by himself, rather than giving up, even though putting his shoes on was a challenge.

**Lindsay** (age five): Will you read to me? I'm bad at reading.

**Leah** (Lindsay's mom): I don't think you're bad at reading. You're still learning how to read, so you don't know very many words yet.

**Lindsay:** Reading is hard.

**Leah:** Reading is hard. It takes a lot of practice. When I was your age, it was hard for me, too.

**Lindsay:** Really?

**Leah:** Yep, but I read a little bit every day and got better and better. Now I love to read!

**Lindsay:** Especially in the bathroom.

**Leah:** That's true. Sometimes I get so excited about a book it's hard for me to stop reading it, even when I'm in the bathroom.

**Lindsay:** Can you read to me now?

**Leah:** How about this—I'll read to you, but if I see one of the words you've been practicing, like "the" or "a" or "cat," then I'll let you read it. That way you can practice, and we can read together.

**Lindsay:** Okay! I know how to read "to" and "and" and "Lindsay."

*What's happening in this conversation:* When Lindsay tells her mom that she's bad at reading, Leah helps her think about the situation in another way. Leah encourages her daughter to think about the fact that she is still learning. She may not be a strong reader yet, but with practice, she can be. The word "yet" can be very helpful in conversations with children. Parents can use "yet" to help children understand that even if they cannot do something *yet*, they can practice and grow.

Using a growth mindset is easier in some instances than in others. We may have preconceived ideas that there are some things we can learn and others that we can't, and sometimes we don't realize it. For example, we might have been told while growing up that *"Allen is the athlete in the family, and Gwen is the artist,"* or that *"The girls in our family have always been good at math, but math skills skipped over the boys."* Statements like these communicate the message that Allen is an athlete, but not an artist. Gwen is an artist, but not an athlete. And in the second family, only girls are expected to be good at math. These statements are counter to having a growth mindset.

It may be true that some people have personality traits or strengths they have cultivated that will give them an advantage at a certain skill, but it doesn't mean that others can't get better at that skill, too. Saying to a child, "you're smart," may not seem problematic. When we say things like this, we mean them, as compliments. We are telling a child that we see something in them that is special. The challenge is that we may also be telling a child that they succeeded because they were smart. The next time they struggle with a task, they might feel that they are not smart anymore and give up rather than sticking with it. Studies have shown that parents who use words to point out the effort children put into a task encourage children to work harder, stick with it, and keep trying (Dweck, 2006). Rather than saying, *"You must be really smart!"* try saying, *"Wow! You must have put a lot of time into that painting. I remember your drawings when you were two—I thought they were great then, but these are amazing. You keep getting better and better!"* In doing so, you are helping children celebrate the time and effort they put into learning a new skill, and this can help children stick to other challenging tasks in the future.

**Sean** (age six): Hi Cory!

**Cory** (age six): Hi.

**Sean:** Are you taking swimming lessons too?

**Cory:** Yes. I'm in level five. What level are you in?

**Sean:** I'm in level one.

**Shaniqua** (Sean's mom): Sean has never taken swimming lessons before. Have you, Cory?

**Cory:** I started swimming when I was four.

**Sean:** Whoa.

**Shaniqua:** So you must have had a lot of practice to get to level five!

**Cory:** Yep. That's my teacher. I have to go.

**Sean:** Mom, he's in level five!

**Shaniqua:** I know. That must have taken a lot of work. He started swimming much younger than you. I bet you'll be in level five someday, too.

**Sean:** Me too. I'm going to get to level five today!

**Shaniqua:** Well, you probably won't get to level five today if it took Cory two years, but you can definitely start learning!

**Sean:** Okay! I got this!

*What's happening in this conversation:* At the community swimming pool, Sean and his mom ran into one of his classmates, Cory. Cory is in a higher swimming level than Sean. Shaniqua points out in a matter-of-fact way that Cory has had more time and practice than Sean to develop his swimming abilities. Talking about swimming as a set of skills that needs to be learned helped Sean approach his swimming lessons with a desire to get better through practice, rather than feel discouraged that he wasn't at the same level as his friend.

**Erika** (Jillian's mom): This is really hard.

**Jillian** (age four): What, mom?

**Erika:** I have to learn a new computer program for my job, but I'm having trouble with it.

**Jillian:** I could help. I know how to type my name on the computer. J-I-L-L!

**Erika:** I know you do.

**Jillian:** Can I type my name now?

**Erika:** No. Not now. I have to figure this out, so I need the computer, but I'm not sure what to do.

**Jillian:** You could ask Aunt Lynn.

**Erika:** Asking for help is a really good idea. I don't think Aunt Lynn knows about this computer program, but I know someone at work who could help me. I'm going to send her an email and see if she can help me learn what I need to do next.

*What's happening in this conversation:* Being comfortable asking for help is an important part of being a learner. In this conversation, Erika shares with her daughter that even as an adult, she has new things to learn. When Jillian suggests asking her aunt for help, Erika uses the conversation to show her daughter that she is comfortable asking for help, something that she often encourages Jillian to do. Demonstrating the qualities related to learning that you would like your child to practice is another way to encourage a growth mindset.

As you support your child's learning, help them realize that there are many different ways to learn and to solve a problem. Sticking with a task and learning how to persevere is important, but continuing to try something in the same way, especially if it is not working, may be frustrating and not helpful. Help your child learn to step back and problem-solve if the approach they are using does not seem to be working. Ask questions like: *"What have you tried already? Do you have ideas for what you could try next?"* Having a growth mindset includes recognizing and being open to trying new and different problem-solving strategies, being able to ask for and accept help and feedback, and feeling comfortable making mistakes along the way.

## MAKING MISTAKES IS PART OF LEARNING

We all make mistakes—children and adults alike. Making mistakes and reflecting on those mistakes is part of the learning process. Teaching children that it is okay to make mistakes can help them feel comfortable talking about their mistakes and seeking help problem solving.

- Making mistakes is part of learning.
- Everyone makes mistakes and bad choices sometimes.

- Your parents can help you learn what to do differently when you make a mistake.
- You are still loved, even when I don't love everything you do.

**Chetna** (Damien's mom): Can you bring me my brown shoes?

**Damien** (age 17 months): (toddles over carrying one brown shoe and one black shoe)

**Chetna:** You brought one black shoe and one brown shoe. Thank you! I'll keep this shoe. Can you go get the other shoe that looks like this?

**Damien:** (brings back the other black shoe)

**Chetna:** Not that one. See the brown one over there? Can you bring me that one?

**Damien:** (brings back brown shoe)

**Chetna:** You did it! It took a few tries, but you brought my two brown shoes. I'm going to put them on. Now can you bring your brown shoes over so we can put those on, too?

*What's happening in this conversation:* Chetna asks her son, Damien, to bring over her brown shoes. Damien likes to be a helper, and Chetna sees this as a fun way to help him learn colors and practice following directions. When Damien brings the wrong shoe, Chetna gently asks him to correct his mistake. As a parent, you might not even consider something like this to be a mistake. When treated matter-of-factly, instances like this one can be seen as natural parts of the learning process. Damien is at a very early stage in learning to identify colors, and Chetna knows that.

**Gwyn** (age three): Wet! My pants are wet.

**Mirtau** (Gwyn's mom): Uh-oh. It looks like you had an accident.

**Gwyn:** I don't like wet pants.

**Mirtau:** I don't like wet pants either—they are uncomfortable. Do you want me to help you take your pants off, or can you get them off yourself?

**Gwyn:** Gwyn do it.

**Mirtau:** You want to do it. Okay. After you sit on the toilet to see if you still need to go to the bathroom, then find some dry clothes to put on.

*What's happening in this conversation:* When Gwyn has an accident, her mom offers help, but allows her to be responsible for sitting on the toilet and changing into dry clothing herself, with gentle guidance and prompts along the way. By being present to serve as a guide, but also allowing her daughter to manage what she is able to on her own, Mirtau helps build Gwyn's sense of independence and autonomy while also teaching her how to respond calmly to mistakes and accidents.

> **Cora** (age four): (holds a pair of scissors with her pointer and middle fingers squeezed through the thumbhole and her thumb stuck in the larger hole)
>
> **Gerald** (Cora's dad): Are you working on a project?
>
> **Cora:** I'm cutting a heart for mom, but the scissors don't work.
>
> **Gerald:** It looks like you might have your fingers in the wrong holes. Would you like me to help you?
>
> **Cora:** I want to do it myself.
>
> **Gerald:** Don't worry. I won't do it for you. I could tell you some things with my words that might be helpful so you can do it yourself if you want.
>
> **Cora:** Okay.
>
> **Gerald:** See how the scissors have two different holes?
>
> **Cora:** Yeah.
>
> **Gerald:** See how there's one small hole? That's for your thumb. Can you put your thumb in that one? The big hole is for your other fingers to go in together.
>
> **Cora:** (adjusts grip)
>
> **Gerald:** Just like that! Does that feel better?
>
> **Cora:** Hey! They work now!
>
> **Gerald:** You did it!

*What's happening in this conversation:* Gerald recognizes that his daughter is holding the scissors incorrectly. He also recognizes that she is determined to fix the problem herself, but that she may not have all the information she needs to do so. He asks if she would like help and then calmly explains to her which fingers are meant to fit in which holes. With her dad's guidance, Cora turns the scissors around, adjusts her grip, and starts cutting on her own. Chances are, Gerald will need to show Cora how to hold the scissors again the next few times she uses them, but he doesn't mind. He understands that repetition is part of her learning process.

**Leo** (age two): A-B-C-D-E-F-G. I-J-lemon lemon P. Q-R-X, T, U, WEE. Double-doo S, Y, and C.

**Ximena** (Leo's mom): I love hearing you sing the alphabet!

**Leo:** A-B-C-D.

**Ximena:** (joins in singing and they continue singing together). Can you say L-M-N-O-P?

**Leo:** Lemon lemon P!

**Ximena:** Try this: L-M-N.

**Leo:** L-M-N.

**Ximena:** You got it! L-M-N.

**Leo:** L-M-N.

**Ximena:** L-M-N-O.

**Leo:** L-M-N-O.

**Ximena:** L-M-N-O-P.

**Leo:** Lemon lemon P!

**Ximena:** (laughs) Almost! We'll keep practicing.

*What's happening in this conversation:* Ximena joins in singing with her son. When they are done, she helps him practice one small section of the song, repeating the letters L-M-N to help him hear the difference between what he is singing and the actual letters of the alphabet. Through practice and repetition in this way a little bit at a time, Ximena knows that Leo will eventually learn the alphabet. After all, he's only two, and it will be a while before he is really expected to understand each individual letter.

**Lin** (age three): (struggles to put on his shirt by himself, with one arm inside out) My arm can't do it!

**Mei-li** (Lin's mom): I see what's happening. Your shirt arm is inside out. Do you want me to show you how to fix it, or do you want to try it by yourself?

**Lin:** Do myself!

**Mei-li:** Okay.

**Lin:** (grunts and struggles) Unh!

**Mei-li:** Do you want me to give you some ideas for what you could try?

**Lin:** NO!

**Mei-li:** Okay.

**Lin:** I said NO!

**Mei-li:** I heard you say no. I'll wait here.

**Lin:** I CAN'T DO IT!

**Mei-li:** I know you want to do it by yourself, so I won't take it from you. It might help if you take your shirt off your head to fix the arms first.

**Lin:** (takes his shirt off and manages to fix the sleeve by himself)

**Mei-li:** You did it! I bet you will be able to put your shirt on now by yourself.

*What's happening in this conversation:* Mei-li realizes that her son, Lin, wants to put his shirt on by himself, so she steps aside to let him work on it. As she watches, she realizes he is growing increasingly frustrated with the approach he is taking. She wants to offer advice, but he's not ready to hear it yet and wants to continue trying on his own. When he continues to struggle, she gently offers guidance without stepping in to allow him to finish the task himself.

Many children don't like being told what to do. They want to be independent, to show us that they can do things by themselves, and to demonstrate that they can make their own choices. Feeling that they can be their own person is an important part of growing up, and this is what we parents want for our children, too. We want them to be able to do things for themselves, by themselves, and to make good decisions when we are not present.

Parents are often eager to jump in and do things for their children or to tell their children what to do. This has been their role since children were born, after all. As children get older, parents have to navigate a tricky balance between providing children with the support they need and standing back to let children try things on their own. By responding sensitively to children's mistakes, missteps, and attempts to take care of themselves, parents can make it easier for children to listen to and ask for help. Part of being a learner means learning to listen to and respond to feedback. Parents can let children know that they are present and able to help, while also acknowledging their child's independence (e.g., *"I know you want to do it your way, but there are things you don't know that might help you."*). Parents can also model openness to feedback in their own lives to encourage children to do the same (e.g., *"I'm really glad we asked that man where to find what we were looking for. It would have taken me a long time to find it by myself."* or *"I'm having trouble with this. Do you have any ideas what I could do? What do you think would help?").*

**Kyra** (age six): Tell me a story about when you were little.

**Jorge** (Kyra's dad): Do you want to hear a story about a time I made a mistake?

**Kyra:** Yeah!

**Jorge:** Well, one time when I was about your age, I wanted to surprise my mom—your grandma—by making her breakfast on her birthday. I poured cereal in a bowl and added milk. I wanted to make it extra special so I climbed up on the counter and found the sugar bowl. I put three big spoonfuls of sugar on top of the cereal and brought it to my mom.

**Kyra:** Did she like it?

**Jorge:** It turns out the sugar bowl was a salt bowl.

**Kyra:** Eww!

**Jorge:** Eww is right. It was very salty and she couldn't eat it.

**Kyra:** Did you get in trouble?

**Jorge:** No. My mom knew it was a mistake. I had good intentions and was trying to do something nice for her. Everyone makes mistakes sometimes. That's part of growing up and part of learning.

*What's happening in this conversation:* By sharing a story about a time when he made a mistake as a child, Jorge lets his daughter know that everyone makes mistakes. Sharing stories with your children about the mistakes you have made in your own life both from when you were a child and now as an adult serves multiple purposes. Not only can stories like these help you build your relationship and bond with your child (most children love hearing stories about their parents!), they also serve as opportunities to share lessons about what you have learned in your own life. Using conversations to talk with your child about mistakes helps a child see that making mistakes is a part of life—not something to feel embarrassed or ashamed of. Children who see mistakes in this way may be better able to talk about their mistakes and consider alternative approaches to challenging situations. They may also be more forgiving of others who make mistakes.

Sometimes we label children's mistakes as **misbehaviors**. The difference between what most people consider a mistake and a misbehavior is the intention. When a child makes a mistake, parents usually see the mistake as a situation where a child meant well, but did not know what to do or was not developmentally ready to do what they were trying to do. In other words, a mistake isn't seen as a child's fault. Mistakes are easier to respond to in a calm way than misbehaviors. A misbehavior is a situation where we think a child has negative intentions. In other words, we think a child is doing something they shouldn't do, even though they should have known better. We might think a child did something bad or wrong on purpose because we have told and shown them what they should have done many times. Or, a child might have shown us that they can respond in a different way to a similar situation in the past so we think they can and should make a better choice now. For example, think of a toddler turning on a light switch over and over even after being asked not to. Are they misbehaving or showing us how they learn?

Whether we label a behavior as a mistake or a misbehavior, it's our responsibility as parents to make sure that children know what they should do in these situations and to make sure that children have the skills and support they need to make a good choice now and in the future. When a child makes a mistake, we can ask ourselves:

> Have I shown my child how to act in this situation?
> Have I taught my child what to do and not just what not to do?
> Does my child have the language ability and the words they need to express themselves in this situation?
> Does my child have the self-control skills they need?
> Have I given my child enough practice and support to succeed on their own in this situation?
> How are my child's feelings affecting them right now?
> Even though I think they should know this skill, is my child too upset or tired to think clearly?
> What skills is my child missing, or what skills need more practice?
> Are the expectations I have for my child reasonable and realistic?
> How are my feelings affecting the way I respond to my child?

As you think through these questions, consider how you can help your child continue to practice the skills they need to manage their feelings and behaviors and to make good choices in the future. This can be harder to do in some instances than in others, especially when our children's behaviors challenge us.

**Olivia** (Rachel's mom): Time to brush your teeth!

**Rachel** (age four): No! You're not the boss of me!

**Olivia:** No, I'm not your boss. I am your mom. And helping kids learn and be responsible is what parents do.

**Rachel:** I don't want to brush my teeth!

**Olivia:** Brushing your teeth is part of how you take care of your body.

**Rachel:** I don't want to!

**Olivia:** I'm going to brush my teeth first, then. I really don't want to get cavities—cavities are little holes in your teeth from sugar. Getting cavities can hurt. Do you want to help me brush my teeth?

**Rachel:** Humph!

**Olivia:** (brushes her own teeth) Okay, I finished brushing my teeth. They feel much better now and so clean and sparkly. Maybe I'll brush my nose next.

**Rachel:** Mom!

**Olivia:** I'm just teasing. Toothpaste isn't for your nose! It's for your chin!

**Rachel:** Teeth! Teeth!

**Olivia:** Ohhh . . . your TEETH! Do you want the blue toothpaste or the pink toothpaste?

**Rachel:** Pink!

**Olivia:** Okay, here you go! I'm so glad you're keeping your teeth healthy and clean!

*What's happening in this conversation:* In the conversation between Rachel and her daughter, Olivia, Rachel relieved the building tension by taking time to brush her teeth first and then using humor to shift Rachel's mood about brushing her own teeth. Conversations like these don't always end so smoothly. If Olivia had firmly refused to brush her teeth, her mother would have had to make a choice. Would she allow Olivia to skip brushing her teeth and let her face the **natural consequence** of putting her teeth at risk for cavities and starting a pattern of poor hygiene, or would she have applied a **logical consequence**, letting Olivia know that if she didn't brush her teeth herself, she would have to do it for her?

Natural consequences are those that happen as a natural result of a situation (Heath, 2012). For example, if your child runs out to play on a cold day without putting on a coat, they will likely be uncomfortable and end up feeling miserable rather than enjoying their time playing—brrrrr! That's a natural consequence.

Let's imagine Rachel and Olivia in another situation using a natural consequence:

**Olivia:** Here's your coat.

**Rachel:** I don't want my coat.

**Olivia:** It's really cold outside. You can choose if you want to wear your coat or not, but check and see if you'll be comfortable.

**Rachel:** I AM comfortable.

**Olivia:** Do you want to stand outside on the porch and see if you're warm enough without your coat?

**Rachel:** Okay.

There are some natural consequences that you may feel comfortable letting your child experience (e.g., feeling chilly on a cold day) but there may be others that you are not (e.g., developing a mouthful of cavities). For instance, a natural consequence of refusing to wear sunscreen is getting a sunburn. If you don't want to put your child at risk for a burn, you might choose to use a **logical consequence** instead. A logical consequence is one that a parent chooses for a situation when a child breaks a family rule (Heath, 2012). A logical consequence is not just any consequence, but one that is connected to the action in a logical way. A logical consequence might look like this:

**Olivia:** It's really sunny outside. I'll get the sunscreen.

**Rachel:** I don't want sunscreen!

**Olivia:** It's important to wear sunscreen when you're in the sun because it protects your body. The sun can burn your skin. It's not good for your body, and getting sunburned really hurts.

**Rachel:** NO SUNSCREEN!

**Olivia:** If you don't have sunscreen on, then you won't be allowed to play outside. I don't want you to get burned. You can make a choice. Do you want to stay inside and play, or put sunscreen on so that you can play outside?

**Rachel:** Fine. Sunscreen.

This particular logical consequence might not work in every situation. What if Olivia's other children are already out the door, and she can't leave her youngest child behind? What if Rachel is on the way to preschool for the day while Olivia goes to work, and she knows they will spend a significant amount of time outdoors?

Another logical consequence that could be used in this situation might look like this:

**Olivia:** It's really sunny outside. I'll get the sunscreen.

**Rachel:** I don't want sunscreen!

**Olivia:** It's important to wear sunscreen when you're in the sun because it protects your body. The sun can burn your skin. It's not good for your body, and getting sunburned really hurts.

**Rachel:** NO SUNSCREEN!

**Olivia:** We have to put it on for school. That's something we don't have a choice about, but you can choose how we put it on. Do you want to help me put it on?

**Rachel:** No!

**Olivia:** Should we start with your arms or legs first?

*(Sometimes offering a choice like this works, and sometimes it doesn't.)*

**Rachel:** None! No sunscreen!

**Olivia:** I need to put sunscreen on your body. You can help me do it and we can make it fun, or I can hold your body and put it on while you're crying. I know you really don't like it when I do that, so you can decide if that's what you want or if you want to try and make it fun.

**Rachel:** Song! Sunscreen song! (crosses arms in a pout)

**Olivia:** Do you want to sing our silly sunscreen song while we do it?

**Rachel:** Yes.

**Olivia:** I think that's a great idea.

When you use natural and logical consequences, your child learns how to connect their actions with those consequences. This approach helps them learn what to expect in situations where they make mistakes or exhibit challenging behaviors. Knowing what to expect from their parents builds trust. A child may not like having consequences, but at least they know that the consequences they face will be consistent, fair, and something their parent thought about and chose carefully. Knowing what to expect makes it less scary to talk to a parent about a mistake, making it easier for children to seek out help when they need it, and easier for children to tell the truth.

**Kenan** (Rose's dad): Did you eat some chocolate?

**Rose** (age two): No chocolate. No chocolate.

**Kenan:** Hmm . . . it looks like you have chocolate on your face.

**Rose:** No, dada. No chocolate.

**Kenan:** Let's look in the mirror. See the chocolate on your face? That tells me that you did have chocolate. And you smell like chocolate—it's all over your teeth. I think you're saying no chocolate because you don't want to get in trouble.

**Rose:** No trouble.

**Kenan:** You know you're not supposed to eat chocolate without asking. From now on, I'm going to put the chocolate in a different place that is out of your reach. If you find the chocolate, please bring it to me and ask me first.

**Rose:** Treat? Dada treat?

**Kenan:** You already had a treat, and one treat each day is enough.

**Rose:** More treat?

**Kenan:** Treats taste good, but they are not very good for your body. Since you already had a treat by eating chocolate, you may not have any-more treats today.

*What's happening in this conversation:* When Kenan asks his daughter if she had chocolate, Rose immediately responds by telling him that she did not. It is not uncommon for young children to respond like this. When children begin to lie or hide the truth, this shows that they are starting to understand that their actions have consequences. Rose realized that eating chocolate without asking might lead to her dad being upset. This is an indication that Rose is thinking about the fact that other people have thoughts and feelings, too. At her age, Rose likely didn't yet have the self-control to stop herself from eating the chocolate that she found while looking for crayons. It wasn't until she finished the chocolate and her dad found her that she realized she might be in trouble. Kenan wants Rose to know that next time she finds chocolate, she should ask him first. He also realizes that it's his responsibility to put the chocolate in a place where she can't reach it until she is able to practice and develop the self-control skills she needs to stop herself from eating chocolate whenever she finds it around the house.

\* \* \*

Using natural and logical consequences is one way to take a conversational approach to discipline. When we take a conversational parenting approach, we let children know what we are thinking and why, even during challenging moments. Taking a conversational approach to discipline is one alternative to using a **punitive approach**. A punitive approach—an approach characterized by harsh words or spanking—can stop or change a child's behavior quickly in some cases, which might make it seem like it's working, but this approach leads to a different outcome. Imagine what it would look like if Kenan had taken a punitive approach with Rose:

**Kenan:** Did you eat some chocolate?
**Rose:** No chocolate. No chocolate.
**Kenan:** Hmm . . . it looks like you have chocolate on your face.
**Rose:** No, dada. No chocolate.
**Kenan:** You know you're not supposed to do that. What's wrong with you? Why don't you ever listen to what I say? Get out of my room and don't come back in here unless I tell you to. (voice rises to a yell)
**Rose:** No chocolate, dada. No chocolate! (growing upset)
**Kenan:** Stay out of the chocolate and don't you touch my stuff again or you'll get spanked.
**Rose:** No spank Dada no! (leaves the room crying)

In this situation, Rose might not come in her dad's room anymore, not because she is doing her best to remember not to eat the chocolate, but because she's afraid of being spanked. Punitive approaches work by making children feel afraid or by inducing shame. Some of the words Kenan used in the last example (*"What's wrong with you?" "Why don't you ever listen to what I say?"*) might make Rose feel like there is something wrong with *her*. When parents use a punitive approach, children learn not to do things out of fear of making their parent upset, or fear of getting in trouble. These fears may lead them to stop certain behaviors when their parents are around (*"If mom sees me do that, she'll yell at me!"*), but the behavior might not change when a parent is not around. (*"As long as nobody is looking, I won't get in trouble."*) Punitive parenting teaches children that aggression is an appropriate way to deal with conflict, and children may feel that they are the problem, rather than understanding that it's their behavior that is problematic. It's important to remember that parents who use a punitive approach aren't doing so because they don't love their children. They are doing the best they can with the strategies they have in their parenting toolbox. As you learn new approaches to parenting, you can add these strategies to your parenting toolbox and use those that work best for your family more and more often.

As you speak with your child, especially when they show challenging behaviors, take time to explain to them what to do and what not to do, and explain why. Help them practice what you would like them to do in the future (e.g., "Next time you find chocolate, can you bring it to me and say, 'Here's the chocolate, daddy!' Want to try that now?"). Model how to be compassionate by using words that you wouldn't mind hearing your child say back to you (or to their friends or teachers). Imagine your child shouting, *"Cut it out! I'm sick of this!"* or *"I told you ten times not to do that!"* We all say things we don't mean when we're upset, but hearing these same words come out of our children's mouths can be surprising and upsetting. It would probably go over better if a child said, *"I don't like it when you do that,"* for example. And we would probably feel better hearing words like that coming out of our own mouths as well.

## Chapter conclusions

The conversations in this chapter focus on building trust between parents and children through compassionate parenting. When parents encourage children to express themselves and then respond in a positive and caring way, children learn that their feelings and needs matter. Children learn to trust their parents and gain confidence in their abilities to share their feelings and ask for what they need, and they learn effective ways to do so. Children also need to learn that their parents trust them to share their feelings honestly, to ask for help when they need it, and to make good decisions, even when their parents are not around.

Trust has to be built with children during the moments when children are easy to get along with, as well as during challenging moments when it's more difficult. For many parents, it's easiest to respond to our children calmly and fairly during moments when they are behaving well. It's much harder during moments when their behaviors challenge us, but it's just as important during those times. When our children learn to trust us even when they are struggling to manage their feelings or behaviors, they will more readily come to us in the future when they face challenges.

Through the relationship they have with their parents, children learn how important it is to consider not only their own feelings, but other people's feelings as well. Children also learn what a positive and healthy relationship looks like. As children learn to build their own relationships, they will use their relationship with you as a model. This model teaches them what to strive to create with others. The skills children learn to express themselves can carry over into their relationships with others at home, in the community, and at school, as well as in their future romantic relationships and eventually in their own families.

As you continue having conversations like the examples in Chapter II, consider these conversation strategies:

1. **Talk, talk, and talk.** Children love to hear your voice, make eye contact, see your face, and have special one-on-one time with you. Whether your child is nonverbal, pre-verbal, or never stops talking, tell him or her about what you see around you and the things you think about. Let your inner voice come out! Your inner voice helps teach your child how to think.

2. **Be creative about what you call a "conversation."** Conversations with children can happen in many different ways, including while running errands, during bathtime, over family meals, in the car, while playing or reading together, and more. Some conversations last for minutes, some only for seconds, and some happen through acting out imaginary scenarios. It is important to make space and time for quiet moments and to play together without words and without an agenda, but it is also important to use the moments you have with your child to creatively integrate intentional conversations.

3. **Make space for children in your conversation.** No matter how old your child is or whether they are very verbal, pre-verbal, or non-verbal, your child can be involved in back-and-forth conversations. A back-and-forth might include taking turns sharing thoughts and ideas; asking or answering questions; or even smiling, scowling, cooing, and babbling. With infants and toddlers, take pauses to make space for their sounds, body movements, and facial expressions. With older toddlers and preschool-aged children, "wonder" out loud (e.g., *"I wonder what will happen next in the story. What do you think?"*). With

school-age children, ask them about their experiences and share stories about your own experiences with the topic (e.g., *"Have you ever had this happen to you? How did you feel when that happened?"*). Allow space in your conversations for silence, too, so that both you and your child have time to share, listen, think, and reflect.

4. **Have conversations outside of emotionally charged moments.** If your child is having a tantrum or a meltdown, or if your child is tired or stressed, this might not be the best moment for a conversation. Learn to recognize when those emotionally charged moments are happening, and use them to connect with your child in the way that they need through listening, hugging, cuddling, or reading a book together. Supporting your child through these types of actions can communicate that you are paying attention to and hearing what they need. If an emotionally charged moment is connected to something you need to address with your child (e.g., your child is throwing a tantrum after hitting another child), return to the conversation once both you and your child have a chance to calm down.

5. **Give yourself the chance for "do-overs."** There may be times when you try to talk about something with your child, and the conversation does not happen in the way you imagined or hoped it would. Your child might not have been interested in the topic or ready to talk about it. You might not have had an answer to one of your child's questions, or you may have said something that you did not feel good about. Whatever the case might be, step back from the conversation, reflect on how you can approach the topic differently next time, and give yourself the chance to try again. When you try a "do-over," let your child know why (e.g., "Yesterday you asked me why I was being mean. I told you to go to your room. I wish I hadn't done that. You didn't do anything wrong. I was feeling upset, and it was about something that was hard for me to talk about because I was so angry." *"Why, mom?"* "Do you want to talk about it with me? I'm feeling a lot calmer now."). Parenting is hard, and we all make mistakes. What matters most to your child is not the occasional slip-up, but the overall pattern in your parenting and how you respond to those slip-up moments that we all have.

### Question and answer: Apply what you learned to parenting challenges

**Q:** My child gets frustrated easily, and in a big way. How can I help him calm down?

**A:** *All children feel frustrated sometimes, but some children get frustrated more easily than others, and some children show their frustration more intensely than others.*

*First, reassure your child (and yourself!) that it is okay to have these feelings:*

*"I can see you are feeling really frustrated. It's okay to be frustrated."*

*"I feel frustrated sometimes too."*

*When teaching your child about a feeling like frustration, it's important to talk about this feeling outside of moments when your child is frustrated. Intense feelings like frustration make it hard to listen, hard to concentrate, and hard to think clearly. It's important to guide your child during these moments too, but your child may learn more when they are feeling calm.*

*When your child is calm, try these strategies:*

- *Talk about what it's like to feel frustrated. Share stories about times when you have felt frustrated, what it felt like in your body, and how you managed your frustration. Ask your child about what their body feels like when they are frustrated. Ask what happens that makes them feel frustrated.*

- *Read books together and talk about what makes the character feel frustrated. How do their faces and bodies look? What do you think their voices sound like? When someone is frustrated, how do they act?*

- *Talk with your child about your family's "emotion rules" for how you would like them to tell you or show you when they are feeling frustrated (e.g., use words to say "I'm frustrated," squeeze a special pillow, or stomp your feet in the corner of the room). Be sure to model these rules yourself!*

- *Role-play using dolls, action figures, puppets, or your own bodies and pretend you are in challenging situations that lead you to feel frustrated. Take turns pretending to get frustrated and showing that feeling in a way that is okay at home.*

*Even after you've practiced these strategies with your child, they likely won't be able to apply them during emotionally challenging moments right away. The more your child practices saying words and choosing actions they can use when frustrated, the easier it will be to use those strategies in those moments.*

*During moments when your child is frustrated, coach your child through their feelings. Let them know that how they are feeling is okay. You can also let them know whether or not the way they are showing their feeling is okay.*

*"It's okay to feel frustrated, but it's not okay to throw the scissors. If you need to show your frustration, you can stomp in the corner, or squeeze your arms together, or say 'I'm frustrated.' "*

*You may have to help guide your child to a safe location where they can continue to tantrum or stop them from doing something that is hurting him/herself or someone else. When ready, help your child think about what they can do to shift their feeling.*

*"Do you still want to feel frustrated for a while, or are you ready to change to another feeling? How about a hug?"*

*You can use these same strategies to help your child express and manage other emotions, too!*

**Q:** I feel myself getting worked up and frustrated when my child is upset. How can I keep my calm? Am I a bad parent if I can't stay calm all the time?

*A: Absolutely not! Feeling worked up when your child gets upset is completely normal! This is one of the ways that our body helps us jump to action when our child needs something. The problem is, when we are upset, it can be hard to think straight, and we might not respond to our child in a way we feel good about. No one has endless patience, and no parent is able to stay calm all the time. Rather than aiming to stay calm all the time, set a more realistic goal to practice strategies to calm down more quickly and to stay calm more often. Pay attention to the feelings in your own body when you start to shift from feeling calm to feeling worked up. How does your body change? How do your thoughts change? When you start to feel them happening, step back, take a deep breath, and think about what you can do in the moment to manage your feelings.*

*Here are a few suggestions:*

***Take a few deep breaths.*** *It only takes a few seconds to take a few deep breaths in and out, but those few seconds can make all the difference. Taking deep breaths is scientifically shown to help calm your body by slowing your heart rate and reducing stress.*

***Drink a glass of water.*** *The amount of time it takes to pour and drink a glass of water can provide space that allows you to collect your own thoughts and make a choice about how to respond to your child following a challenging moment.*

***Use self-talk.*** *Many people have things they say to themselves that help them get through a challenging moment (e.g., "This too shall pass." "I can do this.").*

***Reframe the situation.*** *Try to think about the situation from your child's point of view ("My child is only screaming right now because she didn't sleep last night, and she's probably very, very tired. She's not doing this on purpose to make me upset." "This is the first time he has been to the dentist. It might be very scary for him.").*

*Take time away from the situation.* If "the situation" is an intense moment with your child, trade out with your spouse, partner, co-parent, or other family member if possible.

Share your feelings. Let your child know: "I feel myself getting frustrated right now. I'm doing my best to stay calm, but it's very hard for me." Maybe your child can help you come up with ideas. This helps teach your child important lessons too about managing their own emotions.

*Take care of yourself outside of challenging moments.* Getting enough sleep and finding moments to manage your overall stress level (e.g., exercising, eating well, enjoying hobbies, spending time with friends) can be challenging as a parent. Taking care of yourself, however, is critical to being able to be the parent you want to be, especially during these challenging moments with your child.

Not all these suggestions will work for everyone. Choose and practice those that work best for you. Consider taking this a step further and having a conversation with your child about times when you struggle to stay calm, and share with them what works for you and what doesn't. This is one more way that you can be a role model!

**Q:** What if I make a mistake, or do something I don't feel good about when parenting?

*A:* Everyone makes mistakes. Making mistakes is not only part of growing up, it's part of parenting, too. If you do something you feel badly about as a parent, talk with your child about it. Explain to your child what you did, letting them know you didn't feel good about it. Talk with them about what you should have done instead, what you will do next time, and show them how to make amends.

"I'm really sorry that I yelled this morning. I don't like yelling at you, and I wish I hadn't done that."

"That's okay, mommy."

"Next time I start to get upset, I'm going to stop and take a deep breath and use my calm voice instead. Do you think you can help me practice that?"

"Okay!"

"Thanks, kiddo. I love you. Do you forgive me?"

"I love you too. I forgive you."

Mistakes like these (e.g., raising your voice when trying to stay calm) are not uncommon. Talking about these mistakes can help your child realize they are not alone in making these kinds of mistakes. If you can't seem to stop, or if the parenting mistakes you are making are more serious (e.g., hitting or hurting your child or yourself), it's important to talk with a counselor or doctor to ask about support that is available to help you manage *your own intense emotions and to learn additional parenting strategies that will allow you to parent in a way that you feel good about and that your child needs. All parents can benefit from learning additional strategies and having a supportive community. You might consider looking for parenting groups to join in your community.*

**Q:** What if I told my child they have to do something, but then I realize I shouldn't have said that? Can I take it back without undermining myself as a parent?

*A: Absolutely. Everyone makes mistakes. Sometimes as parents, we say things in the moment that we don't actually mean:*

> *Parent 1: "If you do that, then no TV for a year!"*

*Or we might say something that turns out not to be true:*

> *Parent 2: "I said that we'd get ice cream after dinner? You're right. I did, but I didn't realize how late it was."*

*When children are young, they think in very concrete terms. To many children, what you said must be true, which may be why the child in the first example cries even harder, thinking they have been banned from screen time for a year and the second child starts to scream: "You said that we could have ice cream tonight, so we're having ice cream tonight!" These moments come up for every parent. When you catch yourself saying something you didn't mean to say, or need to make a change because the circumstance has changed, be honest with your child and explain why you were wrong or why there needs to be a change in the plan.*

> *Parent 1: "Earlier when I was upset, I said that you couldn't watch TV for a year. I shouldn't have said that—that wasn't fair. There will be a consequence for not turning the TV off when you were supposed to, but I think having no TV tomorrow is more fair."*

> *Parent 2: "I know I said we could have ice cream after dinner, but I didn't realize how late it was. It's disappointing for me too, but we'll plan to have ice cream tomorrow night. We'll have dinner extra early just to make sure. I know you're still upset about it, but it's too close to bedtime tonight, so we'll have to wait until tomorrow."*

*In the first example, once calmed down, child 1 may be feeling relieved. Child 2 may still be feeling upset, but at least they have heard your reasoning behind why you made the decision you did. Hearing that even parents make mistakes—and seeing you model talking about your mistakes—can help your child feel more comfortable talking about their own mistakes. In addition, using this approach also teaches your child the need to be flexible. Sometimes things change—the situation changes or the information we have changes—and we can use those opportunities to practice managing our feelings and become comfortable with flexibility.*

**Q:** I was spanked/yelled at/taught to respect my elders, and I turned out fine. Why should I do something different with my child?

*A: To spank or not to spank is a tough and very personal question for most parents. The fact is, there is plenty of research that shows positive outcomes for discipline like using natural and logical consequences, but no research has shown positive outcomes from spanking. The research that does exist about spanking has found that spanking is related to an increased risk of many negative outcomes, including low self-esteem, mental health problems in childhood and adulthood, and behavior problems (Gershoff & Grogan-Kaylor, 2016). In general, spanking serves as a quick fix—it stops a challenge in the moment, and that makes it seem like it's working. In the long term, spanking teaches children not to do something out of fear of getting punished, not because they understand why something is wrong. This can lead children to stop a behavior when they think they might get spanked, but it doesn't help them learn to make a good choice by thinking through the reasons for that decision on their own. There are children who are spanked who turn out just fine. These children probably have qualities that will help them thrive no matter what situation they are in. These children are probably doing well despite being spanked not because of it. Sometimes parents rely on spanking when they are not sure what else to do. As you make your own parenting decisions, expand your parenting toolbox so that you have many strategies you can call on when you need them, and use those that work best for you and your child.*

**Q:** People say parents shouldn't be their kids' friends, but isn't that what using a compassionate parenting approach is?

*A: Using a compassionate parenting approach isn't exactly being our kid's friend, but there are some similarities. We would never tell a friend to "be sure and say thank you," or "don't forget to wipe carefully when you're done in the bathroom." In some ways, the relationship we have with our children is like a friendship, but in other ways it is different. One of the similarities is that we value our friends and our children for who they are. We should treat them both with love and respect, and strive to build trust. This doesn't mean you won't experience ups and downs in either type of relationship, but it does mean that when we do have those ups and downs, we approach them with care. One of the differences between a friendship and a parent-child relationship is that when a friend does something we don't like, we make a choice about whether or not to say something and we think about how our words might impact our friendship. Typically, it is not our role to be responsible for a friend's social, emotional, and moral development. This is our responsibility with our children, however. When a child does something we don't like or that we believe is not appropriate, it is our responsibility to help them learn, in a compassionate way, what to do instead.*

**Q:** What if I don't have much time to spend with my child because of work demands or other responsibilities?

**A:** *Depending on your other responsibilities with work, school, volunteering, other children, military deployments, or incarceration, you may have a lot, a little, or no time at all with your child. The good news is that parenting is not about quantity of time, but about quality of time. So long as your child is safe and spending time with caring people who love them, what matters most about the time you spend with your child is quality. If you have limited time with your child, make that time count. Put away electronic devices and be present in the moment. Play games that your child likes to play, and have meaningful conversations and interactions. If you have a significant amount of time to spend with your child during the day, chances are you have other things you need to get done during that time as well. When possible, involve your child. When it's not possible, explain to your child what you are doing and why. If a significant amount of the time you have with your child is spent multitasking, set aside special time to do things with your child when you are not engaging in work or other chores.*

## Extend the conversation through read-alouds

There are many books you can read with your child that emphasize the loving and trusting relationship between children and their parents. Visit your public library with your child and check out books that highlight positive family relationships. As you read together, talk about the different ways families show their children that they love them, as well as how they show them they still love them even when they have challenging moments. Ask your child some of the discussion questions provided, and be sure to share your answers with your child, too!

As you read, talk with your child about the different feelings that characters have. Doing so will show your child that their feelings are normal and that others have these feelings, too. Book characters can be great role models to teach your child about different ways to express their own emotions. Reading books together about different feelings provides an opportunity to problem-solve with your child about what they can do when they have those same feelings. Not all book characters will respond to their emotions in ways that you would like your child to respond. These examples can be learning opportunities, too. When you see a character who doesn't manage their emotions well, talk with your child about what the character did, what they could have done differently, and what you would do instead.

### Books about feeling loved

*All the Love in the World* by Rose Bunting, illustrated by Olivia Chin Mueller

*Daddy and Me* by Karen Katz

*Daddy Hugs* by Karen Katz

*Grandma, Grandpa, and Me* by Mercer Mayer

*Hug* by Jez Alborough

*Hug Machine* by Scott Campbell

*I Love You to the Moon and Back* by Amelia Hepworth, illustrated by Tim Warnes

*The Kissing Hand* by Audrey Penn, illustrated by Ruth E. Harper and Nancy M. Leak

*Llama Llama I Love You* by Anna Dewdney

*Love* by Matt de la Peña, illustrated by Loren Long

*Love from the Very Hungry Caterpillar* by Eric Carle

*Mommy Hugs* by Karen Katz

*On the Night You Were Born* by Nancy Tillman

*The Runaway Bunny* by Margaret Wise Brown, illustrated by Clement Hurd

*Where is Baby's Mommy?* By Karen Katz

### Books about feelings

*Duck & Goose: How Are You Feeling?* by Tad Hills

*Feelings* by Aliki

*Lots of Feelings* by Shelley Rotner

*My Many Colored Days* by Dr. Seuss

*On Monday When it Rained* by Cheryl Kachenmeister, photographs by Tom Berthiaume

*Quiet LOUD* by Leslie Patricelli

### Books about sadness, disappointment, or depression

*The Blue Day Book* by Bradley Trevor Greive

*The Color Thief* by Andrew Fusek Peters and Polly Peters, illustrated by Karin Littlewood

*My Friend is Sad* by Mo Willems

*Not Today, Celeste!* by Liza Stevens

*Pete's a Pizza* by William Steig

*The Princess and the Fog* by Lloyd Jones

*The Rabbit Listened* by Cori Doerrfeld#

### Books about anger, frustration, or stress

*Alexander and the Terrible, Horrible, No Good, Very Bad Day* by Judith Viorst, illustrated by Ray Cruz

*Calm-Down Time* by Elizabeth Verdick, illustrated by Marieka Heinlen

*The Chocolate-Covered-Cookie Tantrum* by Deborah Blumenthal, illustrated by Harvey Stevenson

*Cool Down and Work Through Anger* by Cheri Meiners

*I Was So Mad* by Mercer Mayer

*Llama Llama Mad at Mama* by Anna Dewdney

*Sometimes I'm Bombaloo* by Rachel Vail, illustrated by Yumi Heo

*When I Feel Angry* by Cornelia Maude Spellman, illustrated by Nancy Cote

### Books about worry, fear, or anxiety

*The Dark* by Lemony Snicket, illustrated by Jon Klaasen

*The Little Old Lady Who Was Not Afraid of Anything*

*Llama Llama Red Pajama* by Ann Dewdney

*Wemberly Worried* by Kevin Henkes

*There's a Nightmare in My Closet* by Mercer Mayer

*What a Bad Dream* by Mercer Mayer

*When I Feel Scared* by Cornelia Maude Spelman, illustrated by Kathy Parkinson

*When I Feel Worried* by Cornelia Maude Spelman, illustrated by Kathy Parkinson

### Books about learning and making mistakes

*After the Fall: How Humpty Dumpty Got Back up Again* by Dan Santat

*Beautiful Oops!* by Barney Saltzberg

*But It's Not My Fault* by Julia Cook, illustrated by Anita DuFalla

*David Gets in Trouble* by David Shannon

### *Read-aloud and discussion questions*

- How do the families in the books show their children that they love them?
- How do we show you that we love you?
- How was the character feeling? How do you know they were feeling that way?
- How did the characters show their feelings?
- What happened that made the character feel that way? What happens that makes you feel that way?
- How does your face look when you feel that way? Can you show me?
- How does my face look when I feel that way?
- When do you feel happy? Sad? Excited? Angry?
- What did the character do when they had those feelings?
- What can you do when you have those feelings?
- What could you do to help a friend who is having these feelings?
- How do the families in the book teach their child new things?
- How do the children in the book teach their families new things?
- What do the families do when they make a mistake? What do they do when their child makes a mistake?

## Extend the conversation through family activities

*Share stories with your child about special people in your life.* Children love to hear stories from their parents and caregivers about what it was like when they were growing up. Talk about relationships you had with the special people in your life, as well as the things you loved to do most. If thinking about or talking about your own childhood is difficult, talk about the people who are special in your life now, at home and in the community, and why those people are special to you.

*Spend dedicated one-on-one time with your child.* In addition to using words, you can show your child that you love and care about them with your actions. Set aside time to spend one-on-one time together doing things your child enjoys. For some children, this might include quiet activities like snuggling and cuddling, reading books, or working on art activities. For other children, it might include more active pursuits like playing at the park, exploring, or wrestling. Follow your child's lead and show them that you value them by spending time doing the things they like to do. Introduce your child to things you like to do as well. During these moments, be sure to put aside other distractions, such as household chores or electronic devices, including cell phones. It can be tempting (and sometimes it's necessary) to multitask when spending time with your child, but it is also important to find time when you can focus on being present with one another.

*Go beyond "How was your day?"* Instead of asking one another, "How was your day?" or "Did you have a good day?" try asking about different feelings that your child had. "What happened today that made you feel happy? Did anything happen today that led you to feel disappointed? What was it? How about excited?" Not only is this a great way to help children build their vocabulary, it encourages them to reflect on and share about their day. Take turns choosing feelings and make sure that everyone—children and adults—all have a chance to share.

*Act it out: Play "feelings charades."* Take turns acting out different feelings and trying to guess what feeling the other person is acting out. Make faces (e.g., smiling, frowning) and model body language (e.g., crossed arms, jumping up and down, slumped shoulders). If needed, give clues about things that happen that might lead to that feeling (e.g., *"I wanted to play outside, but it's raining. How am I feeling?"*).

*Make a list of family emotion rules.* Similar to rules about responsibility (e.g., put toys away when finished), create family rules together for different emotions. If someone in your family feels angry, how can they show it at home? For example, is it okay in your house for a child or adult to hit someone else when they are angry? Probably not. Is it okay for a child or adult to yell when they are angry? Most families don't encourage yelling, but maybe saying, "I'm really angry right now!" in a loud voice is okay. Would it be okay for your child to stomp their feet or clench their fists in a way that is not hurting anyone else? That might be a rule that you all agree is an okay way to show anger. What other ways can you think of? Make a list of different challenging emotions, and come up with ways that you agree are okay to show them when you have those feelings in your family. Use that list to help guide your child when those emotions arise (e.g., *"I know you're feeling angry, but hitting is never okay. You can show your anger by stomping your feet or squeezing this pillow if you need to."*).

*Create a list of family activities that promote pleasant emotions.* Together as a family, talk about the feelings you like to have when you are together. When you are having a good time together, how are you feeling? Happy? Loved? Appreciated? Brainstorm together a list of things that your family does or can do more often to foster these feelings. Post your list somewhere so you can see it, such as on the refrigerator. Look at your list together from time to time, and make a plan to do things on your list more often.

*Put items in a "calm down" basket.* Talk with your child about things that help your child feel better or calm down after being upset. What helps your child feel better? Snuggling with a blanket, curling up in a lap and reading a book together, taking deep breaths, a big hug? Gather items to put into a basket, a bag, or a bin of some kind. Practice these calming strategies together and use the calm down basket for ideas when your child has feelings like anger or frustration.

*Create a family music playlist.* Create a playlist of your family's favorite songs. Talk about how each song makes you feel. Find songs that your child likes to listen to when they are feeling happy and upbeat, angry or frustrated, sad or disappointed, and calm and peaceful. Talk about how each song makes you feel.

*Make "what to do when we're feeling blue" cards.* Together with your child, brainstorm things that help your child feel better after feeling sad. Write down each of your ideas on a note card or a Popsicle stick. Use words and pictures together so that your child can "read" the card on their own. When they're finished, place them in a box or other container. When your child is feeling sad, look in the container together for ideas that might help them in that moment.

---

### "What to do when we're feeling blue" card ideas

- Give or ask for a hug.
- Offer a tissue or a drink of water.
- Talk with someone about your feelings.
- Read a book together.
- Listen to your favorite song.
- Cuddle with a stuffed animal.
- Have quiet time.

---

**III**

# You are your own person:
## *Building self-awareness*

"I DON'T RECOGNIZE YOU." This was the first thought I had when my daughter was born. During my pregnancy, I had looked at baby pictures of myself, imagining that this was what my daughter would look like, too. When I held her in my arms for the first time, I was surprised to see that she wasn't an infant version of myself. She was a new person—her own person. It wasn't just her face I didn't recognize, it was everything. I was supposedly a very quiet and content baby. My daughter was anything but that. On our second night home, she cried for hours while my husband and I tried everything we could, from rocking, to singing, to feeding, to changing her in an attempt to soothe and calm her. After nearly three hours, all three of us were in tears. My husband and I joke now that we turned her over to look for her return policy, but that thought didn't seem so funny at the time. From the time she was born, my daughter let us know—loudly and clearly—that she is special. She was and is her own person. We had to set aside our expectations for who we thought she would be to get to know who she actually is and to appreciate who she will become.

When children enter a family, whether through birth or adoption, most parents have expectations for what a child will look like, how they will act, and who they will be. They also might have a vision for what they want their relationship with their child to look like. Daydreaming about our children is perfectly normal and an important part of preparing for parenthood. When we meet our children, however, we often have to look beyond our expectations to get to know our children for who they are.

## YOU ARE SPECIAL

There are many different qualities that define our children. Parents don't get to choose their children's qualities, but they can help them learn about themselves and feel accepted and appreciated for who they are. As children develop self-awareness, parents can teach them about qualities that are part of their identity, including their temperament, sex and gender, race and ethnicity, abilities and disabilities, sexual orientation, and others. Parents can use conversations to let children know that the similarities they share with others—as well as their differences—make them special and let them know they are valued for all their qualities. These conversations are crucial to ensure that children feel safe growing into their personality, their body, and their identity.

Teaching our children self-awareness often begins with conversations that focus on qualities that we can see in our children or expect our children to develop, but these conversations can't end here. In order to create a more compassionate society, it's important for parents to help children learn about qualities that others have (even if their child doesn't share these qualities) so that they can develop a greater understanding and compassion for people who are both similar to and different from themselves.

The conversations in this chapter are examples of topics that parents and children can discuss to promote awareness and acceptance of oneself and others. They are by no means representative of all the possible conversations you might have with your child or inclusive of all the important messages you might share, but they can serve as starting points.

## Key messages for children:
- You are your own person.
- Everyone has strengths and challenges.
- Who you are will grow and change over time.
- Every person has as much value as every other person.
- Sometimes people treat one another differently because of who they are or how they look—sometimes on purpose and sometimes when they don't mean to.
- We should be kind to everyone and treat other people the way they want to be treated.

### Temperament

Every child is born with their own unique **temperament**—the biological foundation for their personality (Berk & Meyers, 2012). A child's temperament includes many different dimensions that shape how a child acts and how they respond in different situations.

Some children are born with an **easy** temperament. These children tend to be easygoing, they don't get upset as easily as other children, and they tend to calm down quickly. If you have a child who smiles and laughs easily and doesn't get upset very often, it's easy to smile back at them. Your child smiles. You smile back. Your child sees you smile, smiles back at you, and the positive cycle continues: smile -> smile -> smile. You meet your child's need for attention and affection, you feel validated as a parent, and a loving and trusting relationship develops. It's not quite as simple as that, but you get the idea. Each time you interact with your child, you have a chance to show how to be compassionate and, with an easy child, it's easy to do. In general, children with easy temperaments have lots of positive interactions with parents and caregivers.

Now imagine a child with a **difficult** temperament—a child who cries easily and often and who is hard to calm down. Each time you pick up your child, the crying continues. There are times when no amount of smiling, singing, rocking, or soothing works. Despite that, you do your best to stay calm and to approach your child with the same compassion you would an easy child. The smiles and laughs that come from time to time help, but it takes a lot of energy and patience to be the parent you want to be for this child. As the adult in the relationship, it falls on you to adjust the way you react and respond to your child to create that loving and trusting relationship, and it can take a lot of effort. Parents who are able to adjust how they respond to their child in a way that meets their child's personality and needs foster what's called a **goodness of fit** (Chess & Thomas, 1991). This can be harder with some children than with others.

A parent's personality and temperament play a role in creating goodness of fit, too. Some parents have endless patience and can sing and rock a child for hours without breaking a sweat; others feel anxious easily, get worked up by the sound of a child crying, and struggle to keep their calm no matter how hard they try. Each of these personality traits is perfectly normal, but it does mean that it takes more work for some parents than for others to be the kind of parent they want to be, and this can be harder or easier depending on their child's temperament. No matter what your personality or your child's temperament, when you have a child, you have an opportunity to strive to be the best possible version of yourself so that you can be the role model that you want your child to have.

**Greta** (age two months): (sleeping)
**Dean** (Greta's dad): I think you are the most easygoing baby there is.

## Dimensions of temperament

**Activity level:** How active your child is in general. Is your child high energy, low energy, or somewhere in the middle?

**Adaptability:** How well and how quickly your child adapts or adjusts to new people, new situations, or new environments. Does your child adapt quickly and easily or take a long time to adjust?

**Approach-withdrawal:** How your child typically approaches new situations. Is your child slow to warm up when introduced to new situations, or ready to eagerly dive in?

**Attention span:** How long your child tends to focus or pay attention to an object, person, or activity. Is your child's attention span longer or shorter than other children's? Are there certain activities that capture their attention better than others?

**Distractibility:** How easily your child can be distracted or redirected from one thing to another. Does your child lose focus when there is a distraction? When they do lose focus, how well are they able to turn back to what they were doing?

**Intensity of reaction:** How strongly your child reacts to both positive and negative situations. Does your child experience and show emotions in a big or small way?

**Quality of mood:** Your child's overall mood or disposition. Does your child tend to be generally in a good mood, upbeat, and optimistic, or negative and pessimistic?

**Rhythmicity:** How regular or unpredictable your child's natural cycles for eating, sleeping, or other natural functions tend to be. Does your child slide easily into a routine, or is it challenging to find a routine that works?

**Sensitivity or responsiveness:** How sensitive your child is to stimuli around them. Is your child easily bothered by lights, noise, or other stimuli?

- What have you noticed about your child's temperament?
- How is your child's temperament similar to and different from your own?
- How is your child's temperament similar to and different from other family members?
- Are there aspects of your child's temperament that you find challenging?
- Are there aspects of your child's temperament that you admire?

**Greta:** (continues sleeping)

**Dean:** Your brother was definitely not like you. Even the smallest sounds woke him up, but you sleep through anything!

**Brian** (Greta's dad): Let's hope you keep on being a good sleeper. One light sleeper in the family is tough enough, but we still love your brother for who he is, just like we love you.

*What's happening in this conversation:* As Greta sleeps, her dads talk about one of the easy aspects of her temperament: the fact that she is not very sensitive to noise and can sleep through anything. In contrast, her brother was very sensitive and woke up at the slightest sounds. Even though this was a challenging aspect of her brother's temperament, Dean and Brian share with Greta that they love both their children for who they are. Having conversations like this one, even before children are able to understand the words they are hearing, sets up a positive pattern of communication that parents like Dean and Brian can carry on throughout their children's childhood.

**Carina** (age three): I don't want to.

**Ibrahim** (Carina's and Rachael's dad): Why don't you go out and give it a try? You've never been to dance class before, so you might really like it. Look at your sister. She ran right out there and is already dancing.

**Carina:** I don't want to.

**Ibrahim:** How about we sit here together and just watch to see what it's like? Maybe that will help you feel more comfortable.

**Carina:** Okay.

**Ibrahim:** When I was about your age, I tried tap dancing for the first time. I sat on the side for the first class with my mom and watched because I was scared.

**Carina:** You were?

**Ibrahim:** Yes I was. But after I watched for a while, it didn't seem so scary anymore because I knew what it was like. And you know what?

**Carina:** What?

**Ibrahim:** Even though I was scared, I had fun and I'm glad I did it.

**Carina:** I just want to watch.

**Ibrahim:** That's okay. We'll stay here and watch together for a while.

*What's happening in this conversation:* Based on their temperaments, children have different comfort levels in new situations. Some children are eager and ready to try anything that comes their way. Other children, like Carina, are slow to warm up and approach new situations with caution. In this conversation, Ibrahim recognizes that his daughter, Carina, needs time to warm up to her new dance class before she will feel comfortable joining the group. In contrast, her sister, Rachael, was ready to join the class immediately. For Rachael, Ibrahim only needed to wave and smile as she ran to join in. For Carina, he gave her the time and space she needed to feel comfortable until she was ready.

**Shane** (Sally's dad): Did you know that you were a really good sleeper when you were a baby? Even if there was loud music playing or people talking, you slept right through it. One time you even slept through the fire alarm!

**Sally** (age four): (laughs)

**Shane:** You don't do that anymore, though. Now, when I think you're asleep and tiptoe out of the room, you always wake up!

**Sally:** (laughs) What else did I do when I was little?

**Shane:** Let's see. You liked to snuggle and cuddle together when you woke up. You still do that now, too. You had a special blanket that you wanted to bring with you everywhere.

**Sally:** I love my blankie.

**Shane:** I know you do, but you don't get upset anymore if we leave it at home like you did when you were two. Now that you're four, you sometimes leave blankie here at home, and that's okay. I wonder what you will be like when you turn five.

*What's happening in this conversation:* Shane shares with his daughter that she is a special person and that who she is has grown and changed over time. By talking with Sally objectively about how she has changed and wondering how she will change in the future, Shane is communicating that it is okay for Sally to be her own person and that he will love her not only for who she is, but for who she will become.

**Marguerite** (Katrine's and Phillipe's mom): Uh-oh. It looks like it's raining outside. We're going to have to wait to go to the park.

**Katrine** (age four): I want to go to the park now!

**Phillipe** (age seven)**:** It's no big deal. We'll just go later. I'm going to read my book.

**Katrine:** (cries) It's not fair. I want to go to the park.

**Phillipe:** Don't be a baby!

**Marguerite:** Phillipe, how do you think it makes your sister feel when you say that?

**Phillipe:** Sorry.

**Marguerite:** It's okay to feel upset, Katrine. It's hard when things don't work out the way you want them to. (hugs Katrine) Maybe we could all think about something else we could do instead of going to the park that would be fun.

**Katrine:** Can we build a fort?

**Marguerite:** Sure.

*What's happening in this conversation:* Marguerite's two children, Katrine and Phillipe, have very different temperaments in many ways. From the time he was very young, Phillipe had been easily adaptable. He was rarely upset by a change in routine or a change in plans, and Marguerite did not have to do much to keep him content. Katrine, on the other hand, had always been highly reactive and got upset easily when a plan changed. Marguerite found that she didn't have to do much for Phillipe when plans changed, but that Katrine needed lots of support. Marguerite always took time to acknowledge Katrine's feelings and let her know that those feelings were okay. She also made suggestions for strategies Katrine could use to manage her feelings, and found that Katrine was starting to use these strategies on her own. As a result, Marguerite noticed that Katrine was spending less time feeling upset in response to change as she got older.

**Abdul** (age five)**:** Tell me a story about when you were little.

**Nasir** (Abdul's dad)**:** Hmm . . . let's see if I can think of a story you haven't heard before. Did I ever tell you about the time that I ran away from home?

**Abdul:** You ran away from home?

**Nasir:** Yes. I was so mad because my mom—your grandma—would not let me eat another cookie. I got really upset and then ran down the sidewalk and sat on the curb until my father came and brought me home.

**Abdul:** I would never run away.

**Nasir:** I know. You're much more cautious than I was when I was growing up. I got upset very easily when I was young so I had to learn to calm down, but you already are very calm most of the time. There are some ways that you and I are different and some ways that we are alike.

**Abdul:** Like what?

**Nasir:** I know we both like cookies.

**Abdul:** Yummy cookies! Can I have one now?

*What's happening in this conversation:* In this conversation, Nasir spends time bonding with his son by sharing about a time when he was young. Through his story, Nasir shares the message that he and his son, Abdul, are different in some ways, similar in others, and that this is okay.

**Genevieve** (Rose's mom): How was school today?

**Rose** (age six): Good.

**Genevieve:** Did anything interesting happen?

**Rose:** Sort of.

**Genevieve:** What was it?

**Rose:** Wade called me a name and I told him that he had to apologize.

**Genevieve:** You did? What did he say?

**Rose:** He said, "Sorry." I told him it wasn't okay and he should never do it again.

**Genevieve:** Wow. I am really impressed that you stood up for yourself like that. When I was your age, I never would have said something like that.

**Rose:** How come?

**Genevieve:** I was very quiet when I was growing up. If someone said something that hurt my feelings, I held it inside. I wasn't comfortable talking about it like you are.

**Rose:** You're not quiet now.

**Genevieve:** Not when I'm around you. I'm quiet around other people though. As I've gotten older, I've learned how to share my feelings better, and now I'm even learning from you how to be brave and speak up for myself!

*What's happening in this conversation:* In this conversation, Rose shares with her mom about an incident that happened at school. When another child called her a name, she asked for an apology. Genevieve was impressed with her daughter's ability to stand up for herself and noted that aspects of her daughter's temperament that were challenging when she was younger were turning into an asset for her now on the playground. She also pointed out ways that their personalities are different from one another in a matter-of-fact way.

＊　＊　＊

Approaching your child's temperament in a nonjudgmental and compassionate way communicates to your child that you love them for who they are. Doing so sends the message that it is okay to be your own person and acknowledges that temperament is part of who we are, rather than something to fight against. Parents can help children learn to understand their temperament by describing what they notice:

> "You seem to be comfortable talking to anyone!"
> "I notice that sometimes it takes a while for you to feel comfortable in a new place."
> "You have very strong feelings when you get upset, and that's okay."

Parents can also talk with children about how their temperament is similar to and different from that of other members of the family.

*"When you wake up, you are always ready to play right away, but your brother needs quiet time in the mornings before he's ready."*

As we get to know our children's temperament, we might find that they remind us of other family members—grandma, grandpa, their older sibling, your older sibling, or maybe even yourself. We often compare our children with the people they remind us of most and this can be a valuable part of strengthening family bonds:

> "You look just like grandpa when you make that face!"
> "Your aunt loved to sing just like you!"
> "I can't believe how much you remind me of your big sister when she was your age."

Positive comparisons like these can help children feel connected with their immediate and extended family and can lead to other great conversations:

*"What else did sissy do when she was my age?"* When children's behaviors challenge us, however, it can be tempting to make negative comparisons.

"You are just like your grandma—she never could control her temper either."

"I hate it when you act like your dad. He did this all the time."

These types of comparisons can send the message to a child that, *"This is how you are and there's nothing to be done about it."* A child may be left feeling that there is something wrong with them. Instead, show your child that you value their individuality. Rather than implying that there are aspects of their personality that need to be changed (e.g., *"I hope you grow out of this phase!"*), focus on skills your child can develop to help them use each aspect of their temperament to their advantage (e.g., *"You have really strong feelings sometimes, and that's okay. It just means that you might have to practice more than other people to calm down when you get upset. I'm really proud of you when you do stay calm, and you use your feelings and your words to stand up for yourself when something is not fair."*). As a parent, you cannot change your child's temperament, but you can help your child appreciate their temperament and learn skills to manage aspects of their temperament that might be challenging at times.

### Race

Race is an important part of an individual's personal and family identity. Conversations with young children about race often begin by talking about physical differences, such as skin color, because these are the characteristics that children notice most easily. These examples focus on how we begin to talk about race, regarding both skin color and physical appearance as well as racial identity, how race defines the way we see ourselves, and how others might view or treat us.

**Audrey** (age three): Mama have blue eyes.
**Kathy** (Audrey's mom): That's right. Mama has blue eyes. What color eyes do you have?
**Audrey:** I dunno.
**Kathy:** Let's look in the mirror.
**Audrey:** Brown!
**Kathy:** Yes. You have brown eyes. What about your sister?

**Audrey:** Brown!

**Kathy:** You both do. Do you know what other eye colors people can have?

**Audrey:** Green.

**Kathy:** Yes. Green. What else?

**Audrey:** Purple?

**Kathy:** (laughs) No, not purple. But they can have gray or green eyes. What about hair? What color hair do you have?

**Audrey:** Brown. Mama's hair is red.

**Kathy:** Mine is red. Actually, mine is starting to turn gray, but I dye it so it still looks red. What other hair colors have you seen?

**Audrey:** White. Yellow hair too!

**Kathy:** We usually call yellow hair blond hair. What other parts of a person can be different colors?

**Audrey:** I dunno.

**Kathy:** What about skin? Have you seen different skin colors?

**Audrey:** Audrey's skin is pink.

**Kathy:** Yes, your skin is sort of pink.

**Audrey:** Charles's skin is brown.

**Kathy:** Yes, your brother's skin is light brown. Remember my friend, Mia? Her skin is a really dark brown that looks almost black.

**Audrey:** Daddy too. Daddy's skin brown.

**Kathy:** That's right. Your eye color, hair color, and skin color are part of you and how you are born. I think it's pretty amazing that people's bodies can have so many different looks.

**Audrey:** And purple eyes too!

**Kathy:** No. There are no purple eyes. (laughs)

*What's happening in this conversation:* In this conversation, Cathy shows her daughter that it is okay to talk about the things that make people similar to and different from one another. She starts by talking about parts of the body that most people feel comfortable talking about (e.g., eye color and hair color) and continues the conversation to include parts of the body that might be less common for people to discuss (e.g., skin color). Audrey has not yet been exposed to stigmas associated with talking about skin color. Hearing her mother talk about the qualities that make each person who they are in a nonjudgmental way teachers her to approach these conversations in the same way.

**José** (age six): Mom, did you know there are other brown kids like me?

**Maria** (José's mom): Yes, I did. Didn't you know that?

**José:** No. At my old school, everyone else was white. At my new school, lots of kids are brown too! Even my teacher is brown. I didn't know brown people could be teachers.

**Maria:** How did it make you feel to find that out?

**José:** I don't feel so different anymore.

**Maria:** I didn't know you were feeling that way. It can be hard to feel like you fit in if you look different from everyone else around you. I feel that way sometimes too.

*What's happening in this conversation:* Even though Maria did not realize it, her son José had noticed that he stood out from his classmates because of his skin color. When the family moved to a new neighborhood and a new school, José noticed immediately that he no longer stood out in the same way because there were now other children who looked like him. He also

---

Vera came home from kindergarten and used a black permanent marker to draw a picture of herself and her friend, Marcus, who was biracial. She drew an outline of herself with the black marker. The white from the paper became the color of her skin. She used the black marker to color in Marcus' skin so that in contrast, he was completely black. The speech bubbles coming out of their mouths said, "I love you," and "I love you too." The only color she had at hand was a black marker, so she and Marcus were drawn in stark contrast as black and white. Although his skin color was closer to hers than to the black of the marker, she used the color she had to make a distinction between the two of them—not a negative distinction in her mind, but a distinction. Because she only had access to a black marker, Vera was forced to make a choice: black or white. So, she put herself and Marcus into these categories. The next day, her mother bought a pack of multiracial skin tone markers and added them to her collection.

- What conversations have you had with your child about similarities and differences between people?

- How well do the toys, books, and art materials that your child has available at home, at school, or in the community (e.g., at playgroups) represent people wih diverse characteristics?

found a new role model in his teacher who showed him that someone who looked like José could be a teacher.

Imagine what life might be like for children who do not feel like they fit in—this might be a child who is in a racial or ethnic minority group, a child who is transgender, a child with a disability, a child struggling with a mental illness, or even a child who looks like everyone else around them, but feels differently on the inside. This child might have difficulty finding role models who look like them and fail to find themselves in the books they read and the images they see in the media, at school, and in the community. Through these types of omissions, a child may receive the message that they are not normal, that there is something wrong with them, or that they are not as valued as others. It isn't just that child's perception of the situation that matters. These same messages are likely being communicated to the people around that child. Others may also view the child as being of lower status or lesser value whether this is a conscious or unconscious belief. These underlying beliefs might impact how they treat that child without them realizing it. Research has shown that this does happen!

For example, in one study, early childhood teachers were shown videos of children in classrooms. Some of the teachers were told they should expect to see challenging behaviors in the video (even though there were no actual challenging behaviors). The results of the study found that teachers who were expecting to see challenging behaviors spent more time watching children in the video who were black/African-American, and especially boys (Gilliam, Maupin, Reyes, Accavitti, & Shic, 2016). Likely without knowing it or meaning to, these teachers demonstrated **implicit bias**. Implicit bias refers to unconscious stereotypes or attitudes that affect our thoughts and actions. What is troubling is that numerous studies have shown that the expectations teachers (or others) have can shape the way they treat children, making it all the more important that we ensure our young children see positive role models of individuals who look like themselves as well as individuals from diverse backgrounds.

**Shana** (age five): My mom's here.
**Missy** (age five): That's not your mom.
**Shana:** Yes it is.
**Missy:** But she's white and you're black so she can't be your mom.

**Shana:** Missy says you can't be my mom because you're white and I'm black.

**Janée** (Shana's mom)**:** We do have different skin colors, don't we? Shana's dad has dark brown skin and I have white skin. When we had Shana, she was born with beautiful brown skin.

**Missy:** I didn't know a white mom could have a brown baby.

**Janée:** They sure can. Some families have many different skin colors. Missy, your skin is a beautiful light brown color, too. What color skin do your parents have?

**Missy:** We're black.

**Janée:** Both my parents had white skin. It's pretty cool that there are so many different skin colors in the world, and even in our own family!

*What's happening in this conversation:* In this conversation, Janée addresses a comment from her daughter's friend, Missy, about the different skin colors within their family. This comment could have been upsetting for Shana to hear, particularly if she hears things like this often—that her mom can't be or shouldn't be her mom. Janée responded to Missy's comment in a matter-of-fact way, using the moment as a teaching opportunity for both Shana and Missy. She shared with Missy that families can include people from different races. She also showed her daughter, Shana, one way to respond to comments like this if and when they come up in the future. Often, it falls on individuals who are in the minority group or who stand out as different in some way to educate others about themselves or their family. If all children and parents had these types of conversations, this responsibility could be shared.

**Bruce** (age four)**:** Walter's eyes are weird. They are squinty like this. (pulls back corners of his eyes)

**Lori** (Bruce's mom)**:** Walter's family is from South Korea. Many people who are Asian have eyes that are the same shape as Walter's.

**Bruce:** Like this? (pulls back corners of his eyes again)

**Lori:** Yes, kind of like that, except that's what Walter's eyes have looked like since he was born. You're using your hands to pull your eyelids back. I know you're just doing that to see what it's like to have eyes that look like Walter's, but if Walter saw you doing that, he might think you were making fun of him. That could hurt his feelings.

**Bruce:** I wasn't trying to hurt his feelings.

**Lori:** I know you weren't. And it's okay to ask about things that you're curious about. Do you remember when you first asked me about skin color?

**Bruce:** No.

**Lori:** You were about two years old and saw someone with black skin for the first time. You thought the man's skin was painted and that's why it was black.

**Bruce:** What did you say?

**Lori:** I told you that people are born with different skin colors and that all skin colors are beautiful. The same is true about having different hair colors or eye colors or eye shapes.

*What's happening in this conversation:* Bruce shares with his mom that Walter's eye shape is different from his own, calling it "weird." His mom, Lori, helps him understand that the shape of Walter's eyes is common among people from some Asian countries, and that this characteristic is part of who Walter is and has been since birth. By responding to Bruce's comment in a nonjudgmental way, she doesn't make Bruce feel badly about his question. She wants to make sure that he feels comfortable asking her questions like this in the future.

**Darwin** (Janelle's dad): Do you know this is Black History Month?

**Janelle** (age seven): Yes. We talked about it at school.

**Darwin:** You did? What did you talk about?

**Janelle:** Rosa Parks and Martin King Luther.

**Darwin:** You mean Martin Luther King, Junior?

**Janelle:** Yeah.

**Darwin:** Do you know why Black History Month is important?

**Janelle:** To celebrate black people?

**Darwin:** Yes, that's part of it. Our country has treated people who are black very poorly for much of our nation's history. Black History Month is a chance to learn about and recognize all the important accomplishments black Americans have been a part of. There's also a National Hispanic Heritage Month to celebrate people who are Latino and Hispanic, and an Asian Pacific American Heritage Month, and others too!

**Janelle:** If there's a Black History Month, is there a White History Month too?

**Darwin:** Most of the history that you learn in school is about people who are white. That's why we need to make a special effort to celebrate minority groups who haven't been recognized as often or whose history has been hidden away.

*What's happening in this conversation:* Having conversations about the role that race plays in our society is important for families of all racial backgrounds. Recognizing events that reflect your own racial heritage as well as those that recognize the racial heritage of others can teach children that people of all races should be recognized and valued equally.

**Caden** (age five): Grandma?

**Siobhan** (Caden's grandma): Yes?

**Caden:** Dylan said I look like a slave. What's a slave?

**Siobhan:** What's a slave? He shouldn't have said that. That makes me so upset.

**Caden:** Why, grandma?

**Siobhan:** Well, a slave is a person who is owned by another person. They don't have control over their lives or what they can do, and many slaves were treated very badly. There was a time when our country had slaves, and many of those slaves had black skin.

**Caden:** Just like me.

**Siobhan:** Yes, just like you, but you are not a slave.

**Caden:** Why were black people slaves?

**Siobhan:** One of the reasons was that people who were black were not valued the same way as people who were white, but we know all people have equal value.

**Caden:** We're equal now.

**Siobhan:** I hope so. It's not legal to have slaves anymore in this country, but sometimes people do treat other people differently even now because of their race, the color of their skin, how they talk, or what they look like. Everyone should be treated equally, but we have a long way to go.

*What's happening in this conversation:* In this conversation, Siobhan is shocked to hear that her grandson, Caden, was told by a neighbor that he looked like a slave. She shares with Caden the definition of what it means to be a slave and that even now people are treated differently because of their race or the color of their skin. She knew Dylan's family well. Dylan and Caden were good friends, and she realized this comment was probably just an observation that wasn't intended to be an insult. In follow-up conversations, she might help Caden learn more about the history of his race, both accomplishments to be proud of as well as challenges faced in the past and those that are ongoing.

For some families, race is a constant and consistent presence in their everyday lives. For other families, it isn't. In general, families who identify as white in the United States spend less time talking about race with their children than families of other races (Hughes et al., 2006). This may be because race doesn't have the same negative impact on the majority of white families as it does for others (although this may not be the case in racially diverse communities or communities where white families are the minority). Families of color are more likely to talk about how their race impacts their lives than families who are white, likely because the impact can be profound. These conversations may include preparing children for bias or prejudice they might face based on how they look. Beyond physically observable differences, race is a very complex topic. Race is not only associated with skin color, but also with values and culture, opportunity or lack of opportunity, historical and modern-day oppression, prejudice and discrimination, and much more. Addressing each of these aspects of race requires building a foundation for having open and honest conversations that foster a child's genuine interest in learning about their own family history and the experiences of others who are like and different from themselves.

Having conversations with all children about race (regardless of their racial heritage) stands in contrast to taking a "color-blind" approach. At face value, sharing with children that race "does not matter" or that we should ignore race and treat all people fairly and equally regardless of the color of their skin sounds like a good idea. The latter part—treating all people fairly and equally—is a message that we want our children to hear and live by. The first part of the message—"race does not matter"—is more problematic. The truth is, race *does* matter in our current society. Children and adults are treated differently in many situations because of the color of their skin and for other reasons as well. Rather than teaching children that race does not matter, we can shift the message to let children know that race *should not* matter, but that it does. Teaching children how to be comfortable talking about race (rather than ignoring the issue of race) can help children become more aware of the role that race plays in our society and set them up with skills they need to actively tackle issues of bias and prejudice.

As you talk about race together, avoid using language that favors one skin color over another. In an attempt to help a child build compassion, it might seem helpful to say things like, "You're really lucky to be born with white skin." In our society, people with white or lighter skin tones often do have an easier time than individuals born with darker skin tones. Without meaning to, however, this message might be interpreted by a child to mean that having white skin is better than having dark skin. Communicate to your child that all skin colors are beautiful and should be valued, but also talk with them about the fact that sometimes people treat one another differently because of the color of their skin and that this is not right. Teaching children about the fact that biases exist can help them become more aware of and prevent discrimination when they see it occur.

### Sex and gender

Is it a girl or a boy? When a new child is born, we have a surefire way to tell. A child born with a vagina is a girl, and a child born with a penis is a boy. We expect girls to act one way and boys to act another—pretty straightforward. Or is it? Our society's understanding of **sex** and **gender** is continually evolving. By definition, sex relates to a child's reproductive anatomy—the body parts they are born with. Gender refers to social roles related to sex—the way individuals express themselves or the way they identify themselves. In most families, the body parts children are born with match how they feel about who they are. There are many different ways that children and adults express themselves and their gender identity. There may be some ways that children follow traditional gender roles and some ways that they do not (e.g., a girl who loves to wear dresses and also loves to play in the mud; a boy who is comfortable talking about his feelings, enjoys playing dolls with his sisters, and loves to wrestle with his brother). Our society is becoming increasingly accepting of children and adults who do not conform to traditional gender roles, but life still tends to be easier for children who fit them most closely.

There are some children who find that they do not fit within society's ideas of what sex means. For example, some children are born with the body parts of one sex, but identify more with the other (e.g., children who are transgender). In relatively rare cases, some children are born with a combination of body parts or body parts that do not fit the description of either sex (e.g., children who are intersex). And, there are children who do not feel that they fit either sex or gender, regardless of their body parts (e.g., children who are gender fluid or nonbinary). This is not the same thing as "going through a phase." Instead, it's a recognition that how you feel and how you identify yourself may or may not match how you look or what others expect from you.

Even from young ages, children notice and are interested in talking about what makes them similar to and different from those around them. Sex and gender are important parts of these conversations. Giving children the space to grow into their own identity (whether your child is a boy, a girl, or neither/ nonbinary) and helping them understand how their identity relates to their body as well as society's expectations for them is an extension of the more traditional *"boys have a penis and girls have a vagina"* conversation.

**Joanne** (James's mom): Do you want to help me give your baby sister a bath?

**James** (age two): Yes!

**Joanne:** Okay, I have the water ready. Let's take her clothes off. Use your gentle hands.

**James:** Where's baby penis?

**Joanne:** She doesn't have a penis. Girls have a vagina.

**James:** Gina?

**Joanne:** That's right, vagina. Can you say vagina?

**James:** Gina!

**Joanne:** Milly has a vagina just like mom, and you have a penis just like daddy.

**James:** My penis is a baby one. Daddy's penis is a big one.

**Joanne:** Your penis will get bigger too, as your body gets bigger. That's part of growing up.

*What's happening in this conversation:* Many children are curious about their bodies and interested in knowing what makes them who they are, as well as how they compare with others. Talking with children about their bodies in matter-of-fact ways and using the names of body parts teaches them to be comfortable having conversations about their bodies. It's common for young children to show interest in how their bodies compare with others (e.g., *"Daddy has a really big penis"* or *"Mommy's vagina has hair on it"*) as well as to wonder what it would be like to have the body parts of the opposite sex (e.g., *"Can I grow a penis too?"*).

For children, each of these statements and questions is a normal part of learning about who they are and how their body compares with others.

**Paloma** (age five): I like that book. I want to be a firefighter when I grow up, too.

**Lucinda** (Paloma's mom): That would be wonderful. Firefighters do a lot to help people. They have to be very strong, so you'll have to exercise and get really strong.

**Paloma:** I am strong! Feel my muscles!

**Lucinda:** Wow! You are strong. I'm glad your book shows both boy and girl firefighters. When I was young, I wanted to be an astronaut, but my books only showed boy astronauts, so I didn't think girls could do it.

**Paloma:** How come they didn't show girl astronauts?

**Lucinda:** It was a different time then. Many people thought that there were some jobs that were only for boys, and that was one of them.

**Paloma:** No fair! Girls can be astronauts too!

**Lucinda:** Yes they can, and firefighters too.

**Paloma:** Like me!

**Lucinda:** Yes, like you.

*What's happening in this conversation:* When Paloma announces to her mom that she wants to be a firefighter, her mom encourages her. In contrast to her own upbringing, during which she was told she could not be an astronaut, Paloma wants Lucinda to grow up believing she can pursue any career she wants. She might follow this conversation with others to talk about the fact that many people still believe that there are some things boys/men should do or should not do, some things girls/women should do or should not do, and some things people who identify as transgender or nonbinary should or should not do. Understanding that bias exists may help Paloma prepare for challenges she may face if she pursues certain career choices. For example, Paloma and Lucinda might talk about the fact that girls can grow up to be firefighters, but there are still many more male firefighters than female firefighters. Even if it is not fair, she might have to work harder than her male colleagues to show that she can do the job because others might not have seen role models of female firefighters before.

**Malcolm** (age three): Can I hold a baby?

**Carley** (age four): The babies are only for girls.

**Malcolm:** Boys can have babies too!

**Carley:** No they can't. Only mommies take care of babies. Mommies are girls.

**Malcolm:** Miss Helen, Carley won't let me play with the babies!

**Helen** (Malcolm's and Carley's preschool teacher): Hmm. It looks like there are four babies and two children, so there are plenty for everyone. Carley, can you offer one of the babies to Malcolm?

**Carley:** Babies are only for girls.

**Helen:** Actually, girls and boys can both take care of babies. Do you remember the book we read today? Remember it was about a daddy who took care of his baby? Would you like to choose a baby to give Malcolm, or would you like me to?

**Carley:** Here. (thrusts baby toward Malcolm)

**Helen:** Maybe you could show Malcolm the way you like to hold your baby.

**Carley:** Like this. (cradles baby in her arms)

**Helen:** That's the same way I see your mom holding your baby sister. Malcolm, can you show Carley how you like to hold your baby? I like the way you are both being so gentle and rocking your babies.

*What's happening in this conversation:* When children say things that promote gender stereotypes, adults can play an important role in letting them know that sex or gender should not be used to determine what others can do or who they can be. Because she is a single parent, Carley's mom is the at-home role model Carley has of a person who takes care of babies. Miss Helen shares with Carley and Malcolm that boys can take care of babies just like girls. In doing so, she is also providing an opportunity for Malcolm to express himself and engage in the kind of play he likes in a supportive environment.

**Arjun** (age seven): Cornelius said there was a girl in his class named Lucy, but now she is a boy named Lucas. Cornelius said he is transgen-something.

**Priya:** Do you mean transgender?

**Arjun:** Yeah. That's it.

**Priya:** Do you know what transgender means?

**Arjun:** I forget.

**Priya:** Well, some children realize that how they feel on the inside doesn't match how they look on the outside. When those feelings are really strong and don't go away, it might mean that they are transgender.

**Arjun:** I look like a boy and I feel like a boy.

**Priya:** That's true. How you feel inside has always matched your body, but it doesn't sound like Lucas feels that way. Being transgender is a different kind of feeling than just wanting to put on dresses for fun, like you used to do with your sisters. Lucas might be going through a transition to change how he looks on the outside to match how he feels on the inside.

**Arjun:** That's weird.

**Priya:** It might just seem weird because this is the first time you have heard of someone who is transgender, but think about how Lucas feels. How do you think it feels for him?

**Arjun:** Maybe confusing or maybe left out because people think he's weird?

**Priya:** I bet that's true. Are there things you or your brother could do to help Lucas feel okay being who he is?

**Arjun:** Maybe we could invite him for a play date sometime.

**Priya:** I think that's a great idea. That would help him feel included and you both could get to know him a little better. You might not think he's so weird then.

**Arjun:** How about tomorrow?

**Priya:** We'll have to ask his parents. I'll call his mom.

Why this conversation is important: When Arjun tells his mom that one of his brother's classmates is transgender, Priya encourages Arjun to consider how Lucas might be feeling and to think about what he can do to be supportive. Priya also realized that she had never had a conversation before with Arjun about what it means to be transgender. Even though her own awareness of sex and gender identities had evolved, she had not thought to talk about this topic with her son before this conversation.

Having conversations with your child about sex and gender is important for multiple reasons. One reason to have these conversations is to help children feel comfortable being who they are and expressing themselves in the way they feel most comfortable. Supporting your child's identity development involves helping your child understand that how they feel is okay—whether they are in the majority of children whose sex and gender match or in the minority of children whose identities do not align with traditional definitions of sex or gender. Even within these groups, there are tremendous differences in how children and adults choose to express themselves. Part of these conversations should include exposing your child to a range of different role models, including individuals who conform to traditional gender roles and norms and those who do not. If children grow up seeing many different role models, they will be better able to find role models with whom they identify.

This may be a conversation that feels very comfortable to you or it may not be. It's important to realize that having a conversation with your child about sex and gender will not lead your child to *choose* to become a boy or a girl if that's not who they are. Instead, conversations like these are intended to encourage children to feel supported simply being who they are. There are choices that children and adults can make related to their preferences and likes and dislikes, including how they dress or activities they engage in, but biology also plays a critical role in shaping your child's identity, and this is something you cannot change through conversations or in any other way. Help your child feel safe being who they are meant to be, and encourage them to be a part of creating a society where others can feel the same.

In addition to helping your child feel comfortable with their own identity, having this conversation can help children learn about the experiences that others have with finding acceptance. Some children may not live in homes where parents openly discuss gender identity. Many children who fall outside of traditional gender norms may struggle to find acceptance inside or outside their homes. Alarmingly, individuals who identify as transgender experience depression at much higher rates than the general population. One study of transgender individuals found that 51 percent of women and 48 percent of men in the study experienced depression (Budge, Adelson, & Howard, 2013). In another study, 56 percent of the participating transgender individuals reported having suicidal ideation in the past year, 45 percent had made a suicide attempt, and 79 percent had seriously considered suicide in the past (Testa et al., 2017). These statistics are concerning, to say the least, and suggest that the challenges children and adults have who identify as transgender can be significant.

One of the factors shown to make the most difference in children's identity development is social support (Wright & Perry, 2006). No matter what your child's sex or gender identity, understanding that they are not alone and that how they feel is normal and okay will help them feel comfortable with who they are. In addition, having this conversation with your child can help provide them with the language and skills they need to offer the support and understanding that may be critical for others.

### Your body

As children gain exposure to others, they pay more attention to the physical attributes that make them similar to and different from one another, including their bodies; skin color; hair color, length, and texture; eye color and shape; height and weight; mobility; features that make them unique (e.g., moles, birthmarks, scars); and other qualities. Aspects of their bodies that are different from others can be sources of pride, embarrassment, or even shame for a child. Early childhood is an opportune time to shape the way children view their own and others' bodies and to help children develop a positive body image. Body image refers to how we feel about our bodies, including size, weight, and the way we move. Children and youth with a positive body image have higher self-esteem, whereas children with a negative body image are at risk for lower self-esteem, anxiety, and isolation (Grogan, 2016). Children who are considered to be overweight or obese, or children who have visible physical differences or disabilities are especially at risk for feeling badly about how their bodies look or move. Talking with children about their bodies and others' in nonjudgmental and matter-of-fact ways may help children recognize that their bodies are part of who they are. Helping children understand that there is no ideal or perfect body, and focusing on what we do to keep our bodies healthy (rather than focusing on the size or shape of our bodies) can help children learn to value their own bodies as well as those of others.

> **Claudia** (Arnold's aunt): You have one, two, three, four, five, six, seven, eight, nine, ten little toes! Your toes are so little, just like your little fingers.
>
> **Arnold** (age four months): (babbles)
>
> **Claudia:** You have very long legs. I wonder if you will be as tall as your dad's family, or maybe you'll be short like your mom and me.
>
> **Arnold:** (babbles)
>
> **Claudia:** You are growing up so quickly. You already look bigger today than yesterday. I can't wait to see how you grow and change next!

*What's happening in this conversation:* During infancy, children's bodies grow and change at a rapid rate. The way we talk about their bodies and the changes we see lets children know that we love them for who they are no matter how they look now and in the future. Even simple conversations, like this one between Claudia and her nephew, can model to children how to view their bodies positively and without judgment.

**Sasha** (Mischa's mom): I like playing dolls with you, but there's something I don't like about these dolls.

**Mischa** (age four): What?

**Sasha:** They don't look the same as real people's bodies. Have you ever noticed that? Do you see any ways these dolls' bodies are different from our bodies?

**Mischa:** They have really huge heads.

**Sasha:** Yes! REALLY huge heads. Anything else that's different?

**Mischa:** Teeny tiny feet?

**Sasha:** I hadn't noticed that, but you're right. It would be hard to balance on those little feet.

**Mischa:** They also have really huge eyes and mouths, but tiny noses.

**Sasha:** You're noticing more things than I did.

**Mischa:** I still like them.

**Sasha:** It's okay to like them, it's just important to know that that's not what a real human body looks like or is meant to look like.

**Mischa:** I know that. Can we get back to playing?

**Sasha:** Of course.

*What's happening in this conversation:* Children are exposed to messages related to body image in many different ways, including through the media (e.g., magazine covers, television) as well as through the toys that they play with. Many toys depict human bodies with unusual or unrealistic proportions, which can contribute to children developing expectations that are not realistic for what their own bodies should look like, potentially contributing to body image dissatisfaction. Body image dissatisfaction starts to emerge in early elementary school for children of all races and genders (Heron, Smyth, Akano, & Wonderlich, 2013). Even through first grade, studies show that children don't think there are noticeable differences between their own body and what they imagine it means to have an ideal body. By second grade, however, children do report noticeable differences between their own bodies and the ideal. Body image is often lower for children who are considered to be obese, as well as for children who have visible chronic illness, such as scoliosis or spina bifida (Puhl & Latner, 2007). It's important to note that feeling dissatisfied with their body does not help motivate children or adults to improve healthy behaviors. On the contrary, having a poor body image is actually linked to behaviors that can put children and youth at risk for weight gain and poor health (e.g., ineffective dieting, binge eating) (Neumark-Sztainer et al, 2006). Conversations that help children appreciate the many different shapes and sizes bodies can be while also focusing on eating well, engaging in physical activities, and healthy sleep habits are more likely to lead to positive health behaviors.

Help your child learn to notice the ways bodies are portrayed, as well as what is realistic and what isn't, as Sasha did with her son Mischa. You might have similar conversations at other times, such as while standing in line at the grocery store. (*"You know what I like about that magazine? It shows people with many different types of bodies. Most magazines only show people who are very tall and thin."*)

**Matilda** (age five): Why do I have brown on my face?

**Staci** (Matilda's mom): That's a birthmark. You've had it ever since you were very young.

**Matilda:** I don't like it. I want to wash it off.

**Staci:** It can't wash off. It's part of you.

**Matilda:** Nobody else has one.

**Staci:** Actually, lots of people have birthmarks. Look, I have one here on my arm and one on the back of my neck, too.

**Matilda:** I have some brown spots on my arm just like you.

**Staci:** Those are moles. Look, we have a matching mole right here in the same spot!

**Matilda:** But you don't have any on your face like me.

**Staci:** No, but lots of people do. We could look up on the Internet later and see if we can find famous people who have moles or birthmarks on their faces.

**Matilda:** Okay.

**Staci:** You know why I like your birthmark?

**Matilda:** Why?

**Staci:** Because it's part of what makes you who you are! Every part of you is special. No one else is exactly like you. And it's my favorite spot to give you a kiss!

**Matilda:** Kiss me there again! Again! (giggles)

*What's happening in this conversation:* Body image isn't always about body size and type. From the shape of our face, to the size of our nose, to moles and birthmarks, there are many different aspects of our bodies that make us unique. Talking about every aspect of your child's body objectively by describing what you see and modeling comfort with your own body, as Staci does in her conversation with Matilda, can help children learn to view themselves through that same lens.

**Alison** (Freda's mom)**:** (looking in the mirror) Hmm . . .

**Freda** (age five)**:** What, mama?

**Alison:** Oh, I was just noticing that I seem to have gained some weight so I don't fit into my swimsuit very well anymore.

**Freda:** I think you look pretty. You're the prettiest mom in the whole world!

**Alison:** Thank you, honey.

**Freda:** I like your big tummy. It's soft and squishy!

**Alison:** (laughs) I'm glad you like it. I like it too, but I would like to do more things to be a little healthier.

**Freda:** How come?

**Alison:** I eat a lot of sugar and treats, and that's probably not very good for me. I need to eat more healthy foods. I don't exercise as much as I should, either.

**Freda:** I exercise on the playground every day! And I eat healthy food.

**Alison:** You do! You eat really healthy food and get lots of exercise. Maybe you could help me remember to do that, too. Maybe we could find some exercises to do together. Could help me with that?

**Freda:** Sure! I'm a good helper. I could show you how we exercise at school.

**Alison:** I would love that.

*What's happening in this conversation:* As parents, we serve as role models in the way we talk about ourselves and the way we talk about others. Even though Alison didn't always feel good about what she saw when she looked in the mirror, she thought carefully about the words she chose when talking about her body with her daughter, Freda. Rather than having a negative attitude toward her body, she focused on healthy approaches to improving her health and well-being, asking Freda to help her exercise more often. Studies have found patterns in the way parents and teachers talk with young children about their bodies, showing that both parents and teachers express concern to children about their own weight (McCabe et al., 2007). One study of preschool children found that the primary messages mothers communicated to their daughters about their bodies were related to losing weight. In contrast, the messages they communicated to their sons focused on increasing their muscles (McCabe et al., 2007). In the study, both girls and boys expressed concern about how they looked, especially related to their hair and clothes, but also related to their weight and muscle tone.

Teaching children to feel confident in themselves and to feel good about their body regardless of their shape or size, is not the same as promoting unhealthy eating or exercise habits. Children can feel good about themselves, but also strive to be more active and to eat more healthfully. If you are concerned about your child's weight or health, rather than focusing on how your child looks, work on developing healthy eating and exercise habits as a family.

By having conversations that normalize different body types, parents can help children recognize that their body is part of who they are. Everyone's body is different and the way bodies look and move should not be used to make judgments about people. Our bodies do not define whether or not we are a good person or a good friend. Help your child appreciate the many different ways that bodies look and move so that they feel comfortable in their own body and help others feel the same.

### Abilities and disabilities

All children (and adults) have strengths and challenges. Some of these strengths and challenges are labeled as special needs, abilities, or disabilities. Some are more pronounced and easier to see than others, and some have a more profound impact than others on a child's or an adult's life. Feeling a sense of belonging and fitting in may be especially hard for children who have visible disabilities, depending not only on their own abilities to make friends, but also on how others approach and respond to them. Helping all children learn to see strengths in themselves and one another can help foster a society in which all children are accepted and valued for who they are.

**Tina** (age 22): Hi! What's your name?

**Naomi** (age four): Naomi.

**Tina:** I'm Tina. That's a pretty dress.

**Naomi:** Thank you.

**Tina:** I'm going to the store all by myself to get a cookie. It's my second time. I have to go straight home when I'm done.

**Doris** (Naomi's mom): That's great, Tina! What kind of cookie are you going to get?

**Tina:** Peanut butter. I love peanut butter, but they didn't have one last time, so I got chocolate chip.

**Naomi:** Chocolate chip is my favorite!

**Tina:** I only get chocolate chip if there is no peanut butter. Bye!

**Naomi:** Bye.

**Doris:** Bye, Tina! Enjoy your cookie!

**Naomi:** Mom?

**Doris:** Yes?

**Naomi:** How come Tina looks like a grown-up, but she talks like a kid?

**Doris:** That's a good question. I think Tina's brain works differently than yours and mine. It takes her longer to learn things than it takes other people, and there are certain things that her brain might never be able to do that yours can do.

**Naomi:** Why is her brain like that?

**Doris:** It might be part of who she has been from when she was born, or she might have had an accident.

**Naomi:** Oh. She always asks me what my name is. She never remembers.

**Doris:** You know one thing I always notice about Tina?

**Naomi:** What?

**Doris:** How kind she is. She's always really nice to everyone she talks to, and I think she really likes children.

**Naomi:** She likes me.

**Doris:** She sure does. And I notice that you are always kind to her too, and that's important. Other kids and grown-ups are not always very nice to Tina. Sometimes they are mean to her or call her names because she is different than they are, and that is never okay.

*What's happening in this conversation:* In this conversation, Doris and Naomi have a conversation with Tina, a woman in their neighborhood. Naomi notices that

Tina asks her what her name is every time they see one another and never seems to remember. She also observes that Tina speaks more like a child than like a grown-up. Although Doris does not know many details about Tina or her life, she does her best to talk with her daughter about Tina in a compassionate and understanding way.

> **Marik** (age five): What's wrong with her?
>
> **Lynn** (Clara's mom): Do you mean why is she in a wheelchair?
>
> **Marik:** Yes.
>
> **Lynn:** Clara was born with cerebral palsy. Have you ever heard of that?
>
> **Marik:** No.
>
> **Lynn:** It's a condition where the part of her brain that helps her muscles move is damaged. It's hard for her to talk, but she really likes to meet other children. Do you want to say hello to her?
>
> **Marik:** Okay.
>
> **Lynn:** Why don't you tell her your name?
>
> **Marik:** I'm Marik.
>
> **Lynn:** Her name is Clara.
>
> **Marik:** Hi Clara.
>
> **Clara** (age eight): (moves her hand)
>
> **Lynn:** That's her way of saying hello. She's learning how to say a few words, but it's harder for her than it is for you.
>
> **Marik:** Want to see the book I checked out?
>
> **Lynn:** Sure, and I bet Clara would like it too. If you hold it right here about this far from her face, it's easier for her to see. Look at that. She's smiling.
>
> **Marik:** I can read it to you. I'm learning to read, but I don't know some of the big words.
>
> **Lynn:** That's okay. I could help you with those. Do you want to read it to Clara?
>
> **Marik:** Sure!
>
> **Lynn:** Some kids are afraid to talk to Clara because she has different abilities than they do, but she loves to make friends, too. I'm really glad you came to say hello.

*What's happening in this conversation:* While at the library, Lynn sees another child, Marik, watching her with her daughter Clara. Clara has cerebral palsy and is not able to initiate interactions on her own, so Lynn helps facilitate these interactions. By inviting Marik to say hello, she also helps him understand more about her daughter's condition and helps him gain comfort and confidence having interactions with children who are different than he is through this positive experience with Clara.

**Arthur** (Jamel's dad): I noticed that there is a girl in your class who has Down syndrome.

**Jamel** (age seven): Yeah, Molly.

**Arthur:** Does your teacher ever talk about what it means to have Down syndrome?

**Jamel:** Yes. She read us a book about Down syndrome, and we take turns being Molly's buddy in class because sometimes she needs extra help.

**Arthur:** I'm really glad to hear that.

**Jamel:** She's really nice. She says funny things sometimes that make other kids laugh, but we don't make fun of her.

**Arthur:** What about on the playground? Are there things you or other kids do to make sure she is included?

**Jamel:** Oh, yeah. Everyone lets her join in. She likes to run around while we play soccer. She can't really follow the rules, but we let her run with us, and we always give her a few turns to kick the ball.

**Arthur:** That's great. Everyone likes to feel included. I think it would be really hard if you were different from your classmates in some way, so I'm glad that you and your class make an effort to help Molly join in.

*What's happening in this conversation:* Arthur asks his son, Jamel, about a classmate named Molly who has Down syndrome. He is pleased to hear that his son's teacher and class make an intentional effort to support and include Molly. If the conversation had gone in another direction (e.g., Jamel shared that he did not know what Down syndrome was or Jamel shared that Molly was often excluded by other children), this could have been an opportunity for Arthur to help Jamel learn more about Down syndrome, consider Molly's feelings, and brainstorm additional ways to help her feel included at school.

**Gregory** (Lena's dad): How was playgroup?

**Lena** (age six): The other kids didn't want to play with me at first. They said only kids with two arms could play.

**Gregory:** What a hurtful thing to say. I'm really sorry that they said that to you.

**Lena:** I told them that kids with one arm were just as good as kids with two arms, and that this is how I was born.

**Marcy** (Lena's mom)**:** You said that? That was a very brave thing to say!

**Lena:** Yes, and then one girl said I could play with her, so I did. And I made a new friend, but I forget her name.

**Marcy:** Wow, Lena. I'm really proud of you for standing up for yourself, and I'm glad you made a new friend.

**Lena:** Me too. She wears glasses and likes to read, just like me.

*What's happening in this conversation:* From the time Lena was born, her parents, Gregory and Marcy, spoke openly with her about the fact that she was born with one arm. They regularly talk about challenges related to having only one arm, and they have learned together new ways that Lena can approach everyday tasks, like putting on her clothes or shoes. They also talk about how other children might react to someone with one arm, and role-play ways to respond if someone asks questions about what it's like to live with one arm or what to do if someone says something hurtful, as the other children did in this situation. These interactions have helped Lena to feel comfortable talking about her disability and to develop advocacy skills to speak up for herself when others do not view her in the same positive light as her parents.

**Klaus** (Jared's dad)**:** Something happened at the restaurant tonight that I wanted to talk to you about.

**Jared** (age six)**:** What, dad?

**Klaus:** Did you see the boy who was waving his hand like this and kept shouting things out loud?

**Jared:** Yeah.

**Klaus:** I think he has autism.

**Jared:** He does. His name's Devon. He goes to my school in Mr. Clark's class. Mr. Clark teaches kids who have disabilities.

**Klaus:** Well, I saw two things happen with other people and his family. One was kind and one was not.

**Jared:** What?

**Klaus:** I heard the family sitting next to them complain to the manager that Devon was bothering them, and they made kind of a mean comment.

**Jared:** What did they say?

**Klaus:** They said he shouldn't be allowed to come to restaurants if he can't control himself.

**Jared:** He can't help it. He does that at school, too.

**Klaus:** I know, but I don't think they realized that how he acts is part of who he is. It might seem strange to people who don't know him, but they weren't being very understanding. You know what the manager said?

**Jared:** What?

**Klaus:** The manager said she was sorry they felt bothered, but that they want all families to be able to come to their restaurant and have a good time. She told the family who complained that they could move to another table if they wanted to, but that she hoped they would be understanding of the other family's feelings. She told them that it was hard for Devon's family to find restaurants where they felt comfortable, but they had been coming to this restaurant every Friday night for five years!

**Jared:** Every Friday?

**Klaus:** Yep! The best part was that the family actually apologized for complaining. I think the manager helped them be more understanding. I bet it would be really hard if you felt like you didn't fit in while in public if you or someone in your family had a disability.

**Jared:** I'm glad I don't have a disability.

**Klaus:** I would love you whether you did or not. You would still be a special part of our family like Devon is to his. That's why we should always be thinking about other people's feelings and what it might be like to be in their shoes.

*What's happening in this conversation:* While out on a father-son dinner date, Klaus and Jared sat near a family with a child named Devon, who had autism. Devon showed behaviors that might have seemed strange or unusual to people who did not know him or who were not familiar with the autism spectrum. In reflecting on what he saw, Klaus wanted to take the opportunity to encourage his son to think about the experience of another family and how it was different from their own. He also pointed out what the restaurant manager said as an example of an accepting attitude and approach. Children are exposed to many

Ellie's son, Ethan, was born with a rare condition. At Ethan's childcare center one day, a group of parents had asked: "So how old IS your son?" The implied message was that he didn't look old enough or big enough to attend his childcare program, especially given that some of their younger children had been turned away. Although this might seem like a potentially innocent question in some contexts, the fact that these parents had never so much as held a conversation with Ellie or made any attempt to get to know Ethan left her feeling deflated. With just a few words, Ethan's value was reduced to his small stature. The other parents did not recognize (or at least did not express recognition of) who this child truly was—a fighter, battling and overcoming serious illness from a young age, and a loving and joyful light in the lives of his family and the community who knew him. These other parents probably didn't have negative intentions, and they probably didn't realize the impact their words had on Ellie in that moment, but this story highlights how important it is to get to know others in our community and to help our children do the same to create a truly compassionate society.

- What could Ellie do to get to know the other parents at her son's school and to help them get to know and appreciate her son for who he is?

- How do you think it would feel as a parent if you were the only advocate your child had?

- What could the parents at Ethan's school do to help Ellie and Ethan feel more welcome?

- What could the teachers and staff at Ethan's school do to foster compassion?

different role models in their communities. Taking time to point out and talk about them, as Klaus did, can help children pay attention to positive examples.

All children have different abilities and strengths, as well as challenges. A significant number of children in the public school system receive special education support. Approximately 6.5 million children (about 13 percent of children enrolled in public school) received support services for disabilities during the 2013–2014 year that impacted their academic performance in some way (National Center for Education Statistics, 2017). Of these children, 35 percent had a learning disability, 21 percent experienced speech or language impairment, 13 percent had health impairments, and 8 percent were autistic. Others were identified as having developmental delays, emotional disturbances, hearing impairments, and other challenges. Whether or not they are identified as needing special education services, a significant number of children can benefit from extra support for the challenges they face. All children deserve to feel as if they fit in and are valued for who they are, no matter their strengths or challenges.

### Sexual orientation

From young ages, children are exposed to true and fictional stories about love. They may see people who love one another in their families, including relationships between their parents, between their parents and other partners, between other adult family members (e.g., aunts and uncles, grandparents), or between other adults in their lives. Just as individuals and families are diverse, so too are relationships. The relationships children see might be between adults of the same or opposite sex, they might involve individuals from different cultural backgrounds, of different races, or of different ages. When talking about the relationships you see around you, help your child learn to focus on the qualities that lead to positive relationships (e.g., getting to know one another well, having positive communication, feeling safe being yourself in a relationship) so that they learn to seek out these qualities in their future relationships, no matter whom they love.

**Jody** (age three): I don't know if I want to marry a boy or girl when I grow up.

**Melanie** (Jody's mom): That's okay. That's not something you have to decide now.

**Jody:** I think I might want to marry Donovan. She's my best friend.

**Melanie:** That's fine so long as you and Donovan both love each other and want to get married when you are older.

**Jody:** I'm not sure. I might want to marry Logan.

**Melanie:** That's okay too. You don't have to decide now. And you might change your mind. Most people marry someone they meet when they are older, and some people don't get married at all and that's okay too!

*What's happening in this conversation:* Jody has a mom and a dad who are married to one another, but she knows that she can marry anyone she wants when she is an adult (so long as they want to marry her as well). Even though her friend Donovan is a girl, considering marrying Donovan, at age three, does not necessarily indicate that Jody is a lesbian, bisexual, or pansexual. This is a typical thought process for a young child as they learn about the world and try on different roles (e.g., being married). The way that Melanie responds shapes Jody's understanding of the world and teaches her about her mom's beliefs. In this scenario, Melanie is communicating to Jody that, in their family, she will be accepted no matter what sex or gender her future partner may be.

**Noriko** (Kyle's mom): Do you know what it means if someone is gay?

**Kyle** (age four): No.

**Noriko:** Being gay means being attracted to someone who is the same sex as you—a boy who wants to marry another boy is gay, or a girl who wants to be in a relationship with another girl.

**Kyle:** Oh. Like Max and Otis.

**Noriko:** Yes! Max and Otis are gay. They are two men who love each other, and we get to go to their wedding soon.

**Kyle:** I've never been to a wedding before!

**Noriko:** I've been to lots of weddings, but you know what?

**Kyle:** What?

**Noriko:** This is my first wedding between two men. I have only been to weddings between a man and a woman before.

**Kyle:** Why?

**Noriko:** When I was young, two men were not allowed to get married to each other. Our country didn't allow it.

**Kyle:** Why?

**Noriko:** I think many people didn't understand that whether you love a man or a woman is part of how you are born. People thought it was something you chose, and that was seen as a bad choice.

**Kyle:** Max and Otis aren't a bad choice.

**Noriko:** No, they are not. They love each other, just like dad and I love each other. I'm glad they can get married now.

**Kyle:** Me too!

*What's happening in this conversation:* Noriko explains to her son, Kyle, what it means to be gay. Although Kyle has positive gay role models in his life, Noriko realized that they had never had a conversation about what it meant to be gay. Even if your child has people who are gay in their lives, having an explicit conversation about what it means to be gay, that being gay is biologically based, and sharing your support for relationships of all forms teaches your child about your own beliefs and helps shape theirs.

**Andrei** (age five): How come grandma was talking about Linda like that?

**Antonia** (Andrei's mom): Grandma doesn't like that Linda is married to another woman.

**Andrei:** Why not? They love each other.

**Antonia:** I know. In our family we believe that it's okay for two women who love each other and are kind to each other to get married, but not everyone feels that way. Some people think that only a man and a woman should get married, not two men or two women. That's what grandma's family believed when she was growing up.

**Andrei:** Why did they think that?

**Antonia:** Well, grandma's parents taught her that if two women loved one another, they were making a choice to turn their back on their religion and their family.

**Andrei:** But that's not true. Your body helps tell you who you love.

**Antonia:** We know that. And there is now science that shows that who you are attracted to is part of your genetics—part of how you are born. They didn't know that when grandma was growing up.

**Andrei:** We could tell her.

**Antonia:** I've tried to do that, but sometimes it's hard for someone to learn about something new if they had a different belief their whole life. I hope she will change her mind someday though.

*What's happening in this conversation:* Although Andrei's mom has taught him that relationships can be between any two people regardless of sex or gender, his grandmother believes otherwise. As children learn about relationships, they may hear different messages about what is acceptable or appropriate from others both inside and outside of their family. In this conversation, Antonia shared with her son what his grandmother believed and why. She did her best to do so in a way that was respectful of her mother and that would not damage the relationship Andrei has with his grandmother (e.g., no name-calling or attacks on her mother's character). Disagreeing with another person's beliefs in a respectful way can teach children that you can still love someone even if you do not agree with them.

Through conversations like these, parents can normalize the fact that people have different sexual orientations by talking about the role of their body and biology in determining sexual orientation. As your child grows and matures, let them know that their body will help them know whether they are straight or heterosexual (attracted to opposite-sex partners), gay or lesbian (attracted to same-sex partners), bisexual or pansexual (attracted to partners who may come from either sex or any gender identity), or asexual (not attracted to others in a romantic or sexual way). Sharing this information with your child from a young age can help normalize for children that there are many different sexual orientations and help them understand that the feelings they have are normal as they grow into their own identity. Neglecting to have conversations about sexual orientation (or race or gender identity, for that matter) means that your child has to guess or make assumptions about how you feel about these issues. Your family's actions, words, and involvement in the community may give your child insight into your values and attitudes toward others. Without having explicit conversations, however, you rely solely on your child to make those connections.

## YOUR FAMILY IS SPECIAL

Most children's earliest relationships occur within the context of family. As self-awareness grows, children start to see how they fit in with their family as well as how their family fits in with society around them. Helping children develop an appreciation for the diversity within and across families begins with teaching a child about the people in their own family, as well as their family values and culture. Parents play an important role in teaching children about who is in their family, what makes a family, and what values are most important to their family and why. In addition, learning about their own family's values can help children understand the importance of culture for not only their own, but other families, too.

### Key messages for children:

- There are many different types of families.
- Even though families can look different from one another, all families care about their children.
- Our family has values, beliefs, and traditions.

- Talking about and sharing our family values can bring us closer together.
- The values other families have are just as important to them as our values are to our family.

### *There are many different types of families*

There are many different types of families. Children are likely to see images in books, advertising, television programming, and movies that communicate to them what a "normal" family looks like. In reality, there is no such thing as a normal family. Children are raised in many different family settings, including families with one, two, or even more parents, grandparents, or other family members. Families can be blended and include stepparents and stepsiblings. Families can include parents of the same or different sexes or genders. Families can be multiracial and multicultural. Families can include foster parents, adoptive parents, and nonfamily caregivers. Families also have many different cultures and beliefs. To each family, the values they have are just as important to them as values are to every other family.

> **Eleanor** (Owen's mom): You are lucky to have so many people in your life who love you.
>
> **Owen** (age one month): (babbles)
>
> **Eleanor:** I can't believe you are one month old today! There were so many people at our party: mom and dad, grandma, aunt Adelajda, uncle Muhamed, all your cousins, our neighbors—so many special people who are part of our family.
>
> **Owen:** (coos)
>
> **Eleanor:** I know you can't understand what I'm saying yet, but you will someday. All these people are a special part of our life. We are lucky to have them and they are lucky to have you. And I know you loved having all that attention today!

*What's happening in this conversation:* Even though Owen can't understand her words, Eleanor is bonding with him and providing opportunities for Owen to spend time with the community that surrounds them. Recognizing all the different people who can be part of a family sends the message to a child that they are part of a special group of people who love them—their family.

**Malik** (age four): Tell me the story about when you became my mama.

**Jenn** (Malik's mom): Well, your mommy and I wanted to be parents, and we decided that the best way for us to have a child was to adopt a boy or girl who needed a family to be part of our family.

**Malik:** And I was that boy.

**Jenn:** That's right! You were five months old when we brought you home. Mommy and I loved you from the first time we saw you. We didn't always know what to do because we had never been parents before, so sometimes we made mistakes . . .

**Malik:** Like that time I threw up in the car and you had no clothes for me?

**Jenn:** Don't remind me! That was a big mess.

**Malik:** (laughs)

**Jenn:** But we learned and we keep learning every day how to be the best parents for you we can be.

*What's happening in this conversation:* Many children love to hear about how they became part of their family. Children may enjoy hearing stories like this over and over again. This conversation may look different, depending on whether a child was adopted, born into a family, or came into a family in another way. Share with your child how they joined your family, whether it was through adoption, being a foster child, or a biological process involving mom and dad or a donor. Talk with your child about the different ways other families grow and come together, and highlight how you felt about your child joining your family.

**Elliott** (Miguel's dad): You're a very lucky kid to have two parents who love you so much.

**Miguel** (age five): You only had grandma.

**Elliott:** That's true. I did. My dad died when I was very young. Grandma was a great mom, and I was very lucky to have her too.

**Miguel:** Did you miss your dad?

**Elliott:** Probably, but I didn't remember him very well so it never seemed strange to me that our family was just mom and me. It was tough sometimes, but all families have tough times, and we were happy being a family together—just like we are now.

*What's happening in this conversation:* Elliott shares with his son, Miguel, about his own experiences growing up in a single-parent family in contrast to

Miguel growing up in a two-parent household. Although he mentions that there were challenges, he also points out that all families can have tough times and that he had a loving family, just like their family does now. Recognizing the diverse family forms within your own extended family is one way to begin having conversations about different family types, using people and contexts that are already familiar to your child.

> **Aurelia** (Julie's older sister): Who are all the people you can think of who might be in a family?
>
> **Julie** (age six): A mom and dad.
>
> **Aurelia:** Yep. Lots of families have a mom and a dad. What about two moms or two dads?
>
> **Julie:** Like Jordan's family.
>
> **Aurelia:** Yes—he has two moms. Who else can you think of?
>
> **Julie:** Maya has a stepmom.
>
> **Aurelia:** Okay, so stepmoms and stepdads too! What about foster parents? Have you ever heard of foster parents?
>
> **Julie:** No.
>
> **Aurelia:** Foster parents are people who take care of children for a short time or a long time when their own parents are not able to take care of them.
>
> **Julie:** Oh. I know another one we forgot.
>
> **Aurelia:** Who?
>
> **Julie:** Big sisters! They're the best!
>
> **Aurelia:** Aww, thanks. What's most important is that kids have people who love them and take care of them.
>
> **Julie:** I know. I know.
>
> **Aurelia:** I know you know. I just wanted to say it again so that you knew it was okay to have families that look different from your friends at school and so you could help other kids feel good about their families, too.

*What's happening in this conversation:* In addition to conversations that emerge naturally with a child about what it means to be a family or who is in a family, the parent in this conversation (Julie's older sister, Aurelia) is bringing up the topic intentionally with her younger sister. Worried that her sister might feel that her family is lesser than other families because she does not have a mom or a dad in her life, she holds conversations often with Julie to talk about how different families can be.

**Kimmy** (age seven): Neveah said our family is weird because we have five kids. Hers only has one.

**George** (Kimmy's stepfather): Weird? I guess every family might seem a little weird to someone else because each family is different. Mom and I love all our children very much. Don't you like having brothers and sisters to play with whenever you want?

**Kimmy:** Sometimes. But I wish I had my own room.

**George:** I understand that. It's hard to find quiet time in a big family. I bet there are times that Neveah feels lonely and wishes she had other brothers and sisters to play with.

**Kimmy:** Yeah.

**George:** There are lots of different kinds of families—big families, little families, families with one parent, families with two parents, families with grandparents, families with no children—so many different kinds. No family is better than any other. All families have good things about them, and they have their challenges too. But I know one thing that all families have in common.

**Kimmy:** They love each other?

**George:** Hey! That's what I was going to say!

*What's happening in this conversation:* From early ages, children begin to notice differences between themselves and others. Some children ask about or point out these differences in ways that communicate interest and curiosity. Other children point out differences in ways that might be hurtful. In this conversation, George responded to a potentially hurtful comment by talking about their own family and Neveah's family in a nonjudgmental way, pointing out that all families come in different forms, and each has strengths and challenges.

✳ ✳ ✳

There was a time in the United States when a two-parent family (a family with one mom and one dad) was the most common family form, but it isn't now. There is no one dominant form of family in the United States. Each family form comes with its own unique strengths and challenges, but positive outcomes are possible for children, no matter what form their family takes. Consider these statistics about families in the United States (Pew Research Center, 2017):

- 46 percent of children live with two parents who are in their first marriage.
- 15 percent of children live with two parents who have been remarried.
- 7 percent of children live with cohabiting parents.
- Approximately 130,000 same-sex couples are raising 250,000 biological, step, foster, or adopted children (same-sex couples are four times more likely to raise an adopted child or child in foster care than opposite-sex couples) (Williams Institute, 2017).
- 26 percent of children live with a single parent.
- 5 percent of children do not live with either of their parents (many of these children are being raised by grandparents).
- 16 percent of children live in blended families.
- 8 percent of children in blended families live with a stepparent.
- 12 percent of children in blended families live with stepsiblings or half-siblings.
- 2 percent of children in the U.S. are adopted (either through foster care or international services) (Child Trends Data Bank, 2015).
- Nearly half a million children are in the foster care system at any given time (Child Welfare Information Gateway, 2015).

These statistics give an example of the many different types of families in the United States. Having conversations about the fact that families can look differently from one another, and focusing on the support families give their children as what defines a family can help children learn to appreciate their own family and others. Speak objectively and without judgment with your child about how your family came to be, as well as the ways other families are formed. If your child feels comfortable having conversations about your family as well as exposure to a wide range of family types, they may be better able to approach conversations about other families without judgment, and contribute to shaping more accepting societal attitudes related to family diversity.

### All families have beliefs, culture, and values

Families are diverse, not only in makeup, but also in terms of cultural beliefs and values. Every family has a culture, including values, beliefs, and traditions that are important to them. Teaching your child about your family's culture is called **cultural socialization** (Oakley, Farr, & Scherer, 2016).

There are many different ways that cultural socialization happens, including involving your child in special events and traditions, reading culturally relevant books, talking about historical or cultural figures, celebrating holidays, cooking and eating ethnic foods, listening to music, and modeling your family values. The conversations you have with your children along the way can help them understand where your family culture comes from and why it is important to you. Having an appreciation for the role culture plays in your own family can help children understand the importance of culture for other families as well.

Cultural socialization is related to many positive outcomes even in preschool, including higher language abilities, better pre-academic skills, and fewer behavior problems (Baker, Tichovolsky, Kupersmidt, Voegler-Lee, & Arnold, 2014; Caughy & Owen, 2015). Cultural socialization also relates to better science and social studies outcomes in older children. Most research on cultural socialization has focused on children from minority families (e.g., black/African-American families, Latino families). This may be because families of color are more likely to spend time talking about their family culture and how their family relates to the dominant culture (Priest et al., 2014). In minority families, conversations about culture are not used only to promote pride in and knowledge of one's own culture, but also to help children prepare themselves for bias or prejudice they may face in society. If more children had an appreciation for one another's cultural values, conversations about bias might become less necessary.

**Roccio** (Stella's grandma): Te amo. I love you.
**Stella** (age six months): (babbles)
**Roccio:** Te amo es español. I love you is English.
**Stella:** (babbles)
**Roccio:** Nose, nariz. Eyes, ojos. Ears, orejas.

*What's happening in this conversation:* Even though Stella is pre-verbal, Roccio lets her know in English and in Spanish that she is loved. Roccio is also introducing her native language to her grandchild, which is part of cultural socialization, and one way that she can share their family's cultural heritage.

**Duc** (age four): Anna says you talk funny.
**Hoa** (Duc's mom): That's probably because I have an accent. I didn't learn

how to speak English until I came to the United States when I was a teenager, so my English isn't as good as yours.

**Duc:** You didn't learn English until you were a teenager?

**Hoa:** No, we spoke Vietnamese when I was growing up. And now you're lucky because you are growing up learning Vietnamese and English!

**Duc:** Why is that lucky?

**Hoa:** Well, you know two languages, and most people only know one. Don't you think that's lucky?

**Duc:** I guess.

**Hoa:** You also get to talk with your grandparents, who only speak Vietnamese. You get to listen to grandpa's funny stories about when he was growing up.

**Duc:** And grandma's stories about when you got in trouble.

**Hoa:** (laughs) If that's what she's telling you, maybe it's not such a good idea for you to learn Vietnamese after all!

*What's happening in this conversation:* In this conversation, Hoa talks with her son about the value of learning her native language (Vietnamese). With older children, like Duc, there will be more intentional sharing about why family culture is important than with an infant like Stella in the previous example. Sharing language is one of the ways families can participate in cultural socialization and often gives children a lens into other aspects of their family culture, including access to family stories and traditions through extended family members.

**Cecily** (Paul's mom): How about we make noodles together for your birthday dinner?

**Paul** (age five): Do we have to have noodles? I want pizza.

**Cecily:** We could make pizza too. Do you know why I always make noodles for your birthday?

**Paul:** Why?

**Cecily:** Because in our culture, eating long noodles means having a long life.

**Paul:** Oh! I thought you just liked noodles.

**Cecily:** Well, that too!

**Paul:** I guess I want noodles and pizza.

**Cecily:** That sounds like a good plan!

*What's happening in this conversation:* In this conversation, Cecily shares with Paul why their family makes noodles as part of birthday celebrations. She later extends the conversation by involving Paul in learning how to make noodles, talking about how she learned to cook noodles, who first told her about their special meaning, and why that tradition is still an important part of their family. Conversations about culture, like this one between Cecily and Paul, can help children understand not only *what* their family values, but also *why* these values are important to the family. Sometimes we take for granted the rituals, traditions, or customs that children see on a daily basis. Although regular exposure to cultural traditions may make them part of what your child experiences as "normal," taking time to explain to your child why these traditions are important to your family can help strengthen their understanding of your family values and provide children with the vocabulary to talk about their home culture with others. Learning about the values of other families can help strengthen a child's understanding of their own culture and help them learn how their family culture is both similar to and different from others, while teaching them to appreciate and see value in the beliefs of all families.

**Jeremy** (Billy's dad)**:** Look at this! Next week your school is having a multicultural celebration!

**Billy** (age seven)**:** I know, but we don't have a culture.

**Jeremy:** Why do you say that?

**Billy:** Because we don't. Samuel's family is Jewish. They celebrate Chanukah and stuff like that. Ke is Chinese. He does Chinese New Year. Kamal is from Sudan. His family has special clothes. They all have cool holidays and stuff. We're just regular.

**Billy:** That doesn't mean we don't have a culture. We have lots of special holidays we celebrate, like Thanksgiving and Christmas. Can you think of other special traditions we have in our family?

**Jeremy:** We have family taco and movie night on Fridays.

**Billy:** That's true! Spending time together can be part of our family culture and values. What about the things that are important to our family? What's our number one family rule?

**Jeremy:** Always be kind.

**Billy:** That's part of our family culture too.

**Jeremy:** I never thought of it like that.

*What's happening in this conversation:* Families who come from the dominant culture (for example, families in the United States who identify as white) are less likely to spend time engaging in cultural socialization than families from minority cultures. This does not mean that they do not have a culture. All families have traditions, values, and beliefs that are important to them. From his son's comments, Jeremy realizes that although their family has values and beliefs, they have not spent time explicitly talking about them, and he makes an effort to begin shifting that. By intentionally pointing out the beliefs and values important in your own family, you can help your child develop an appreciation for the role of culture in their own lives. Having this framework may help children understand how important culture is in the lives of other families as well.

**Jane** (Nadya's aunt): Look at this! Next week your school is having a multicultural celebration! I think that is so wonderful.

**Nadya** (age six): Why?

**Jane:** When I was growing up, schools didn't do things like that. My parents—your grandparents—actually tried to hide our family culture because it was different from everyone else's. They made me practice speaking like an American so that I wouldn't stick out at school, and they wouldn't even speak Russian in front of me at home.

**Nadya:** Why did they do that?

**Jane:** They didn't want me to be treated badly because we were different from other families. Some people were afraid of people from other cultures when I was a kid—some people still feel that way now.

**Nadya:** That's weird. How come people are afraid of other cultures?

**Jane:** Maybe they just never learned about other cultures. Sometimes people are afraid of things they don't understand. I felt like I missed out on our family culture. That's why it's so important to me to teach you about our family traditions and for you to learn about other families too.

*What's happening in this conversation:* In this conversation, Jane shares with Nadya one of the reasons she feels so strongly about making sure that she learns about her own family cultural heritage as well as the cultures of other families. Although this conversation focuses on events from Jane's childhood, many families have conversations with their children related to discrimination they have faced, or that they worry their child might face, in our current society.

**Madeleine** (John's mom): Esther invited us to light the menorah with her family tonight as part of their Chanukah celebration.

**John** (age four): What's a menorah?

**Madeleine:** It's a special candle holder that has nine candles—one for each of the eight days of Chanukah, and one more to light the other candles.

**John:** Is it like birthday cake candles? Can I blow them out?

**Madeleine:** To be honest, I don't know very much about it. How about if we join them tonight and we can ask more about it?

**John:** Okay.

**Madeleine:** I never knew anyone who was Jewish growing up, so I'm excited to learn more about Chanukah and other Jewish traditions.

**John:** Me too. I like candles!

*What's happening in this conversation:* In this conversation, Madeleine models to her son, John, an interest and openness to learn about another family's cultural traditions. Modeling open-mindedness is one way to show your child how to approach learning about another family's beliefs with curiosity and without fear or threat that learning about another family's traditions will lead to rejection of your own family values.

As you help your child learn about other cultures, avoid taking a tourist approach to sharing other cultures with your child. A tourist approach is one that limits what we talk about with children to holidays or special events, rather than exploring the full richness that comes along with a culture. Exposing children to many different facets of a culture shows them that each family's cultural beliefs and values are likely as deep and complex as your own.

## Chapter conclusions

Together, the conversations in this chapter aim to help children and the special adults in their lives get to know themselves and develop an appreciation for what makes them and their family special. Through these conversations, children develop self-awareness and learn to appreciate the diversity that exists within and across individuals and families. There are many other conversations you can have with your child to continue to build self-awareness and foster empathy. You might talk about your home and the different types of homes families live in as well as families who do not have a home. You might talk about the different jobs people have and the different roles people play inside and outside of a family. You might share your spiritual or religious views, what they are and why they are important to your family. You might talk about where you live and the importance of your community in your family life.

Even as the content of your conversations change, the underlying principles and strategies you use will likely stay the same:

1. **Use an objective and nonjudgmental tone.** Using a calm and objective tone when you have conversations about the qualities your child has and the qualities that others have can help your child learn to approach these topics in a nonjudgmental way. As adults, we recognize that some topics have stigmas attached to them (e.g., body type). Other topics might feel embarrassing to talk about (e.g., bodily functions or certain feelings). And still there are other topics that we just don't know how to talk about because nobody talked with us about them when we were growing up (e.g., gender identity, race). For young children, these negative connections might not exist yet. The conversations we have with our children shape how they feel about these topics. Rather than perpetuating feelings of embarrassment, shame, or fear, we can help foster our children's natural curiosity and teach them how to talk openly about a wide range of topics.

2. **Focus on shared feelings.** As you talk about different individual and family characteristics, focus on shared feelings. No matter an individual's race, religion, sex, gender, culture, abilities or disabilities, or life experiences, everyone has feelings. Help your child focus on the fact that we all have feelings as a way to build compassion and understanding. Stopping to think about how another person feels can help your child build a connection with that person and focus on what they have in common, while also appreciating their differences.

3. **Extend the golden rule.** Many of us are taught that we should follow the golden rule and treat others as we want to be treated. Oftentimes this is misinterpreted to mean that everyone wants to be treated the same way—just like you. The problem is that this is simply not true. Some people want to be hugged when they are upset, but others want to be left alone. Some people could spend all day in a

large crowd, while others need long periods of quiet time. Help your child understand that we should treat people the way *they* want to be treated. This interpretation of the golden rule is sometimes called the "platinum rule." It's also important to make the point that we can guess how someone else might feel, but the only way to know for sure is to ask. In order to know what others need, we have to get to know them.

4. **Choose conversations that align with your family values, but if you choose not to have a conversation ask yourself:** *Why not?* This book provides suggestions for many different conversation topics. Some of these topics will appeal to almost every family, but there are other conversations that might not. You know your child and family best, and I encourage you to decide which conversations you are comfortable discussing with your child and which conversations you are not. If you choose not to have a certain conversation, however, take a moment to ask yourself: *Why not?* Do you believe the conversation topic is too advanced for your child? If so, is there benefit to introducing the topic to your child in a simplified way? Or would it be better to wait until your child is a little older or more mature? Does the conversation stand against your own family values? If so, consider that having that conversation could help your child learn to see value in others, even when they have differing viewpoints, opinions, or ways of life. Understanding the values and viewpoints of others in society may even help strengthen your child's understanding of your own family's values and beliefs.

5. **Have conversations more than once.** Remember that children learn through repetition. Having conversations more than once helps children learn different aspects of a topic. In addition, what children are able to remember and understand at different ages and stages will change over time.

## Question and answer: Apply what you learned to parenting challenges

**Q:** What if someone else makes fun of my child for who they are?

*A: Unfortunately, as children come into contact with other children and adults inside and outside the family, the likelihood that they will be made fun of or teased increases. Whether a comment about your child is made unintentionally or with negative inten-*

*tions, words can be hurtful. Depending on the words as well as their temperament, a child may respond in different ways. Some children shrug and let hurtful words roll off of their shoulders without another thought. Other children hear hurtful words and think about them again and again and again, letting those words impact how they feel about themselves. And still other children respond explosively, attacking right back.*

*When your child hears words that are hurtful to them, let your child know that it's okay to be upset or hurt by these comments. Share with them how it makes you feel to hear (or hear about) someone saying those words to your child.*

*"I don't like that he said that. Those words were really hurtful. It makes me feel angry when anyone says words like that, especially to someone in my family."*

*Reassure your child that the words spoken are not true.*

**Christy** (Autumn's mom): When Julianna said your skin is ugly, that was not a kind thing to say. You know that wasn't true, right?

**Autumn** (age six): I know, but it made me feel bad.

**Christy:** I can understand that. It makes me upset just thinking about it.

**Autumn:** And it made me feel embarrassed.

**Christy:** It would make me feel embarrassed too. It's not right that she said that. Your skin is beautiful and I don't want those words to change how you feel about yourself.

**Autumn:** It doesn't, but I'm still mad.

**Christy:** Me too.

*Talk with your child about why people might say hurtful words. For example, they might not know their words are hurtful. They might think they are being funny or trying to get attention. They might be angry or upset and trying to make someone else feel that way too. Let children know that no matter what the reason, it's still not okay to say words that hurt someone else on purpose. You can't always control what other people say to your child, but you can help your child feel secure in who they are so that hurtful words do not impact how they feel about themselves.*

**Q:** What if I hear my child making fun of someone else?

**A:** *If you hear your child say or do something that might be hurtful to someone else, help your child think about the other person's feelings.*

*"I heard you laughing earlier at the way Miles was walking. How do you think that made him feel?"*

*Talk with your child about the importance of thinking about how their words and actions make other people feel, and encourage them to stop and think about those feelings before speaking. Outside of these situations, help your child practice thinking about other people's feelings by talking about the feelings characters have when you read together or watch television shows or movies. Model thinking about other people's feelings yourself. The more practice your child has stopping and considering another person's feelings, the less likely they will be to intentionally say something hurtful. When they do make hurtful comments, help them think about what they can do to make amends.*

**Q:** What should I do if my child stares at or points at someone who is different from them in public?

**A:** *Children have a natural curiosity about others. When they stare, point, or ask questions about someone who looks different than they do, we often tell children that what they are doing is not polite:*

*"Don't stare."*

*"It's not nice to point."*

*"Shhhhhhhh."*

*These messages communicate to children that talking about people who are different than they are is not okay. Gossiping about other people is something we should discourage, but getting to know others and learning about what makes us different as well as what makes us similar is something we should encourage in our child. The next time your child shows interest in another individual while in public, whether at the park, the grocery store, or the library, consider supporting their curiosity. Think about what you can say to help your child connect with someone with whom they might not have connected otherwise. You could help your child brainstorm questions to ask or to encourage them to say hello to someone new. If your child is feeling brave, he or she may want to ask questions him or herself. Here are a few examples:*

*"Excuse me, my son was interested in your wheelchair and wanted to know if he could ask you about it."*

*"We saw that you have two babies in the same stroller. My daughter has never seen twins, so she was wondering if she could say hello to them."*

*"I noticed that you were wearing a medical ID bracelet on your wrist. Would you mind showing it to my kids so I can teach them what it means?"*

*"I'm really sorry about that. I told my daughter that asking someone about their*

weight isn't very polite, but if she wanted to say hello and make a new friend, that would be okay."

"My son noticed your uniform and was wondering why you were wearing it. Could you tell him about it because I don't know what it's for, either. We were just interested."

"My daughter noticed the tattoos on your arms so I was explaining to her what tattoos are. Do you mind if we ask you about yours?"

You may be surprised at how positively most people will respond if they believe you have good intentions. When asked with genuine interest, most people will take the time to have a conversation, and likely enjoy it. Making a connection with another human being can also come with risks. There may be times when someone you approach doesn't have the time or interest to talk, or even takes offense at your greeting or question. It's also possible that you may be asking someone about something they feel self-conscious about, which can cause embarrassment.

When approaching another child or adult, it's important to realize that even with the best intentions, those intentions may not come across in the way that you intend.

Even without meaning to, asking questions may communicate to another family that you are asking:

"What's wrong with your child?"

"Can we examine/observe your child so that I can teach my child about him/her?"

The messages you want to share instead are:

"We are interested in getting to know you and your child."

"I want my child to learn about everyone's value and strengths."

If an interaction doesn't start positively, be prepared with a response for that too:

"I'm so sorry to bother you."

"I didn't mean to offend you. We really were asking out of interest and care."

The example you set for your child in each of these situations models important life skills and shows them how to interact with others in the community. Interactions like these teach conversation skills and teach children to approach others with interest, acceptance, and compassion.

**Q:** If my child is from the dominant culture, should I still teach them about prejudice and discrimination, even if I don't think they will ever face these issues?

*A: Absolutely. In order for us to move toward a more compassionate society, all children need to understand what prejudice and discrimination look like as well as the negative impact these types of words and actions can have on others. Knowing this will help our children recognize when they are being treated unfairly. In addition, conversations about these topics can help children avoid being participants in perpetuating injustice and help them think about how they can serve as an advocate for others.*

**Q:** Will talking about values and cultures that are different from ours be confusing to my child, or lead them to choose different values or values that we don't believe in?

**A:** *Talking with children about values and cultures different from your own family's does give your child exposure to other ways of thinking and other ways of life. It's important to realize that your child will be exposed to many different values in society, whether you introduce them to your child or not. Choosing to have these types of conversations with your child allows you to teach your child that you can still appreciate and get along with others who have different beliefs than you or your family. Understanding how their own family culture and beliefs fits in with others may actually contribute to a stronger sense of self-worth and pride in your family values.*

**Q:** How can I learn about other people's life experiences and other cultures and beliefs so that I can teach my child about them?

**A:** *There are many ways that you can learn about other people's life experiences. Several ideas are shared in the Family Activities section at the end of this chapter. It would be impossible to get to know every type of life experience, every culture, and every language that exists, but the more we learn about others, the more likely we are to approach them with interest, openness, and compassion.*

### Extend the conversation through read-alouds

Read many different books with your child that show diverse characters. Across these books, help your child find characters they relate to, and talk about how each character expresses who they are. Finding role models in storybooks that are both similar to and different from your child can help them as they develop their own identity (Kim & Tinajero, 2016). Use these stories as opportunities to talk with your child about the importance of being who you are, even if who you are is different from who other people want or expect you to be. Talk with your child about the differences you notice between characters in how they look, think, and act, and the experiences they share, as well as those that are unique to them. Find commonality across all characters by talking about how they feel. Point out to your child that no matter how similarly or differently people look from one another or how different their experiences may be, everyone has feelings.

In addition, look for books that show families of different types, celebrating different cultural traditions, and living in different types of communities. You may not be able to find one perfect book that shows all the different ways families live, so instead read a collection of books that highlight this diversity. With each book, talk with your child about how each family is similar to or different from your own, as well as what each family does to show they care about one another. Reading books about families that are like your family in some way can help normalize your own family's experiences for your child. Reading books that show families that are different from yours can help your child understand just how diverse families can be while still providing love and support for one another. Both messages are important. Help your child connect with your own family's culture and experience through reading and learning about others' values and beliefs. Ensuring that all children, whether they are members of the dominant culture or a minority culture, learn to value their own culture and those of others can help increase appreciation for the importance of culture, ultimately reducing prejudice, and increasing compassion.

### Books about being who you are

*I Am Enough* by Grace Byers, illustrated by Keturah A. Bobo

*I'd Know You Anywhere, My Love* by Nancy Tillman

*I Like Me!* by Nancy Carlson

*I Like Myself!* by Karen Beaumont, illustrated by David Catrow

*I Love My Hair* by Natasha Anastasia Tarpley, illustrated by E. B. Lewis

*Marvelous Me: Inside and Out* by Lisa Bullard, illustrated by Brandon Reibeling

*Mostly Monsterly* by Tammi Sauer, illustrated by Scott Magoon

*Only One You* by Linda Kranz

*The Story of Ferdinand* by Munro Leaf, illustrated by Robert Lawson

*What I Like About Me* by Allia Zobel and Miki Sakamoto

*Whoever You Are* by Mem Fox, illustrated by Leslie Staub

*Owen* by Kevin Henkes

### Books about nontraditional gender roles/identities

*I am Jazz* by Jessica Herthel and Jazz Jennings

*It's Not the Stork: A Book about Girls, Boys, Babies, Bodies, Families, and Friends* by Robie H. Harris, illustrated by Michael Emberley

*Jacob's New Dress* by Sarah Hoffman and Ian Hoffman, illustrated by Chris Case

*My Name is Not Isabella* by Jennifer Fosberry, illustrated by Mike Fosberry

*The Story of Ferdinand* by Munro Leaf

*Who Has What? All About Girls' Bodies and Boys' Bodies* by Robie H. Harris, illustrated by Nadine Bernard Westcott

### Books about race, ethnicity, and diversity

*All the Colors of the Earth* by Sheila Hamanaka

*All the Colors We Are/Todos los colores de nuestra piel* by Katie Kissinger

*The Colors of Us* by Karen Katz

*Crescent Moons and Pointed Minarets: A Muslim Book of Shapes* by Hena Khan, illustrated by Mehrdokht Amini

*Golden Domes and Silver Lanterns: A Muslim Book of Colors* by Hena Khan, illustrated by Mehrdokht Amini

*Happy in Our Skin* by Fran Manushkin, illustrated by Lauren Tobia

*Islandborn* by Junot Díaz, Leo Espinosa

*It's a Small World* by Richard M. Sherman and Robert B. Sherman, illustrated by Joey Chou

*Let's Talk About Race* by Julius Lester, illustrated by Karen Barbour

*More More More Said the Baby* by Vera B. Williams

*People* by Peter Spier

*Same, Same but Different* by Jenny Sue Kostecki-Shaw

*Shades of People* by Sheila M. Kelly, photographs by Shelley Rotner

*The Skin You Live In* by Michael Tyler, illustrated by David Lee Csicsko

*We All Sing with the Same Voice* by Philip Miller and Sheppard Greene, illustrated by Paul Meisel

*Whoever You Are* by Mem Fox, illustrated by Leslie Staub

*Whose Toes are Those?* By Jabari Asim, illustrated by LeUyen Pham

*Who We Are! All About Being the Same and Being Different* by Robie H. Harris, illustrated by Nadine Bernard Westcott

### Books about abilities and disabilities

*Autism is . . .?* by Ymkje Wideman-van der Lann, illustrated by Rob Feldbman

*A Picture Book of Helen Keller* by David A. Adler

*A Friend Like Simon* by Kate Gaynot

*Ian's Walk: A Story About Autism* by Laurie Lears, illustrated by Karen Ritz

*I See Things Differently: A First Look at Autism* by Pat Thomas

*Leo the Late Bloomer* by Robert Kraus, illustrated by José Aruego

*Making Friends* by Fred Rogers

*My Brother Charlie* by Holly Robinson Peete and Ryan Elizabeth Peete, illustrated by Shane Evans

*My Friend Isabelle* by Eliza Woloson, illustrated by Bryan Gough

*We'll Paint the Octopus Red* by Stephanie Struve-Bodeen, illustrated by Pam DeVito

*Why Johnny Doesn't Flap: NT is OK!* By Clay Morton and Gail Morton, illustrated by Alex Merry

### Books about your body

*Amazing You! Getting Smart About Your Private Parts* by Gail Saltz, illustrated by Lynne Avril Cravath

*Brontorina* by James Howe, illustrated by Randy Cecil

*From Head to Toe* by Eric Carle

*The Going to Bed Book* by Sandra Boynton

*My Amazing Body: A First Look at Health and Fitness* by Pat Thomas, illustrated by Lesley Harker

*Shake a Leg!* by Constance Allen, illustrated by Maggie Swanson

*Toes, Ears, and Nose* by Karen Katz

### Books about different types of families

*A Chair for My Mother* by Vera B. Williams

*All Families Are Special* by Norma Simon, illustrated by Teresa Flavin

*All Kinds of Families* by Mary Ann Hoberman, illustrated by Marc Boutavant

*And Tango Makes Three* by Justin Richardson and Peter Parnell

*Daddy, Papa, and Me* by Lesléa Newman, illustrated by Carol Thompson

*Grandma, Grandpa, and Me* by Mercer Mayer

*The Great Big Book of Families* by Mary Hoffman, illustrated by Ros Asquith

*How to Babysit a Grandma* by Jean Reagan, illustrated by Lee Wildish

*How to Babysit a Grandpa* by Jean Reagan, illustrated by Lee Wildish

*Kids Need to Be Safe: A Book for Children in Foster Care* by Julie Nelson, illustrated by Mary Gallagher

*Love is a Family* by Roma Downey and Justine Gasquet

*Mommy, Mama, and Me* by Lesléa Newman, illustrated by Carol Thompson

*One Family* by George Shannon, illustrated by Blanca Gomez

*Oscar's Half Birthday* by Bob Graham

*Tell Me Again About the Night I was Born* by Jamie Lee Curtis, illustrated by Laura Cornell

*The Relatives Came* by Cynthia Rylant, illustrated by Stephen Gammell

*Who's in a Family?* by Robert Skutch, illustrated by Lauren Nienhaus

*Who's in My Family? All About Our Families* by Robie H. Harris, illustrated by Nadine Bernard Westcott

### Books about cultural traditions and values

*Bee-Bim Bop!* by Linda Sue Park, illustrated by Ho Baek Lee

*Golden Domes and Silver Lanterns* by Hena Khan, illustrated by Mehrdokht Amini

*One Green Apple* by Eve Bunting, illustrated by Ted Lewin

*Round is a Mooncake: A Book of Shapes* by Roseanne Thong and Grace Lin

*Mooncakes* by Loretta Seto, illustrated by Renné Benoit

*My Name is Yoon* by Helen Recorvits, illustrated by Gabi Swiatkowska

*What We Wear: Dressing Up Around the World* by Maya Ajmera, Elise Hofer Derstine, and Cynthia Pon

*Two Mrs. Gibsons* by Toyomi Igus, illustrated by Daryl Wells

*Yoko Writes Her Name* by Rosemary Wells

### Books about neighborhood and community

*Counting on Community* by Innosanto Nagara

*Last Stop on Market Street* by Matt Peña, illustrated by Christian Robinson

*Places in My Community* by Bobbie Kalman

### Read-aloud and discussion questions

- How are the characters in the book like you? How are they different from you?
- What makes each character special? What do you think they are most proud of?
- What makes you special? What are you most proud of?
- Have you ever had someone tell you that you couldn't do something because of who you were or how you looked? How did that make you feel? What could you do if you saw this happen to someone else?
- What can you do to help others know that you like them for who they are?
- What are some of the things that are special to the family in the book?
- How is this family like our family? How is this family different from our family?
- How did the family members in the book show that they care about each other?
- How does our family show that we care about each other?
- Is there anything the family in the book does together that you think we should try, too?
- Even though the family in the book celebrates the same holidays/traditions we do, did you notice anything they do that is different from our family?
- Even though the family in the book celebrates different holidays/traditions than we do, did you notice anything they do that is the same as our family?
- What did the character like best about their neighborhood/community?
- How is their neighborhood/community like ours? How is it different?

## Extend the conversation through family activities

*Draw self-portraits.* Use crayons, colored pencils, or paint to draw self-portraits together with your child. Look at pictures of yourselves or use a mirror as you draw. Talk about the different colors of your skin and try to match your skin, hair, and eye color in your artwork. Make sure your child has access to art materials at home and school that allow them to create artwork that depicts their own skin tone as well as the full range of skin tones.

*Draw a family portrait.* Help your child draw a picture of the people in your family. Talk about what makes each member of your family special. Display your family picture in a place you can see it often.

*Create a photo album of the special people in your child's life.* Include family members, friends, teachers, or anyone else in your child's life they see regularly. Look at the book together and talk about each person and why they are special to your child and family.

*Conduct family surveys.* Help your child think of a question to ask family members (or friends) as a way to start conversations about similarities and differences. Ask questions about personal qualities (e.g., hair color, eye color) or likes/dislikes (favorite vegetable, favorite season, favorite game). Help your child write each person's response, and talk about ways members of your family are similar and different from one another.

*Make a "my favorite things" collage.* Help your child make a collage of their favorite things by cutting out pictures from magazines, printing them from the Internet, or drawing them together. Talk about why your child chose each item. Make a collage of your favorite things as well and share with your child what you chose and why. Talk about the things that you and your child like that are the same and those that are different. Talk with your child about the importance of being who you are and feeling good about who you are.

*Book scavenger hunt.* Use the books you have at home, or visit your public library. Try to find books that have different types of people and families in them: families with two parents (one mom and one dad, two dads, two moms), families with one parent (one mom, one dad), families with grandparents, families with adopted children, multiracial families, stepfamilies, and others. See how many different kinds of families you can find. As you read each book together, use the read-aloud questions provided in this chapter. In addition, talk about the types of families that were easiest to find in books, and the types of families that were the most difficult to find. Were there any types of families that you could not find in a book? Why do you think that is? How do you think it feels to families who cannot find books showing families that are similar to their own?

*Seek out stories with role models from similar and different racial and cultural backgrounds from your own family.* Giving children exposure to others from the same racial and cultural backgrounds as your own family provides role models that your child can connect with and relate to. Children who come from the dominant or majority race will likely already have exposure to many different role models from their same racial background. This may not be true for children coming from minority backgrounds or communities of color. Intentionally finding and seeking out these role models can be especially important. Take time to intentionally expose your child to role models and stories of individuals from different racial backgrounds from your family as well. Seeing role models from different racial backgrounds can help normalize the message that children and adults of all races and cultures have equal value.

*Look for community activities to attend that celebrate and recognize the contributions of diverse groups.* There are specific days and months dedicated to celebrating diversity in the United States when events may be happening in your community, including African American History Month (February), Asian Pacific American Heritage Month (May), Pride Month (June), National Hispanic Heritage Month (September 15 to October 15), National Native American Heritage Month (November), and others. Community and cultural centers, universities and colleges, and many other nonprofit organizations can be a great resource for community activities that may be open to the public.

*Cook family meals together.* Many cultures have traditions involving cooking together or sharing meals as a family. Talk with your child about the role food plays in your family's culture by involving your child in the kitchen. Even from young ages, children can help scoop, pour, and stir. Older children can be involved with measuring or basic cooking with supervision. Time in the kitchen together can be quality bonding time, and allows you the opportunity to have conversations with your child as well as to talk about what you are eating and why.

*Model inclusiveness in your own life.* Serve as a role model for your child in the way you talk about and approach others with disabilities in your community. Provide your children with opportunities to be exposed to many different people with different abilities and disabilities. When children have exposure to people from many different backgrounds as well as the opportunity to interact with and get to know others who are similar to and different from themselves, they become more comfortable having interactions in the future. Through practice, they can gain the confidence, comfort, and skills necessary to approach and respond positively to others. Look for events in your community to participate in with your child that are inclusive and accessible (e.g., Paralympics).

*Neighborhood accessibility walk.* Take a walk through your neighborhood and talk with your child about what it might be like to take that same walk if you had challenges seeing, hearing, talking, or walking. Talk with your child about what that might it feel like. What challenges might you face? Are there supports in your community (e.g., wheelchair-accessible ramps, audio crosswalks) that are designed to help? What else could be done in your community to improve accessibility for everyone? Try taking a walk on another day and thinking about what it might be like to walk through your neighborhood with a different skin color, with a different sexual orientation, or as a different gender. How would that impact how others viewed you, approached you, or responded to you?

*Embed different relationships and family forms into play with your child.* During conversations with your child or during play, use language that acknowledges many different relationships and family types. For example, when playing together with dolls or action figures (or during imaginary role playing), act out stories with families that resemble your own as well as families that are different from your family:

*"I'm going to pretend this boy was adopted just like you."*

*"Today let's imagine you're the dad and I'm the mom."*

*"Let's pretend we're two sisters who take care of each other and live with their grandma."*

*"I'll be the daddy and you be the papa."*

Normalizing many different family types can help your child expand their understanding of what it means to be a family and focus on the importance of relationships within a family rather than developing a mindset around who *should be* in a family.

*Tell your child stories about how you learned about your own family culture when you were young.* Share stories about your own childhood to teach your child about what was important in your family when you were young. Which of those traditions have you kept? What new traditions have you added to your family? Give each family member a chance to share about their experiences to help your child see where the many different cultural traditions in their family came from.

*Involve your child in sharing your family traditions with others.* As you teach your child about the traditions important to your family, look for opportunities to share these traditions with others. Invite friends and neighbors to join you in your family traditions (when appropriate) and involve your child in helping teach others. This may involve sharing favorite foods through a neighborhood potluck, inviting others to join you for special family holidays, or teaching a friend a favorite family song. Giving your child the opportunity to help teach others allows them to take ownership over your family culture, values, and beliefs and strengthen their own understanding of the importance of these values. Importantly, look for opportunities to introduce your child to the traditions of other families as well. Seek out opportunities in your community to participate in community-based cultural activities or ask friends or neighbors to share their traditions with your family. Talk with children about how others' cultures are similar to and different from your own.

## IV

# You are part of the world around you:
## *Fostering resilience*

MAYA GOLD WAS A TEENAGER with a big heart. She was well liked by her peers, had close relationships with her family and friends, and had dreams of working with orphans in Nepal after graduating from high school. Before Maya had a chance to pursue that dream, she took her own life. Maya was 15. Her family and the community she left behind were stunned and heartbroken. Maya did not exhibit any of the warning signs that are often related to being at risk for suicide. She was not clinically depressed or socially isolated. Her untimely death was related to the use of a psychoactive combination of over-the-counter drugs popular among some teens in Maya's high school. Parents and teachers alike had no idea how widespread the problem was.

Maya's family turned their grief over the loss of their beloved daughter to positive action and created the Maya Gold Foundation, which aims to "empower youth to access their inner wisdom and realize their dreams." I had the honor of co-hosting a workshop on emotional intelligence sponsored by the foundation. The workshop was an opportunity to bring parents and teens in Maya's community together to share feelings and practice positive communication. My own daughter had just turned six. When she asked me where I was going and what I was doing, I debated how much to tell her about Maya. In the end, I decided to tell her everything I knew about Maya, from her life goals to her loving family to her suicide. Other families might not have made this same choice, but I saw this as an important opportunity to talk with my daughter about something that might be every parent's worst nightmare—the death of their child.

Talking about suicide or death with a young child can be a scary thing. Most parents don't like to see their child feeling sad, scared, depressed, or hopeless, and these are the feelings that a topic like suicide can bring up. We would prefer that our children live in a world where they feel happy, loved, and supported at all times, but unfortunately, this isn't the world we live in.

It's impossible for a parent to know all the challenges their child will face, but there are things parents can do to foster **resilience**. Fostering resilience means arming children with skills that will help them navigate challenges and adversity. Children who demonstrate resilience are those who bounce back from challenges, or even thrive as a result of them. Fostering resilience doesn't have to begin with a conversation about suicide. There are many things parents can do and many conversations parents can have to arm their children with **protective factors**—factors that minimize the negative impacts of adversity. Protective factors linked to resilience include warm and responsive parenting, having a secure and trusting relationship with an adult, being able to manage intense emotions and cope with stress, and having the skills needed to create lasting friendships and build networks of social support. Building these protective factors is the focus of many of the conversations in this book!

This chapter includes examples of conversations between parents and children on a range of topics that might be considered challenging. Conversations about challenging topics will look different at different ages, and will vary based on what you feel your child is ready for and what you feel comfortable sharing with your child. As you read over the conversation topics and examples, you may decide to share some of these topics with your child, save some for a later time, and choose to never talk about some of them. That is okay.

Just as we discussed in Chapter II, creating a home base (or secure base) for children helps them know that they have a safe place to go. Through conversations like these, your child will learn that they can come to you to talk about anything, knowing that you will give them honest and open answers to their questions. One of the benefits of introducing challenging topics to children at young ages is having the opportunity to shape the way your child is exposed to a topic, rather than relying on a friend at school or the news to inform your child. If you have reservations about introducing a specific topic to your child, think about how you would feel if your child heard about a topic from someone else first. Another benefit to having conversations about challenging topics when children are young is that we can help them learn and practice words and strategies that might be helpful when and if those situations arise for them in the future.

As you read through the conversation in this chapter, you may come across topics that you feel are not relevant to your child (e.g., *"My child is not in a divorced family," "My child is not at risk for abuse."*). Whether or not you think a particular conversation relates to your child, the conversation may still be worthwhile. Your child may know other children for whom the topic is important. Building compassion means not only supporting your child's needs, but also arming them with awareness of the experiences and challenges that others have. Doing so will better enable your child to recognize when others might need help or support.

## YOU CAN TALK TO YOUR FAMILY ABOUT ANYTHING

### Key messages for children:

- It's okay to talk with your parents about anything.
- I don't have the answers, but I will do my best to answer your questions openly and honestly.
- Learning about challenging situations now can help us think about good choices we can make in the future.
- Learning about challenging situations can help us understand other people's life experiences better.

The conversations that follow are examples of conversations about a range of challenging topics between parents and young children at different stages of development.

### *Love, relationships, and sex*

Conversations about sex often stem from children's questions about where babies come from. Your child's age and developmental level will affect how you approach this topic, as well as what your child is able to understand. Conversations about sex can be introduced at any age or stage, but the conversation will likely look very different at each age. When your child is an infant or toddler, early conversations about sex might not be about sex at all. Instead, these conversations might focus on showing your child love and affection so that they learn how to recognize what positive, supportive relationships look like. In preschool, conversations about sex might stem from questions about where babies come from and focus on anatomy (boys have a penis, girls have a vagina), or safe and unsafe touches. As your children get older, you might choose to share more details with them about details related to sex (e.g., how people have sex), why people have sex, positive and safe ways to have a physical relationship, safe sex practices, and how to avoid unsafe situations. As part of these conversations, it's important to talk about how love and positive romantic relationships develop as well.

> **Eli** (age four): I set up a trap to find my true love.
> **Pavel** (Eli's dad): What do you mean?
> **Eli:** I put a tricycle on the path and waited to see who would touch it first. I like riding tricycles, so whoever touches it first will be my true love.
> **Pavel:** What happened?
> **Eli:** Nothing. No one touched the bike, so I didn't find my true love.
> **Pavel:** That's disappointing. It's a good start to find someone who likes the same things you do, but you have to get to know someone, too. You can't just trap a true love!
> **Otis** (Eli's dad): That's right. Your dad and I met in a cycling club because we both liked riding bikes—just like you! But that's not the only reason we fell in love. We went on lots and lots of dates to get to know each other. We dated for five years before we got married, so that we could make sure we got along and wanted to spend our lives together.
> **Pavel:** And that we would be good parents together for you and your sister!
> **Eli:** You're the best dads in the whole wide world.

*What's happening in this conversation:* Eli came home from school days earlier talking about finding his true love. Apparently, many of the children in his preschool were staging marriages on the playground. His dad, Pavel, had talked with him about the importance of finding someone who liked the same things you do. Eli had taken this conversation very literally and set out to find his true love with a "trap." Together, Pavel and Otis extended this conversation to expand Eli's understanding of what it means to be in a relationship, using their own relationship as a model. Although Eli's perception of what it means to love someone will grow and change over time, having these types of conversations and exposure to models of relationships in his own life can help shape what he looks for in his future relationships.

> **Lars** (Mika's dad): I don't really like this show.
> **Mika** (age seven): Why not? It's funny.
> **Lars:** The parents in the show don't treat each other very nicely. They yell at each other a lot and make fun of each other. I wouldn't like being in a relationship with someone who treated me that way.

**Mika:** Me neither.

**Lars:** I'm glad we don't treat each other that way in our family.

**Mika:** Me too! But can I still watch my show?

**Lars:** Sure. So long as you realize that's not an okay way to act in our family.

**Mika:** I know, dad.

*What's happening in this conversation:* As a parent, it's up to you to decide what types of media you feel comfortable sharing with your child and at what age. There are many family-focused shows that depict a mix of positive messages, as well as messages that we might not be so thrilled about sharing with our child. As Mika watches one of her favorite sitcoms, Lars points out that the family members in the show treat one another in a way that he would not want to be treated and would not want his daughter to be treated. In another family, a conversation about the same show might have had different results. Another parent might watch the show with their child and say, "I love that this family doesn't take themselves too seriously. They can tease one another without hurting each other's feelings. That's exactly what we do in our family." And in another family, children might not even be allowed to watch the show. An important point to acknowledge is that there is no perfect type of relationship. What every family wants and needs will vary based on the individuals within that relationship. What matters most for your child is that they find a relationship as an adult (if they want to be in a relationship) where they feel loved and supported for who they are.

There are many different ways that parents contribute to their children's understanding of what it means to be in a relationship, both friendships and romantic relationships. Parents can use their own relationships as models (e.g., modeling positive interactions as well as appropriate ways to resolve conflict), share family values, and discuss other relationships that children are exposed to in the community or media. Your words and actions can shape not only the types of relationships children seek out in the future, but also the skills they have to navigate these relationships. Talk with your child about the different types of relationships that exist (e.g., romantic relationships, friendships) as well as other family values related to relationships, such as family beliefs about dating (e.g., *"I wasn't allowed to go on dates until I was 16." "In our family culture, boys and girls are not allowed to go on dates by themselves. They can go places together as long as an adult is with them."*). Have conversations with your child about each of your specific beliefs and values. Share what your family rules are as well as why these rules are important and where they come from, whether they are based on cultural, religious, or personal values.

**Kenny** (age five): Where do babies come from?

**Zoey** (Kenny's mom): Babies grow inside their mom's uterus and then come out through their vagina.

**Kenny:** How does the baby get in there?

**Zoey:** Women's bodies make eggs and men's bodies make sperm. When an egg and sperm get together, they start to grow into a baby.

**Kenny:** How do the egg and sperm get together?

**Zoey:** One way is for a man and a woman to have sex.

**Kenny:** What's sex?

**Zoey:** Sex is when a man puts his penis into a woman's vagina.

**Kenny:** Eww! That's gross.

**Zoey:** It seems gross now, but it might not seem gross when you're older. Maybe we could get a book for kids from the library that talks about and shows pictures of how babies grow.

**Kenny:** Okay.

*What's happening in this conversation:* Kenny asks his mom, Zoey, about where babies come from. This is a fairly common question for young children when their family or someone else's family they know is expecting a new baby. These questions may even come up out of the blue. What you decide to tell your child may depend on your child's age, as well as your comfort level in discussing the topics of sex and pregnancy. What's most important is addressing children's questions and sharing information in a way that they can understand and in a way that encourages them to continue coming to you with their questions without fear of judgment or punishment.

**Tomas** (age three): Look at this, dad!

**Tarek** (Tomas's dad): Oh! Please pull your pants back up. Touching your penis is something you can do in private. Definitely not something we do in the grocery store.

**Tomas:** Look it's stretchy! I like it.

**Tarek:** I know you do, but touching or playing with the private parts of your body, like your penis, is not something we share with other people in public. Put your pants on and when we get home, you can touch your penis when you are by yourself in your room.

**Tomas:** Okay, dad, but watch. It's funny!

**Tarek:** Tomas!

**Tomas:** Okay.

*What's happening in this conversation:* In this conversation, Tomas discovers a new way to play with his penis in the grocery store while shopping with his dad, Tarek. Tarek does his best to respond calmly, letting his son know that exploring his body is okay, but that there is an appropriate time and place to do so (not at the grocery store).

Being curious about and wanting to touch and explore different parts of their bodies is perfectly normal for young children. When a child first discovers and sucks on their fingers or fist, many parents ooh and aah. When a child discovers their toes and pulls them up to their face, many parents smile and take a picture. When a child discovers their penis or vagina, the reaction they get from their parents isn't always so positive. For a child, exploring body parts considered to be private may not seem much different from exploring any other part of their body, aside from the reaction they get from parents and caregivers. When responding to a child who is exploring their body, stay calm and matter-of-fact. Let children know what is allowed, what is not, and why. Societal values and beliefs will play a role in this conversation, along with your own personal, family, and cultural beliefs.

If children are interested in touching and exploring their body parts, let them know what would be an appropriate time and place to do so (e.g., *"It's okay to do that in your room or the bathtub when you are by yourself."*). If you have cultural or religious beliefs that do not allow these types of actions, explain those to your child as well, providing rationale behind why this is important in your family, as well as strategies for what to do instead when they have an urge to explore.

**Stephanie** (age four): Mom, can I use your phone to take a picture?

**Sylvie:** What do you want to take a picture of?

**Stephanie:** My vagina. Sam is going to have a baby sister and he doesn't know what a vagina is, so I told him I would show him a picture of my vagina.

**Sylvie:** That's really nice of you to want to help your friend learn about vaginas, but that's a private part of your body. You should only show your vagina to your parents or your doctor. If Sam wants to know what a vagina looks like, he could ask his mom, and she can show him a picture. Okay?

**Stephanie:** Okay, mom!

*What's happening in this conversation:* Stephanie was surprised to hear her daughter ask to use her phone to take a picture of her vagina for her friend. In stepping back to think about it, she realized that from her daughter's point of view, taking a picture of her vagina probably didn't seem any different from taking a picture of any other part of her body. The request was not sexual in nature, but rather a generous offer to help a same-age friend who had questions in preparation for his new baby sister's arrival. A similar conversation might occur upon finding two children playing doctor or showing one another each other's body parts. In this case, a parent can let them know that there is nothing to be ashamed of, but that the private parts of our bodies are meant to stay private outside of our families until children are older.

**Allen** (age six)**:** They said "sex" on TV.

**Charlie** (Allen's dad)**:** Yes, they did.

**Allen:** Are they trying to make a baby?

**Charlie:** Maybe. But people have sex for other reasons too.

**Allen:** What other reasons?

**Charlie:** Sex is one way that grown-ups show that they care about and love each other. People also have sex because it feels good.

**Allen:** Oh.

**Charlie:** But sex is something that is not for kids. It's something grown-ups do when they are older and in a special relationship.

**Allen:** Like you and mom?

**Charlie:** That's right.

*What's happening in this conversation:* When Allen heard a reference to sex on TV, his father explained to him that sex is something adults do, not just to have children, but also because it feels good. This is a message that is often left out of conversations that adults have with children. As Allen gets older, his father can extend this conversation by talking about making good choices related to having sex (e.g., the importance of being in a caring and trusting relationship) and safe sex practices (e.g., using birth control and protection from sexually transmitted infections).

**Masha** (Elsa's mom): In our culture, it is very important for women and men to wait until they are married to have sex.

**Elsa** (age 10): I know, mama.

**Masha:** Do you know why?

**Elsa:** So you won't have kids before getting married?

**Masha:** That's part of it. But it is also so that when you become married, you and your husband will be the only person you have been with together in that way, making your marriage that much more special.

*What's happening in this conversation:* Individuals and families have many different values related to sex. Whether you believe that teenagers should have sex only if they are taking precautions and using protection, or that they should not have sex at all, share your values with your child and explain to them why those values are important to you.

\* \* \*

There are many different messages parents might want to share with children related to sex and relationships. Some conversations might not even be about sex directly at all. For example, parents may talk with children about how to be in a positive relationship that is supporting and caring; learning how to express what you want and how to express when you don't want something; watching for other people's cues of what they want and don't want and responding appropriately; and how to break up or end a relationship that is not going well. Conversations with children about sex can be uncomfortable or challenging to navigate, but when these conversations begin at a young age, parents can shape what children are exposed to and how. In addition, having conversations about sex when your child is young can make these conversations more comfortable and remove some of the stigma that occurs when parents wait to have these conversations until their children are adolescents.

In general, research has shown that parents choose to talk with their children about issues related to sex after children have already had exposure to these topics through other sources, whether through sex education in school, the media, or even personal experience. In many cases, youth have already engaged in sexual activity by the time their parents initiate a conversation about sex. Talking with children about sex at earlier ages relates to higher prevalence of safe sex practices, including condom use (Beckett et al, 2010). When surveyed, parents have also reported that it is easier to talk with children about sex when they are younger than it is when they are older (Wilson et al, 2010).

Parents have different levels of comfort talking about sex, and approach talking about sex in different ways. For example, mothers are more likely to talk with their daughters about sex than fathers. Mothers are also more likely to talk with their daughters than their sons about topics related to sex, including romantic relationships. One study found, however, that mothers were less likely to talk with children about pleasure associated with sex, or abuse (Martin et al., 2010), even though children in the study expressed interest in learning more about these issues. Importantly, a survey conducted with girls in their late teens found that 80 percent of teens interviewed wished their fathers had played a bigger role in talking with them about sex. Specifically, daughters wished their fathers had spoken with them about dating, ways to deal with pressure around having sex, and their own values and expectations for their children (Hutchinson & Cederbaum, 2011).

### *Divorce*

**Natalia** (Petr's mom): Matthew's parents are getting a divorce.

**Petr** (age three): What's divorce?

**Natalia:** A divorce is when two people who are married decide they are not going to be married anymore.

**Petr:** Why won't they be married anymore?

**Natalia:** I don't know—I didn't ask them. There are lots of reasons that people get divorced. Maybe they aren't getting along very well or want to do different things in their life. No matter what, they still love Matthew though, and they will always be his parents. They won't live together anymore, though.

**Petr:** Where will they live?

**Natalia:** Matthew's dad is moving into an apartment not too far away, so Matthew will spend some days staying in his mom's apartment and some days staying in his dad's apartment. He will have two homes.

**Petr:** Are you and dad going to divorce?

**Natalia:** No. Dad and I are very happy being married together. We are not planning to get a divorce.

**Petr:** Tomorrow will you?

**Natalia:** I sure hope not! Sometimes things change in people's relationships, but right now you don't need to worry about that.

**Petr:** I don't want you to divorce.

**Natalia:** I don't want that either, and neither does your dad. I wonder how Matthew is feeling about his parents getting a divorce. It might be a hard time for him, so we could think about things we could do to be helpful to him.

*What's happening in this conversation:* In this conversation, Natalia introduces the concept of divorce to her son, Petr. She begins by explaining what divorce is, as well as some of the possible reasons for and consequences of divorce. She also reassures Petr that there is no immediate risk of his own parents divorcing. When learning about other people's experiences, children may wonder about how those experiences might impact their own life and family. Having questions and even worries and fears is normal. Reassure your child and help them think about what they can do to be a support for their friends who are experiencing situations you are discussing.

**Tia** (age six)**:** Is mom going to pick me up today or tomorrow?

**Simon** (Tia's dad)**:** Your mom's coming to pick you up tomorrow after school, and you'll stay with her for the rest of the week.

**Tia:** Okay. Can I bring my teddy bear to mom's?

**Simon:** Of course you can bring your teddy bear. You can bring anything you like, but remember, you have toys at your other home too.

**Tia:** I know.

**Simon:** You know, even if we don't want to be together anymore, your mom and I both love you very much. We want you to have everything you need at each of your homes, especially all the love you need! That way, even if you miss some of your things, you'll still have us.

*What's happening in this conversation:* As Tia adjusts to a new way of life for her family, her dad does his best to help her feel comfortable across her two homes.

Even though her parents are no longer together, they each let Tia know that she is loved when they are together and when they are apart. Having loving and supportive relationships with each of her parents will help Tia adjust to the changes that come with divorce.

**Luna** (Addison's mom): Do you want to talk about how you're feeling?

**Addison** (age six): No.

**Luna:** That's okay. I just want you to know that it's okay to talk about it when you want to.

**Addison:** Okay.

**Luna:** I've been feeling kind of sad lately.

**Addison:** Why?

**Luna:** Well, even though I think getting a divorce is the best thing for our family, it's still a big change for our family, and it doesn't mean I like everything that is happening.

**Addison:** Oh.

**Luna:** Do you ever feel sad about it?

**Addison:** Sometimes. I miss you when I'm at dad's. Or I miss dad when I'm here.

**Luna:** I can understand that. You spent most of your life until now in one house with both of your parents. This is a big change to get used to. It's okay to feel sad about it.

*What's happening in this conversation:* When Luna checks in with her daughter about how she is feeling, Addison lets her know that she doesn't want to talk about her feelings right then. Luna lets her know that that is okay. She models sharing her own feelings with Addison in case that helps her feel more comfortable opening up, which it does. Another way that Luna could use her feelings to help Addison is by talking about what she is doing to manage her feelings (e.g., *"I feel sad too, but thinking about how much I love you and how much your dad loves you, even though we're not together, makes me feel better."*). Sharing strategies for ways that she is managing her own feelings may help Addison try these strategies herself.

**Finn** (age five): Is it because of me?

**Clay** (Finn's dad): You mean is it your fault that we are getting divorced?

**Finn:** Uh-huh.

**Clay:** No. It's not your fault. Dad and I do disagree sometimes about the best way to be a good parent, but that's our issue. We aren't getting divorced because of you. Dad and I both love you so much, even though we're not getting along with each other.

**Finn:** I wish you got along.

**Clay:** I know you do. And we tried our best, but sometimes things don't work out. It's important for you to know it is not because of you—it's definitely not your fault, and we both love you so much, no matter what.

*What's happening in this conversation:* Young children may need reassurance that separation or divorce is not their fault. Disagreeing on issues related to parenting is not uncommon, and if children have heard their parents have these types of disagreements, they may worry that their parents' separation or divorce is happening because of them. In this conversation, Clay reassures Finn that this is not the case. Finn may need to be reminded of this fact multiple times over days, weeks, or even months.

If your family is experiencing or has experienced divorce, it may be harder to talk with your child about divorce than if you are introducing the idea of divorce to your child hypothetically. Many of your own feelings will likely be closely tied to the topic of divorce. When possible, work together with your co-parent to decide what you think it is appropriate to share, when, and how. This is not always possible, depending on the approach and mindset of your co-parent. You may want to avoid sharing negative thoughts that you have about the other parent with your child, but it's okay to share your general feelings with your child. Let your child know if you are feeling sad, disappointed, angry, or even relieved. More likely than not, you and your child will have many of the same feelings associated with divorce—some pleasant and some unpleasant. Talking with your child about their feelings and your own helps them know that their feelings are okay. You can also help one another talk about ways to manage those feelings.

Divorce can impact children in different ways depending on the situation, as well as on your child's age and temperament. Some children manage changes better than others. For children who experience a significant number of changes, having conversations with and support from one or both parents may help them adapt more easily to those changes. Parents who respond compassionately to their children, recognizing that they may express their emotions by regressing to behaviors they had when they were younger (e.g., wetting the bed, sucking their thumb) or an increase in challenging behaviors (e.g., acting out) can give their child the time and support they need to adjust to new family routines.

### Peer pressure

Many people—children and adults alike—want to fit in and belong. There is nothing wrong with feeling this way. Belonging and having friends is important. Friends can be a positive influence on our lives in many ways. Friends can help us problem-solve when we face a challenge, introduce us to new ideas and experiences, or help us feel brave trying something new. In fact, having friends and social support is one of the strongest predictors of resilience. But sometimes friends or peers can have a negative impact on us as well. **Peer pressure** occurs when a child (or adult) feels influenced in some way by members of their peer group. Usually the term "peer pressure" is used to describe negative pressure, such as pressure to misbehave, engage in smoking, drinking, drug use, or sexual activity. In some cases, peer pressure might be the pressure to do something positive, but maybe something you just don't feel like doing (e.g., going for a run). Most parents hope that their children will gain all the benefits they can from spending time with their peers, while also having the skills they need to make a different choice if and when peers exert pressure or have a negative influence. Fortunately, there are factors that decrease the impact of negative peer pressure, namely having a positive relationship with parents and caregivers (Chan & Chan, 2013; Simpson, Duarte, & Bishop, 2016).

**Danica** (Xavier's mom): Do you want to have a red Popsicle or a purple Popsicle?

**Xavier** (age four): What color Popsicle is Judy having?

**Danica:** She chose red.

**Xavier:** I want red too.

**Danica:** Okay, but last time you had red you didn't really like that kind.

**Xavier:** I might like it now.

**Danica:** You might. And it's okay to try it again to see if your tastes changed. But you don't have to choose something just because your friend did. You'll still be friends and have fun together even if you have different color Popsicles.

**Xavier:** I know. Maybe I'll just have purple.

**Danica:** You can choose whichever one you want.

**Xavier:** Okay. Purple!

*What's happening in this conversation:* When Danica asks her son if he would like a Popsicle, he first stops to consider what color Popsicle his friend, Judy, is having. His mom points out that he can still have fun with Judy even if they choose different colored Popsicles. She hopes that Xavier will gain confidence making his own choices and come to realize that good friends will like him for being who he is.

From birth, we encourage children to learn through copying and imitating the role models in their lives. Early on, parents serve as children's primary examples, but as children start spending more time outside the home and with peers, the number of possible role models increases. Through conversations like this one, parents can teach children about when it is helpful to be like others and when it is important to make their own decisions.

**Gabriela** (Jillian's and Felix's mom)**:** Uh-oh. What is happening in here? I see water all over the floor and two children holding empty cups.

**Jillian** (age four)**:** He poured water on the floor on purpose.

**Felix** (age six)**:** She did it too.

**Jillian:** You did it first.

**Gabriela:** It sounds like you were both involved. It doesn't matter who did it first. You both did something you shouldn't have done, so I would like you both to help clean it up.

**Felix:** Yes, mom.

**Jillian:** Okay.

**(after cleaning is completed)**

**Gabriela:** Jillian and Felix, come sit down with me.

**Jillian:** What?

**Gabriela:** I want to talk about what happened earlier with the water. No matter who started making the mess, it wasn't okay to do. If you see someone doing something that they shouldn't be doing, that doesn't make it okay for you to do it too. Just because someone else is doing it doesn't make it right. You still have to be responsible for your own actions.

**Felix:** I know, mom.

**Gabriela:** I didn't like you pouring water on the floor, but that's not a really big deal. No one got hurt—it just made a mess. But what if someone was doing something more serious, like smoking or doing drugs or hurting someone else?

**Felix:** We wouldn't do that.

**Gabriela:** I know, but I want you to think about it. Sometimes when someone else starts doing something wrong, it makes it easier to join in—kind of like today.

**Jillian:** We won't do it again, mom.

**Gabriela:** I know, honey. What do you think you would say if you saw someone doing something wrong that they wanted you to do with them?

**Felix:** No thanks!

**Jillian:** Yeah. No thanks!

**Gabriela:** I think that's a great answer. Even if someone else asks you to do something—if it's not a good thing to do, it's still your fault and your responsibility if you join in.

*What's happening in this conversation:* In this conversation, Gabriela discovers her children pouring water on the floor—something she knows they know they shouldn't do. She asked them to clean it up and then continued the conversation, encouraging them to think about taking responsibility for their own actions. Studies have shown that children assign less blame to someone influenced by peer pressure when they do something wrong than if they are acting on their own. This may mean that they see the behavior as not the person's fault if someone else is doing it too or encouraging them to do it (Scott, Miller, Kelly, Richman, & Park, 2016). Having conversations like the one between Gabriela and her children can help children learn to take responsibility for their own actions. Parents can also help children practice words and strategies they can use if they ever find themselves facing peer pressure in the future.

**Magna** (Mason's mom): Have you ever heard of "peer pressure"?

**Mason** (age six): No.

**Magna:** Do you know what a peer is?

**Mason:** No.

**Magna:** A peer is someone who is like you in some way. It might be someone who is the same age as you, like someone in your class at school. Are all the kids in your class friends?

**Mason:** No. Erika and Liam are friends, but I'm not really friends with Claude.

**Magna:** Since you're all the same age and in the same class, they are all your peers—even if they are not friends.

**Mason:** Got it.

**Magna:** Peer pressure is when peers—people your own age or in the same group as you—want you to do something you don't want to do.

**Mason:** Then I just say no.

**Magna:** It's always okay to say no, but sometimes kids feel embarrassed about saying no, or don't know how to say no.

**Mason:** Like when?

**Magna:** Well, if someone who they want to be friends with asks them to do something, and they want to fit in.

**Mason:** I would still say no.

**Magna:** I'm glad. It can be really hard to do, but good friends will never make you do something you don't want to do. That's something important to remember—if someone asks you to do something and you don't feel good about doing it, good friends will understand.

**Mason:** Hiro always understands when I don't want to play soccer. We're still friends.

**Magna:** Hiro is a good friend.

*What's happening in this conversation:* Magna introduces the concept of peer pressure to her son, Mason. As he gets older, she might extend the conversation by sharing stories about times that she experienced peer pressure growing up, common circumstances that children might face where they have to make tough decisions, and brainstorm with Mason ways that he can respond if he ever faces these situations himself. She might also talk to him about the importance of being a good friend to others and never forcing someone else to do something that makes them uncomfortable.

**Zach** (age seven): Have you ever smoked a cigarette before, dad?

**Andrew** (Zach's dad): Yes, I have. One time when I was about 13, a boy that I went to school with took some cigarettes from his mom's purse and brought them to school. He asked me to smoke them with him. I didn't want to, but I did it anyway.

**Zach:** Why did you do it if you didn't want to?

**Andrew:** I don't know. I guess I worried he would think I wasn't cool or that he would make fun of me. What do you think you would do if that happened to you?

**Zach:** I would say no for sure. Smoking is gross.

**Andrew:** I'm glad. It is really bad for you, and it was gross. I wish I had been brave enough to say no. Now I realize I could have just said, "No thanks," or "I'm not interested," but I didn't know that then. I'm glad you do.

*What's happening in this conversation:* Zach shares a story with his son about a time when he gave in to peer pressure. Sharing stories about your own experiences with peer pressure can help your child understand that saying "no" isn't always easy. As a parent, it's up to you to decide how much to share with your child about your own experiences growing up. Sharing with children about mistakes that you made can be one way to bond with your child and help them know that you understand the challenges they face from your own experiences. These conversations can also serve as opportunities for you and your child to brainstorm together ways to respond if and when they face situations like these in the future.

✳ ✳ ✳

Indirectly, many of the earlier conversations in this book relate to peer pressure. Having a warm and trusting relationship helps establish positive patterns of communication that will help your child feel more comfortable talking with you about challenging situations that arise, without fear of punishment or shame. Building children's self-awareness, along with their confidence and self-esteem, helps children see that their value and worth does not have to be defined by others. Learning to accept themselves and others for their strengths and weaknesses also encourages children to think about the quality of friendships that they have. From birth, children are encouraged to learn from others, and especially the parents and caregivers in their lives. Think about the shift that occurs throughout childhood. As children spend more time with people outside their family, including teachers, friends, and peers, whom they learn from begins to shift. As they get older and gain autonomy, children can play a role in deciding who to watch and learn from, who to watch and ignore, when to step up and lead or teach others, and when to follow. Teaching children about positive relationships and making good choices provides them with tools to use that can help them make these types of decisions.

### Bullying

In early childhood, an essential skill is learning how to get along with others. When very young children have trouble getting along, we view this as part of their learning process. At some point, however, a shift occurs, and society starts to label children who struggle with social and emotional skills as "bullies." Once a child is labeled as a bully, we are no longer approaching that child as a learner. We no longer see them as someone who has the potential to learn and grow. I originally named this section "Bullies and Bullying," but after giving it some thought, I changed it to just "Bullying" to focus on the behavior as the focal point—not the child. **Bullying** is unwanted or aggressive behavior between school-aged or older children. When children struggle to get along during their early years, this isn't considered bullying. By the time a child reaches school age, we often move the focus from the role parents and teachers play in teaching children social skills to putting the focus on the child. In other words, society stands behind the message that a child should know better by school age (whether that is true or not). What makes bullying different from other challenges between kids is that the behavior happens repeatedly, and there is a power imbalance at play. A power imbalance can be that one child has greater physical strength than another, or that one child has power over another child in some other way. For example, one child might know something embarrassing about another child and use that information against them, or one child might be more popular than another and use that popularity to hurt the other child's reputation or social standing. Bullying is not a new challenge, but the way bullying happens has evolved over time and with advances in technology.

> **Mrs. Jeffers** (early childhood classroom teacher): I notice Jeremiah sitting over on the side of the room by himself. So many fun things are happening in our class. Who would like to go over and invite him to join in with them?

**Simone** (age four): Me!

**Mrs. Jeffers:** Thank you, Simone!

**Simone:** (stands next to Jeremiah and smiles)

**Mrs. Jeffers:** You could ask, "Do you want to play with me?" or "Do you want to build with me?"

**Simone:** (to Jeremiah) Do you want to build with me?

**Jeremiah** (age four): Okay.

**Simone:** I was building a castle.

**Jeremiah:** I want to build a bridge.

**Simone:** You can put it on my castle.

**Jeremiah:** Okay.

*What's happening in this conversation:* This conversation is one example of how an early childhood teacher might promote positive interactions between children in preschool. Promoting children's social and emotional skills relates to many positive outcomes for children, including increased positive behaviors and improved academic performance (Durlak, Weissberg, Dymnicki, Taylor, & Schellinger, 2011). These skills are also critical to preventing and reducing incidences of bullying at later ages.

Bullying impacts an estimated 30 percent of school-aged children in the United States in some way, either through their own participation in bullying or being a victim of bullying, or both. Approximately 21 percent of children between 12 and 18 report that they have been bullied and 16 percent report that they have been a victim of cyberbullying. Bullying and cyberbullying have many negative effects on children, including increased likelihood of drug and alcohol use, skipping school, poor grades, low self-esteem, and more health problems (U.S. Department of Health & Human Services, 2017). Bullying is not a new phenomenon. Our society has tackled bullying in different ways. Programs encouraging schools to take a zero-tolerance policy, in other words, programs that suspend or expel children for bullying, generally don't work. These approaches focus on punishing children rather than teaching them the skills they need to have positive relationships with others. Teaching children to have empathy and to stop and think about the impact that their words and actions have on others is a critical part of preventing bullying and a key ingredient of programs that effectively reduce bullying in older children. Children who bully others haven't developed key skills. There is no exact "recipe" that leads a child to bully, although research has helped identify trends and patterns in children's lives that might make them more likely to engage in bullying. In general, children who bully are more likely than others to come from homes that use physical punishment or physical abuse as a form of discipline. Children who are in households in which their parents are not attentive or use punitive types of discipline are at risk for receiving messages that reinforce bullying. They may see role models who use force or intimidation and use these same techniques when interacting with others, or they may not have positive role models at all.

**Kalea** (age four): Gavin kept pushing me at the park. I didn't like it.

**Agatha** (Kalea's mom): I saw that happen. I also saw that you told him, "I don't like that. Please stop." I thought that was a really good way to handle it.

**Kalea:** But he didn't stop, so I went to play on the swings instead to get away from him.

**Malachi:** (Kalea's grandpa): Oh, he probably just pushed you because he likes you. That's what boys do.

**Agatha:** I sure hope not. It's possible, but if he was trying to show that he liked you, then that was not a kind way to do that.

**Kalea:** I don't like him.

**Agatha:** I can understand that. I wouldn't like being pushed either. I'm proud of you for letting him know how you felt and moving away from him when he didn't listen. I hope he learns how to be a better friend.

*What's happening in this conversation:* Kalea shared with her mom and grandpa that a boy at the playground, Gavin, was pushing her. When her grandfather told her he was probably pushing her because he liked her, her mom was concerned about her daughter hearing that message. Telling children that someone treats them poorly because they like them may communicate the message that it doesn't matter how someone treats you as long as they mean well. When children are young, have special needs, or struggle with social skills, they may in fact try to interact with your child or try to get their attention by doing something that is hurtful (e.g., hair pulling, hitting, pushing). The child doing these things may or may not realize they are hurtful. Rather than saying to your child, "He's just doing that because he likes you," acknowledge that the action was not okay. "He should not have said that to you. It wasn't kind, and I understand why it hurt your feelings." It is possible to show compassion to the other child while also acknowledging that what they did was not right. "I wonder why she did that. Do you think she was trying to get your attention and didn't know how?"

**Katya** (Reed's mom): Do you know what bullying is?
**Reed** (age six): It's being mean.
**Katya:** Sort of. It's hurting someone's body or their feelings more than once—over and over.
**Reed:** Like hitting and punching?
**Katya:** Sure. Like hitting and punching or breaking someone's things. Calling names or making fun of someone is bullying, too.
**Reed:** I don't like those things.
**Katya:** I don't like those things either. How do you think it would feel if someone did that to you?
**Reed:** Bad. I wouldn't like it.
**Katya:** Me neither.

*What's happening in this conversation:* Teaching children what bullying means can help them learn to recognize the different forms that bullying might take in their own lives or in the lives of others. Bullying comes in different forms. Three main types are: 1) verbal bullying (e.g., teasing, name-calling, threats); 2) social or relational bullying (e.g., spreading rumors, public embarrassment, leaving someone out intentionally); and 3) physical bullying (e.g., hitting, kicking, punching, taking or breaking someone's things) (Völlink, Bolman, Dehue, & Jacobs, 2013). Understanding what bullying looks like can help children learn to identify instances of bullying in their own lives and in the lives of others. Teaching children to recognize bullying should happen in combination with teaching children skills related to empathy and considering other people's feelings.

**Christa** (Silas's mom): Do you ever see kids getting bullied at school?
**Silas** (age eight): I don't know. Sometimes maybe.
**Christa:** I saw someone get bullied at school when I was growing up.
**Silas:** You did?
**Christa:** Yes—Melba. Every day, a boy named Reuben would take her lunch from her and step on it. I felt really badly for her. He made fun of her a lot and pushed her around.

**Silas:** Did you tell a teacher?

**Christa:** No. I didn't do anything.

**Silas:** How come?

**Christa:** I didn't really know what to do. Do you know what you would do if you saw someone do that at school?

**Silas:** I would tell them to stop!

**Christa:** I'm glad. That can be hard to do. I wish I had helped Melba, but I was too afraid of Reuben.

**Silas:** You could have told him to stop or told a teacher.

**Christa:** Do you think you would feel comfortable telling someone to stop if you saw them bullying someone else?

**Silas:** I know I could.

**Christa:** I'm glad. It's a very brave thing to do, but it can be hard, especially if no one else is speaking up. But if you say something, it might help other people say something too. What if you didn't feel like you could tell them to stop. What else could you do?

**Silas:** Tell a teacher?

**Christa:** That's definitely a good idea. Other adults could help. If you ever asked an adult for help and they don't help you, then it's important to find another adult and keep trying until you find someone who will help. Is there a teacher that you think would be able to help if you saw someone being bullied?

**Silas:** Mr. Petersen would definitely help. He always listens to us when we tell him things.

**Christa:** Those are the best kinds of teachers. I think it's also important to be a helper to the person being bullied. How do you think it feels to be bullied?

**Silas:** Bad.

**Christa:** Yeah, really bad.

*What's happening in this conversation:* Christa uses an example from her own childhood to talk with her son about bullying. She feels badly that she never spoke up when she saw Melba being bullied, and she wants to help Silas learn skills that she lacked to be able to stand up for others.

**Olga** (Aria's mom): I love this picture of you! Is it okay with you if I put it online to show my friends?

**Aria** (age seven): Let me see it.

**Olga:** Here it is.

**Aria:** No. I don't like that one.

**Olga:** How about a different picture? What about this one?

**Aria:** Okay. I like that one.

**Olga:** When I put it on online, that means anyone on the Internet can see it. Probably the only people who will see it are friends of mine, but other people might see it too.

**Aria:** That's okay. What did they say?

**Olga:** What did they say about your picture?

**Aria:** Uh-huh.

**Olga:** I don't know. I haven't put it up yet. Do you want to help me do it?

**Aria:** Yes!

*What's happening in this conversation:* This conversation isn't specifically about bullying, but it touches on a related topic: Internet safety. In this conversation, Olga models to her daughter the kind of behavior she would like to see her use when she eventually has her own social media accounts. Olga asks Aria if it's okay before posting a picture of her online. In doing so, she considers her daughter's feelings, letting her know that she would never post a picture of her without her permission. Follow-up conversations might focus on applying this rule to others outside of their family and only posting pictures of other people with their permission. In addition, they could talk about strategies for what to do if someone ever posted a picture that she didn't like or said something online that was unkind about her.

Technology has led to an evolution in bullying and the emergence of **cyberbullying**. Cyberbullying is bullying that takes place with technology, through computers, tablets, smartphones, or other devices. Cyberbullying can happen through social media, email, text messages, or other methods. One of the problems related to cyberbullying is that bullying is no longer restricted to face-to-face interactions during or after school. Cyberbullying can happen at any time, day or night. A child can be exposed to cyberbullying in their own home, even in the safety of their own bedroom. This is alarming, and all the more reason to help children understand what cyberbullying is, how to avoid hurting other people in online settings, and what to do when they are being bullied or hurt in this way.

**Landon** (Uri's dad): I just read a news article about a girl who got in trouble for doing something called sexting.

**Uri** (age seven): What's sexting?

**Landon:** Sexting is when you send someone pictures or videos that show your private parts.

**Uri:** Eww.

**Landon:** It sounds gross now, but it's something that some older kids think is cool or fun to do. The problem is they don't realize that anything you put on the Internet or send with your phone is there forever. Even if you think you're sending a picture just to one friend, they can share it with lots of other people.

**Uri:** I would never do that, and my friends wouldn't do that either.

**Landon:** That's why I'm telling you about it now. Then you'll know what can happen and help make sure it doesn't happen to others. This girl sent a picture of herself when she was naked to just one person, who told her they would never show anyone. That person lied to her though, and sent it to their whole school. She feels really embarrassed, and she's now in trouble for it. So are the kids who shared it.

**Uri:** Did she erase it?

**Landon:** She tried, but she couldn't. It's important not to share something electronically that you don't want other people to see. Even if you think it won't last or that you can erase it, you really can't. It stays on the Internet forever.

*What's happening in this conversation:* Children are growing up with exposure to technology at younger ages than generations in the past. Because of this, children's beliefs about the Internet and other technologies are formed at early ages. Talking with children, as Landon does with Uri, about the benefits and the risks associated with using technology can help children develop good habits in the hope that these habits will carry on in the future. Although, at age seven, Uri is likely not thinking about sexting or cyberbullying, when he is allowed to send text messages or emails, his dad can talk to him about the importance of thinking about what you share as well as what you do with information that others share with you. In addition, his dad can talk with Uri about the fact that everyone makes mistakes and bad choices. The kids in this scenario are not bad kids, but they made bad decisions. If Uri makes a bad choice, his dad would probably want him to feel comfortable telling him so that he could help Uri through it. This is a message that it is important to communicate to children repeatedly. If children believe that their parents will be there to support them, even when they make mistakes, they will be more likely to seek out support when they do.

### Safe and unsafe touches (abuse)

Abuse is another topic that no parent wants their child to need to know about. There are a number of reasons this conversation is important, however. First, we want to keep our children safe and help them learn to identify potentially dangerous situations, both now as well as when they are older. Second, we can use these conversations to empower children to help others if they see or hear of a friend or classmate who might be in an abusive situation.

**Magna** (Dakota's mom): I love our Saturday morning snuggle time in bed.
**Dakota** (age two): Me too.
**Magna:** How about we read one more book together before we get up?
**Dakota:** Two more books!
**Magna:** Okay. Two more, but then we have to get up and have breakfast.
  I'm hungry!
**Dakota:** Me too.

*What's happening in this conversation:* As part of their Saturday morning routine, Magna and her son, Dakota, spend time reading books in bed together before getting up. Through actions and routines like this one, parents can model to their children how they should expect to be treated, and what it means to be in a positive and loving relationship. Such examples are foundational to conversations about child abuse or neglect of any kind because children need to have an understanding of what a positive and appropriate relationship looks like. Children are adaptive. They learn what to expect from the environments they live in. If a child is accustomed to receiving positive attention and hearing kind words, they will learn that this is *normal*. Hearing a lot of yelling as part of family life, or experiencing neglect and a lack of attention, teaches children that this is what they should expect. Think about what you would like your child to think of as normal during your daily interactions, and strive to have those types of interactions most often.

**Cedric** (age three): Hug, hug, hug. I love hugs.

**Amber** (age three): Me too. Hug, hug, hug.

*(the two children hug and then continue playing together)*

**Cedric:** Hug, hug, hug.

**Amber:** Stop it!

**Cedric:** What? I want huggies!

**Amber:** No huggies!

**Cedric:** Huggies!

**Amber:** No!

**Corinne:** (Amber's mom): Amber, just give Cedric a hug. You love hugs and couldn't stop hugging him earlier.

**Amber:** No more hugs!

**Roland** (Cedric's dad): Cedric, did you hear Amber's words? She said she didn't want any more hugs. When someone says stop, it's important for you to stop.

*What's happening in this conversation:* Although Corinne thought it was relatively harmless to encourage her daughter, Amber, to hug Cedric, Cedric's dad wanted his son to realize that it was time to stop when Amber said "No." Helping children practice listening to other people's words and responding to their cues teaches them how to treat others with kindness. These are messages we should share with our children, regardless of their sex and gender. All children should learn that they have control over their own bodies and should not be forced to interact with someone if they are uncomfortable or don't want to. In addition, they should learn how to communicate their needs and learn to offer others that same respect that we want them to receive.

**Miranda** (Vivienne's aunt): Come give auntie a big hug and kiss.

**Vivienne** (age two): (pulls away)

**Miranda:** Don't be shy. Mwah! Mwah! Just one more kiss and hug!

**Vivienne:** (squirms and pushes away)

**Clyde** (Vivienne's dad): That's okay. If you don't feel like a hug and kiss right now, you don't have to have one. How about giving Aunt Miranda a high five?

**Vivienne:** (high fives with aunt Miranda)

*What's happening in this conversation:* The same message, discussed in the previous conversation, is relevant here, although this time the example is between a child and an adult. There are many different types of conversations that might arise where we tell and show children that their bodies belong to them and they should be able to make choices about who touches their bodies, when, and in what way. When a power difference comes into play (such as between a child and an adult), a parent may need to step in and advocate for their child if they are not able to do so for themselves. In this conversation, Clyde sees that his daughter, Vivienne, is trying to pull away from her aunt. He gives her permission to do so and helps encourage her aunt to step back and give her space.

**Gustav** (Whitney's dad): You have your check-up today!

**Whitney** (age four): Let's play doctor again!

**Gustav:** Okay, I'll pretend to be Dr. Harrison.

**Whitney:** A A A A A A H H H H H H.

**Gustav:** Oh good! You're already opening your mouth. Let me take a look. Okay, now I'll look in your ears and your eyes. Okay, let me listen to your heartbeat. I'll pretend this paper towel tube is a stethoscope. Good, good. Now take a deep breath, and I will listen to your back.

**Whitney:** Do my tummy!

**Gustav:** Okay, please lie down and let me feel your tummy.

**Whitney:** (laughs) Tickles! Too tickly, daddy!

**Gustav:** Oh sorry! You know what else the doctor might do?

**Whitney:** What?

**Gustav:** The doctor will probably want to look at your vagina to make sure everything is healthy. So she might ask you to take off your underwear, but I won't do that now.

**Whitney:** Okay.

**Gustav:** The only people who you should show your private parts to are your parents when we are helping you wipe or keep clean.

**Whitney:** Or if I have an owie.

**Gustav:** Yes, sometimes we check if you feel like you have a rash. Or when a doctor asks to look at your private parts to make sure you're growing and healthy.

**Whitney:** Okay, daddy.

**Gustav:** But it's your body, so it's important for you, now that you're getting older, to decide if it's okay when you show your body to mom and dad or the doctor. If you don't feel comfortable, you can say so.

**Whitney:** Okay, daddy.

*What's happening in this conversation:* As they prepare for Whitney's upcoming doctor's appointment, her dad, Gustav, reinforces the message that Whitney's body is her own and that she should have the right to determine who touches and sees her body, even in safe scenarios. There are times when adults may have to touch children, even when they don't want to be touched. For example, if a child is having a meltdown in the parking lot on the way back to the car, a parent might say, *"This is not safe. You can move your body yourself, or I will pick you up,"* and then follow through by picking up their child and carrying them, kicking and screaming, to safety. Whenever possible, adults can help children learn that they are, and should be, in control of their bodies—so long as they are not in danger.

> **João** (Max's dad): Hitting your brother is never okay.
>
> **Max** (age five): But he took my toy!
>
> **João:** I know that he took your toy. He shouldn't have done that, but you still should not have hit him. Just because he did something wrong doesn't mean you should do something wrong, too. Have you ever seen mom and me hit each other when we get upset?
>
> **Max:** No.
>
> **João:** That's right. We use our words. We would never hit each other even when we disagree, and I want you and your brother to learn that same thing. Is there something you could do instead of hitting?
>
> **Max:** Give me my toy!
>
> **João:** Using your words is a good idea, but that's not a very kind way to ask. What about asking, "May I have my toy, please?"
>
> **Max:** "May I have my toy please?" (takes toy back) Thank you!

*What's happening in this conversation:* João continually reinforces to his two sons that hitting is not the way that they solve problems in their family. Although his sons continually resort to pushing and hitting, he realizes that changing these patterns and encouraging his sons to find another way to settle their disputes will take time and practice.

**Annette** (Hilde's mom): Do you know what abuse means?

**Hilde** (age seven): No.

**Annette:** Abuse is when someone hurts someone else on purpose.

**Hilde:** Like when Carl hits me?

**Annette:** Well, Carl is only three and he is still learning, so we don't call that abuse. But if an older kid who knew better, or a grown-up ever hurt you on purpose, that would be abuse.

**Hilde:** Oh.

**Annette:** I'm telling you this because it's important for you to know that it's never okay for adults to hurt kids—not to hit them or push them or kick them or anything else like that. If someone ever hurt you on purpose, get away from them and tell another grown-up right away.

**Hilde:** I already know that, mom.

*What's happening in this conversation:* As mentioned in an earlier conversation, children learn what is normal through the interactions they have with their parents and family members. For children who grow up without exposure to abuse, parents may have to decide when they feel it is best to introduce the idea to their child that sometimes adults hurt children. A critical part of this message is that when this does happen, it is not okay. As Annette continues this conversation (either now or at a later time), she may also let Hilde know that an adult who hurts children needs help to stop, and that adults who are hurting children sometimes tell children things that are not true:

**Annette:** Sometimes grown-ups who hurt children trick them. They tell them that something bad will happen if they tell anyone. They might even tell children they will hurt them more, or hurt their family, or even kill them. When someone says that, it's a trick because they don't want to get in trouble. It's really important for you to tell a grown-up if someone ever hurts you. If the grown-up you tell doesn't listen to you or doesn't believe you, tell someone else. You can always tell mom and dad. We will always believe you, but the most important thing is to tell someone and find someone who will help you.

Letting children know that abuse can and does happen will help them be better able to seek out help if they recognize that this is happening. In the

United States, approximately 700,000 children are abused annually. The most common form of abuse is neglect, with 75 percent of children who are abused experiencing neglect, approximately 17 percent suffering physical abuse, and approximately 8 percent suffering sexual abuse. Younger children are more likely than older children to be abused, with 37 percent of abuse victims falling in the 0–6 age range, 37 percent falling in the 7–12 age range, and the remaining 26 percent falling in the 13–17 age range. More often than not (in 78 percent of abuse cases), a child's parent is the perpetrator of abuse (National Children's Alliance, 2015). In these instances, it may be extremely difficult for a young child to ask for help, making it all the more important that all children and families strive to be a support for one another.

**Chuck** (Nathan's dad): I wanted to talk to you about something.

**Nathan** (age five): What?

**Chuck:** I just read a story about a girl who was being abused by one of her family members. That means one of her family members was hurting her on purpose.

**Nathan:** Why did they hurt her?

**Chuck:** I don't know why. Adults should never, ever hurt children on purpose. Adults who hurt children need help learning how to stop. They might have been abused, so that's how they learned how to manage problems, or they might have drug or alcohol abuse problems. There are lots of reasons.

**Nathan:** How come she didn't tell them to stop or tell her teacher?

**Chuck:** Even though her mom was hurting her, it was still her mom. She was afraid that her mom would get in trouble.

**Nathan:** Will her mom get in trouble?

**Chuck:** Yes, probably, but she will also get help so that she doesn't hurt her daughter anymore.

*What's happening in this conversation:* This conversation and the ones that came before provide examples for ways to talk about abuse with children who have not personally experienced abuse. Conversations with children who have experienced abuse are likely to look differently, and should be approached with caution and with support from counseling professionals.

### Substance use and abuse

Families have many different beliefs related to substance use, from cigarettes to alcohol to drugs (legal and illegal). Children learn and develop attitudes about substance abuse from young ages and can be profoundly shaped by the behaviors they see in their family, as well as the conversations they have. Think about the messages you would like your child to learn from a young age, and what you can do through both conversations and behaviors to teach those messages to your child.

**Rhiannon** (age four): What are you drinking?

**Trisha** (Rhiannon's mom): It's wine.

**Rhiannon:** Can I have some?

**Trisha:** No. It has alcohol in it so it's not for kids.

**Rhiannon:** What's alcohol?

**Trisha:** Alcohol is something that some adults like to drink. It's not for kids because it can change the way your body feels, or even change the way you think.

**Rhiannon:** It changes the way you think?

**Trisha:** Yes. It might make you feel more relaxed. For some people, it helps them feel less shy. Some people get more upset or angrier when they drink alcohol. If you have too much, it might make it hard to think straight.

**Rhiannon:** I don't want it. I'm never never never going to drink it. You can't make me.

**Trisha:** You don't have to have it. Drinking alcohol or not drinking alcohol is a choice you can make when you're an adult. It's not something you have to do.

*What's happening in this conversation:* In this conversation, Trisha talks with her daughter Rhiannon about alcohol. This conversation may look very different, depending on your own family's use of and beliefs about alcohol. You may instead share with your child that alcohol is something you do not drink, and share your reasons why, or you may have other values related to drinking alcohol, such as that alcohol is appropriate for certain occasions only. Whatever your beliefs may be, share them with your child, as well as the reasoning behind them. Follow-up conversations might include talking about the age at which it is legal to drink alcohol, and making good decisions about drinking (e.g., not driving while drinking).

**Bea** (age four): What is that man doing?

**Polly** (Bea's mom): He's smoking a cigarette.

**Bea:** What's a cigarette?

**Polly:** A cigarette has tobacco inside. Some people like to smoke them. They light them on fire and breathe in the smoke.

**Bea:** Why?

**Polly:** Some people like how it makes them feel. Tobacco has nicotine in it, and nicotine is very addictive. That means your body wants more and more and more when you try it.

**Bea:** It smells bad.

**Polly:** I think so too, and it's really bad for your body.

**Bea:** Yuck. I don't like it.

**Polly:** Breathing in that kind of smoke is bad for your lungs. It can make it hard to breathe, and if you do it a lot it can make it easier for you to get sick.

**Bea:** I don't want to smoke cigarettes.

**Polly:** You don't have to. Smoking is something people choose to do if they want to, but it's definitely not a good choice.

**Bea:** Why do people do it?

**Polly:** When I was young, kids thought it was cool to smoke cigarettes.

**Bea:** Did they know it was bad?

**Polly:** Yes, but they didn't care. They just wanted to look cool. The problem was, once they started smoking, it was hard to stop, so some of them kept doing it.

**Bea:** I'm never going to smoke!

**Polly:** I sure hope you don't!

*What's happening in this conversation:* Although Bea has seen other people smoking cigarettes in the past (and she may have had a similar conversation with her mom in the past), she asks once again about smoking. Her mom answers her questions openly and even talks about why kids might choose to smoke (because it has been associated with looking cool). Follow-up conversations might include talking about how to say no, and ideas for what to do if saying no feels hard to do.

**Eldon** (Vic's dad): Do you see that picture of a leaf?

**Vic** (age five): Yes.

**Eldon:** That's a marijuana leaf. That billboard is an advertisement for people to buy marijuana.

**Vic:** What's marijuana?

**Eldon:** It's a kind of drug. It used to be against the law, but now it's legal in our state. Do you remember what drugs are?

**Vic:** Medicine from the doctor?

**Eldon:** Medicines are a kind of drug, but a drug is anything you put in your body that changes it in some way. It might change how you're thinking or how you're feeling. If you take medicine from the doctor, it can help you feel better when you are sick.

**Vic:** Is that medicine?

**Eldon:** Marijuana? Some people use it as medicine, but a lot of people who smoke marijuana are not sick. They use it because it changes the way they feel and they like that.

**Vic:** Do you smoke marijuana?

**Eldon:** No. I don't. I tried it a few times when I was in college, but I didn't like feeling differently. I like to feel like I'm in control of my body.

**Vic:** Me too.

*What's happening in this conversation:* As they are driving down the street, Eldon points out a billboard with a picture of a marijuana leaf and uses the opportunity to talk with his son, Vic, about drugs. Talking with children about what drugs are, as well as the impact they can have on your body, provides them with information that may help them make informed decisions related to drug use as they get older.

**Marie** (age six): Why is that man doing that?

**Marnix** (Marie's dad): What do you mean?

**Marie:** He's walking funny and yelling at people over there.

**Marnix:** Oh, I see what you mean. I think he might be using drugs or he might have a disability or mental illness. Do you see how he's having trouble controlling his body?

**Marie:** Yeah. He can't walk very well. He keeps falling down.

**Marnix:** That can happen when you take a lot of drugs. You can lose control of your body. Drugs are really bad for your body.

**Marie:** I never want to take drugs.

**Marnix:** I know, and I hope you won't change your mind when you're older.

**Marie:** I won't change my mind.

**Marnix:** I believe you. Sometimes older kids take drugs because they want to see what it's like, so it can be really hard to say no if all your friends are doing them.

**Marie:** I know, dad.

*What's happening in this conversation:* Marnix and his daughter, Marie, see a man in their community who appears to be impaired. Marnix uses this opportunity to talk with his daughter about what can happen to your body when taking drugs. Follow-up conversations might focus on reasons why people start taking drugs, reasons why it is hard to stop taking drugs, and ways to say no to drugs, especially in challenging situations. Importantly, studies have shown that conversations between parents and children about drug and alcohol use and abuse can impact children's attitudes (Huansuriya, Sigel, & Crano, 2014; Kuntsche & Kuntsche; 2016). Having conversations that acknowledge the challenges that children and adults might face related to drug and alcohol use can better prepare children for these challenging situations if and when they do arise.

### Death

When children first learn about death and reflect on death throughout their childhoods, they may have many different emotions. It is important to let children know that the many different feelings they have related to death are normal. Some children are exposed to death earlier than others. Some experience death in a way that is timely and expected, such as through the loss of an aging pet or the loss of an elderly grandparent who enjoyed a long life. Others experience death in a way that is unexpected or tragic, such as through the loss of a friend, family, or community member through serious illness, violence, an accident, or suicide. The example conversations included here focus on teaching children about the concept of death, as well as basic coping strategies. Children who have experienced trauma related to death will likely need additional support from pediatricians, teachers, or counseling professionals.

**Isa** (Hannah's mom): This part of the book is a little sad. The character dies.

**Hannah** (age four): What happens when you die?

**Isa:** When you die, you're not alive anymore.

**Hannah:** Why do people die?

**Isa:** Everyone dies. That's part of living. Our bodies are only meant to live for so long. Some people live until they are 50 or 60 or even 100. But at some point when we get old, our bodies stop working.

**Hannah:** I don't want my body to stop working. I don't want to die.

**Isa:** Thinking about dying can be sad or scary and that's okay. Sometimes it helps to think about things we can do to live a long and healthy life. If you keep your body healthy and safe, you'll probably live a really long time. Grandpa lived until he was 87, and Grandma lived until she was 96! You might be able to live that long too, or even longer.

*What's happening in this conversation:* Hannah explains to her daughter Isa that death occurs when a person's body stops working and stops living. Children who understand death from a biological perspective tend to have lower levels of fear about death than those who do not (Slaughter & Griffiths, 2007). In addition to sharing with your child what death means biologically, share your personal, family, religious, or spiritual beliefs about death with your child so that they learn how your family celebrates and mourns when someone dies.

**Fiona** (age five): I don't want to die.

**Carlos** (Fiona's dad): I don't want to die, either.

**Fiona:** Will I die?

**Carlos:** Yes. Everybody dies, but you probably will not die for a very, very long time.

**Fiona:** Will you die?

**Carlos:** Yes. Someday, but also not for a very long time.

**Fiona:** I'm afraid to die.

**Carlos:** It's okay to feel afraid. I feel afraid about dying sometimes too, but do you know what I do when I feel that way?

**Fiona:** What?

**Carlos:** I think about all the things I can do to make sure that I live for a very, very long time.

**Fiona:** Like what?

**Carlos:** Like keeping my body safe by looking both ways before I cross the street. Or making sure I eat healthy foods and exercise to keep my body strong. You can do those things too!

**Fiona:** My body is already strong!

**Carlos:** Yes it is, and if you keep taking care of your body, you'll probably live a really long time.

**Fiona:** I'm going to live to be a million!

**Carlos:** No one has ever lived that long before, but some people live to be a hundred.

**Fiona:** I'm going to live to be two hundred!

**Carlos:** (laughs) You can sure try. If you do, you might be the oldest person who ever lived!

*What's happening in this conversation:* When children first learn about death and when they reflect on death throughout their childhoods, they will likely have many different emotions. In this conversation, Carlos lets his daughter, Fiona, know that her feelings are okay and shares his own feelings with her as well. Death is a phenomenon that we have little control over. By helping children focus on what they can do (e.g., keeping their bodies healthy and safe), parents can help children feel that they are taking control of the aspects of death that they can influence.

**Saif** (age seven)**:** I'm scared about dying.

**Sahyid** (Saif's dad)**:** It's okay to feel afraid about dying. Actually, it may even be good for you to feel a little afraid about dying.

**Saif:** Why?

**Sahyid:** Well, feeling a little afraid about dying might help you keep your body safe. If you're a little bit afraid, it means you won't do things that are too dangerous, like walking in the street when there are cars coming. I bet when you're older, though, you might not feel so afraid anymore.

**Saif:** How come?

**Sahyid:** I was really afraid of dying when I was young, but as I've gotten older, it doesn't seem so scary anymore. You might feel that way, too. When people have lived a long time and feel like they have had a good life, death doesn't always seem too scary anymore.

**Saif:** I don't think I will ever want to die.

**Sahyid:** I hope you will live a very, very long life.

*What's happening in this conversation:* Children may bring up the topic of death in different ways at different times in their lives. Saif shares with his father that he's feeling scared about dying. Sahyid lets him know that this feeling is okay, but also shares with him his own feelings and how his feelings have changed over time.

**Cybele** (Anya's mom)**:** I have some sad news to share with you.

**Anya** (age six)**:** What?

**Cybele:** Darcy's sister, Valerie, died today.

**Anya:** Oh.

**Cybele:** Darcy won't be at school tomorrow and may not be there for a while.

**Anya:** Her sister was going to have an operation.

**Cybele:** I know. They didn't know if the operation would work or not, and it didn't.

**Anya:** I'm sad for Darcy.

**Cybele:** Me too. I wonder if there is anything we can do to help their family.

**Anya:** Maybe I could draw her a picture to make her feel better.

**Cybele:** That would be a nice thing to do. It's a very sad thing when someone you love dies. A picture might not help Darcy feel better, but it shows her that you care about her.

**Anya:** What can I do to help her feel better?

**Cybele:** There might not be anything we can do to help her feel better— people can feel sad for a long time when someone they love dies, and that's okay. But we can do things to help their family and show them we care. How about if we make a lasagna so that they have food for dinner and don't have to cook? We'll drop it off at your house along with your picture.

**Anya:** Okay. Can I help?

**Cybele:** You bet!

*What's happening in this conversation:* In this conversation, Cybele shares with her daughter, Anya, that her classmate's sister died. Even though Anya didn't know Valerie (the girl who died), she is friends with her sister, Darcy. Her mom encourages her to think about what she can do to be helpful to the family. When Anya starts thinking about ways to help her friend feel better, Cybele lets her know that it's okay for Darcy to feel sad, and that there may not be a way to help her feel better right away, and that's okay.

**Evan** (age five): What happens when you die?

**Barack** (Evan's grandfather): No one really knows for sure. I think when you die that it's like going to sleep for a really, really long time and not waking up again.

**Evan:** Do you dream?

**Barack:** I don't think so. Your body stops working, so I think it's probably like being in a deep sleep where you don't dream or have any thoughts.

**Evan:** How do you know that?

**Barack:** I don't know for sure. We do know that when you die, your body stops—even your brain. Some people think that your body has a soul—a part of your body that keeps living, even after you die. Some people think your soul goes to heaven.

**Evan:** What's heaven?

**Barack:** Heaven is a special place where people who die go to be at peace and watch over the people you love. Some people believe heaven is real. Some people don't. But it's nice to think about.

**Evan:** I like heaven.

**Barack:** Me too.

*What's happening in this conversation:* There are many different individual, religious, and spiritual beliefs about what happens when someone dies. Share your family's beliefs with your child, but also consider sharing with them the beliefs that others have. Doing so helps your child learn that death is something everyone experiences, and that when someone dies, there are many different approaches to celebrating and mourning life and death.

**Alice** (Craig's mom): We're going to have a funeral for grandpa.

**Craig** (age four): A funeral for grandpa? Is a funeral a toy?

**Alice:** A funeral is a time when people get together to remember someone who died. People might tell stories about that person, or share pictures or special memories. There are lots of different ways to have a funeral.

**Craig:** Like what?

**Alice:** Some funerals are very sad and a time for people to cry together or feel sad together. There's a special kind of sadness when someone dies or you lose something important to you—that's called grieving. Can you say grieving?

**Craig:** Grieving.

**Alice:** Funerals are a time for people to grieve together. Some funerals are a celebration. That's what I want when I die! I want to live a really long time and then have people come together to celebrate that I had a good life and share funny stories and happy memories about me. Maybe even dancing.

**Craig:** Like a party?

**Alice:** Yes! Like a party!

**Craig:** Is grandpa's funeral going to be a party.

**Alice:** It'll probably be a little sad and a little party too, knowing our family.

*What's happening in this conversation:* Funerals or celebrations of life can be important ways to grieve and celebrate the death of a loved one. Before bringing a young child to a funeral, it is important for a parent to think about whether or not the funeral will be a helpful experience for that child. For example, will there be adults present who are able to help the child understand what is happening and manage the child's emotions while the adult manages their own? Will the adult be able to leave with the child if the funeral becomes too overwhelming? Whether or not to include children in funerals and at what age is a family decision that should be made based both on the child's needs as well as on the family's comfort level.

**Madison** (age four): I miss grandma.

**Patel** (Madison's dad): Me too. Do you want to come sit next to me and have a big hug?

**Madison:** Okay.

**Patel:** Sometimes when I miss grandma, I like to think about some of the good memories I have with her. Do you want to hear a story about grandma from when I was a little boy?

**Madison:** No story now.

**Patel:** Okay, then we can just sit and have a hug.

*What's happening in this conversation:* When young children experience a death or a loss, it's not uncommon for them to revisit that loss from time to time, even months after the loss has occurred. In this conversation, Patel lets Madison know that her feelings are okay and that he has those same feelings. In addition, he offers a strategy (sharing good memories) that helps him manage the feelings he has that might help her as well.

Death is a hard concept for children and adults to understand, but a reality that everyone faces. Help your child understand what death is, as well as the beliefs your family has related to death. These conversations can help children understand that death is something everyone experiences, and that there are things you can do to live a healthy and meaningful life.

### Suicide

Suicide is a topic most parents never want to think about or consider being a possibility for their own child or anyone else's. The sad reality is that suicide does occur and is a real risk for children, whether we like it or not. There are different approaches that parents can take to talking about suicide, and the approach you take may differ based on your child's exposure to the topic. If a child is grieving the loss of someone they know or love who has committed suicide, the conversation will likely be very different than when introducing the topic as a preventative measure. Children who have conversations with parents about suicide may also be better equipped to help a friend or peer who shows warning signs at a later time.

**Georgia** (Ruby's aunt): I noticed that you seemed a little quieter than usual today. Are you thinking about something?

**Ruby** (age six): No.

**Georgia:** Just having a quiet day?

**Ruby:** Yeah.

**Georgia:** That's okay. Sometimes I have quiet days too.

**Ruby:** I just like being quiet.

**Georgia:** I understand. Do you want to come sit on the couch with me and just snuggle?

**Ruby:** Okay.

**Georgia:** If you decide you want to talk about anything at all, I'll be right here. I love you, and anything important to you is important to me too.

**Ruby:** I love you, Aunt Georgia.

**Georgia:** I love you too.

*What's happening in this conversation:* Having ups and downs is a normal part of life. Letting a child know that you notice their ups and downs while offering support (without pushing or prying) communicates to children that they are valued. When Ruby tells her aunt Georgia that she doesn't want to talk, Georgia respects that request while also letting Ruby know that she wants to support her if and when she needs and wants that support. Many of the early conversations in this book promote warm and positive interactions and open communication between parents and children. This conversation is another example of how a parent or caregiver can let their child know that they are loved and available to talk about anything that matters to them, no matter how big or how small.

**Pablo** (Javier's dad)**:** I just heard about a show that teenagers are watching about suicide, so I wanted to talk to you about it. Do you know what suicide means?

**Javier** (age seven)**:** No.

**Pablo:** Suicide is when someone takes their own life—someone makes themselves die or kills themselves.

**Javier:** Oh. I don't like that.

**Pablo:** I don't like it either. It's very sad when that happens.

**Javier:** I would never make myself die.

**Pablo:** I'm glad. That would be the saddest thing I could imagine in the whole world. When people die from suicide or try to kill themselves, it is very, very sad for the people who know them and love them. There's always something else you can do to make things better, rather than suicide. Even if things feel hopeless, it's important to talk to someone.

*What's happening in this conversation:* Sometimes the topic of suicide arises because a family or community experiences a loss. Rather than waiting for the topic to arise in your child's life, consider proactively teaching your child what suicide means, using words that your child can understand. In this conversation, Pablo brings up the topic after reading about a popular show highlighting suicide. Even though his son is young, he realizes that Javier may be exposed to the topic through his older brothers and sisters and wants to make sure he is not confused or scared by what he hears. Pablo also wants to plant the seed while Javier is young that there are always alternatives to suicide.

**Heather** (Florian's mom): Something very sad happened.

**Florian** (age six): What?

**Heather:** Do you remember Frank from my work?

**Florian:** Does he have the cowboy belt?

**Heather:** Yes—that's Frank! Something sad happened in his family. His brother died from suicide yesterday.

**Florian:** He died?

**Heather:** Yes. He killed himself. Frank didn't come to work today so that he could be with his family.

**Florian:** Why did he kill himself?

**Heather:** They're not sure. There are lots of reasons why someone dies from suicide. They might be depressed. Do you remember what depression means?

**Florian:** No.

**Heather:** It's when someone is really, really sad and can't help it. They might not know why they are sad. So maybe he was depressed. Sometimes drugs or alcohol lead people to make bad choices. I don't know why Frank's brother died from suicide. But I know that Frank wishes that his brother would have told him he was sad and asked for help.

**Florian:** Is he the one who helped me fly my kite at the picnic?

**Heather:** Yes, that was Frank's brother. I forgot that you met him.

**Florian:** He was nice.

*What's happening in this conversation:* Like Pablo and Javier in the previous conversation, Heather brings up the topic of suicide with her son, Florian. In this conversation, however, she is sharing with her son about a death that happened in their family's community. Florian remembers Frank's brother as being someone who was nice. Talking about suicide can carry a stigma and the message that anyone who dies from suicide has a problem. Having met Frank, Florian has seen that even people who are nice and appear to be happy in life may need help.

**Hunter** (Jessica's dad): I was thinking about your aunt Joan again.

**Jessica** (age 10): Why, dad?

**Hunter:** I miss her. I wish she would have talked to someone instead of hurting herself. I keep wondering if I could have changed things if I had known what she was going through. I hope you know that even if you ever make a bad choice or get in trouble for any reason, you can always talk to me about it. I might not like it, but I will always do my best to help you—no matter what.

**Jessica:** I know, dad.

**Hunter:** I know you know. I just wanted to remind you and make sure. I love you so much, and nothing could be as bad as losing you.

**Jessica:** I love you, dad.

**Hunter:** I love you too. If you ever hear someone talking about wanting to kill themselves, it's really important to talk to them and make sure they get help.

**Jessica:** I know.

*What's happening in this conversation:* Suicide happens for many reasons. It's impossible to know when someone dies from suicide if there was something that could have been done to change the outcome. Hunter speaks with his daughter, Jessica, about her aunt's suicide. He lets her know that he will always be there for his daughter—no matter what.

\* \* \*

Although suicide is a topic that no parent wants their child to have personal experience with in any way, the likelihood is high that a child will, at some point in their life, know someone who attempts suicide or who dies from suicide. Alarmingly, suicide is a leading cause of death for children ages 12 to 19, ranking above cancer, heart disease, influenza, and pneumonia. Suicide is also on the rise for younger children. Even though suicide in children under 11 does not receive much attention, it does happen. From 1993 to 2012, 657 children in the United States between the ages of 5 and 11 dies from suicide. It is important to know that talking about suicide with children is not related to increased suicidal thoughts or motivations. As you consider talking with your child about suicide, realize that early conversations about suicide may not be about suicide at all. Building a secure and trusting relationship with your child and establishing a positive pattern of communication can help your child effectively manage their emotions and feel comfortable asking for help when they need it.

## Incarceration

Depending on exposure and life experience, the messages children learn about incarceration can be very different from one another. Some children may have direct experience with incarceration through family members, neighbors, or friends. Other children may know nothing about incarceration, or know only what they see in books, stories, movies, and through pretend play. Regardless of their personal exposure, children may find incarceration to be an interesting topic and one that leads to a multitude of questions about who is incarcerated and why.

**Emile** (Grace's dad): Uh-oh. There are police lights behind us. I must have been driving a little too fast.

**Grace** (age six): Do you have to go to jail?

**Emile:** No, but when you see flashing police lights, it's important to pull over and talk to the police officer. I'll probably get a ticket and a fine, though.

**Grace:** What's a fine?

**Emile:** When you do something that's against the law, like speeding, there is a consequence. When you speed, you usually get a ticket that says you have to pay a certain amount of money. That's called a fine.

**Grace:** How much money?

**Emile:** It depends on how fast you were going. It's supposed to be a way to stop people from doing things they shouldn't do, and teach them to be more careful next time.

*What's happening in this conversation:* Staying as calm as Emile did while being pulled over for speeding may not be realistic for all parents, but doing so can help your child understand what is happening and why. Just like the consequences children experience at home, when consequences are logical and make sense, they are less scary. Talking through the consequences that adults face teaches children about how their experiences fit in with the larger society around them.

**Brann** (age four): What's that building with the big fence.

**Karen** (Brann's mom): That's a prison.

**Brann:** What's a prison?

**Karen:** A prison is a place where people have to go if they commit certain crimes. It's like a jail.

**Brann:** Have you ever been to prison?

**Karen:** No.

**Brann:** Has daddy ever been to prison?

**Karen:** No. Only bad guys go to prison.

**Brann:** Only bad guys go to prison?

**Karen:** Well, maybe I shouldn't have said it like that. People in prison are not necessarily bad guys, but usually people who have done something they should not have done. Most people aren't bad guys. Most people are good most of the time, but sometimes good people make bad choices.

**Brann:** Sometimes I make bad choices.

**Karen:** Me too. But when you're a grown-up, there are certain mistakes that you're not supposed to make anymore, especially hurting other people in some way. When you make really bad mistakes—mistakes that are against the law, that's when you might have to go to prison.

*What's happening in this conversation:* When Brann asks his mom if only bad guys go to prison, she encourages him to think about the fact that most people aren't "bad guys," but that even good people make bad choices. This conversation may be especially important for children who experience the incarceration of a loved one.

These conversations give rise to questions about how to best talk with children about an issue like incarceration. Do we tell children that only "bad guys" go to jail so that they won't worry about going to jail themselves? What kind of message would this communicate to the child in the previous scenario—telling him that his brother is bad? He likely loves and looks up to his brother. Hearing that his brother is bad may be confusing and may make him feel bad as well, or lead him to believe that being bad is not such a bad thing. His brother probably has many good qualities, but that doesn't mean he didn't make a mistake. We all make mistakes. Rather than focusing on good guys and bad guys, parents can focus on the fact that everyone makes mistakes, but certain mistakes are worse than others, and certain mistakes have more serious consequences than others.

One afternoon, I arrived at a childcare center to be greeted by a teacher, Ms. Becker whom I knew well.

"Thank goodness you're here," she said. I just had a conversation with Corey and I didn't know what to do." Ms. Becker went on to explain that she had noticed four-year-old Corey in her class sitting to the side of the room with his head down. When she approached him, he shared that he was feeling sad because he missed his brother. "Don't worry," she replied. "You'll see your brother after school."

"No I won't. He's in jail."

Ms. Becker shook her head and shared with me, "I wish they wouldn't have told him that. They should have told him that his brother was on vacation." Ms. Becker let Corey know it was okay to be sad, but made sure not to talk about the topic around the other children in the class in order to protect Corey and prevent him from feeling embarrassed or ashamed.

At another school in a neighboring community, children set up a pretend jail in the imaginary play corner of their classroom. Several of the children in the class had incarcerated family members. They showed the other children how to walk through the pretend metal detectors and sign in for a visit. Their teacher, Ms. Diaz, allowed the children to play in this way, as she saw it as helpful for all of them. The children who had incarcerated family members had a chance to talk about their feelings and saw that they were not alone. The children who did not have exposure to incarceration had a chance to learn more about their classmates' lives and see that each person's life experience was filled with different challenges.

One of the children in this classroom, Carla, (a child who had no previous experience with incarceration) came home and asked her mom about jail.

"Will I have to go to jail some day? Will you have to go to jail? What about daddy?"

As her daughter's list of questions grew, her mother told her not to worry. "Jail is only for bad guys."

Carla thought about this a while and then asked, "Is Avery's brother a bad guy? He's in jail."

Her mom had to think about how to answer this question. Was Avery's brother a bad guy? Maybe, but perhaps the issue was more complicated than that. Maybe

continued

he was a good guy who made a bad choice, or maybe he was incarcerated for something he didn't do. She felt torn wanting to reassure her daughter that she was safe, but also wanting her to understand the issue was complicated.

• How would you answer these questions for your own child?

Incarceration is a consequence adults face if they engage in certain illegal behaviors. For children to feel safe, consequences should make sense. They should be logical, they should be fair, and they should help them learn what to do next time. At face value, this argument sounds good, but in practice, the logic can break down. If incarceration paralleled effective parenting, going to jail or prison would represent facing a consequence for a bad behavior (crime), learning from that mistake, returning to society (if and when allowed), and learning what to do differently next time. Sometimes, however, individuals are incarcerated unfairly or for something they did not do. Unfortunately, incarceration is not a consequence that is applied equitably in the United States. There are racial disparities in the numbers of incarcerated adults by race. For example, black/African-American adults and specifically males are incarcerated at a rate that is five times higher than the rate of white/Caucasian-American males. In addition, studies including hundreds of thousands of prisoners in the United States have shown that recidivism rates are very high. One study found that within 3 years of release, approximately 68 percent of prisoners were rearrested. By the end of 5 years, the number rose to nearly 75 percent (National Institute of Justice, 2014). These statistics call into question whether or not incarceration and the programs associated with incarceration are serving as effective ways to make sure people have the support they need to make good choices and improve their lives for the better.

Young children who experience incarceration of a parent or a family member may also be experiencing separation, loneliness, stigma, chaotic or unstable home environments and childcare arrangements, stress, and many other factors (Murray, Farrington, & Sekol, 2012). Given these challenges, children who experience incarceration in their families may be an especially critical group to support compassionately at home, at school, and in the community.

## Guns and violence

There are many reasons a family might want to own one or more guns, including for recreational shooting, hunting, protection, for a job requirement, or because they own a relic or piece of family history. There are also many reasons why a family might not want to own a gun, including the many dangers associated with accidental shootings. Guns are responsible for 30 percent of pediatric trauma fatalities (Lee, Moriarty, Tashjian, & Patterson, 2013). The American Pediatric Association asserts that the most effective measure to prevent suicide, homicide, and unintentional injuries to children and youth is the absence of guns from homes and communities (American Academy of Pediatrics, 2012). No matter how your family feels about gun ownership, guns are prevalent in the United States. All parents should strongly consider teaching their children about gun safety within and outside of their homes. A survey of teachers found that the majority believed gun safety should be taught at school (62 percent), with 28 percent believing awareness should begin in preschool (Obeng, 2010). Schools have a range of policies related to teaching children about guns and gun safety. Some schools include gun safety as a required part of the curriculum, while others don't include it at all, leaving conversations about gun safety up to parents.

> **Diego** (age four): I'm going to shoot you!
> **Matthias** (age five): I'm going to shoot you first!
> **Sebastian** (Diego's and Matthias's dad): Who's shooting whom around here?
> **Diego:** Dad, they're just sticks! We found them in the backyard.
> **Sebastian:** You know our family rule, no shooting other people—even for pretend. You can pretend to shoot targets, but not people.
> **Matthias:** Okay, dad.

*What's happening in this conversation:* Many families have strong feelings about children's imaginary play with guns. Some families may believe that children should not even pretend to play with guns or other weapons, no matter what the circumstances. Other families may believe imaginary gunplay is fine with certain restrictions (e.g., no shooting people) or with no restrictions at all. Whatever your family rules are, have a conversation about them with your child.

**Wyatt** (Suzie's dad): I want to show you something.

**Suzie** (age six): What?

**Wyatt:** This is a gun.

**Suzie:** Whoa! Can I touch it?

**Wyatt:** Yes, but only right now, when I'm with you. There are no bullets in it, and it has this lock so it can't hurt anyone right now.

**Suzie:** It's heavy.

**Wyatt:** I wanted to show you so that you would know what this was.

**Suzie:** Okay, dad.

**Wyatt:** I'm going to put it away in a locked safe. I wanted you to know it was here because it's very important that if you ever find it, you need to tell me right away.

**Suzie:** Okay, dad.

**Wyatt:** I don't want you to ever touch it on your own. If you find it, leave it where it is and come tell me or another grown-up. Got it?

**Suzie:** Got it.

**Wyatt:** This is true if you ever find a gun anywhere—in our house or someone else's house. Don't touch it, leave it where it is, and tell a grown-up right away. This is very important because kids can get hurt with guns, and even die.

**Suzie:** Okay, dad! I know what to do!

*What's happening in this conversation:* Whether you have a gun in your home or not, having a conversation with a child about what to do if they ever see or find a gun is an important safety precaution. Approximately one third of households in the United States have a gun. Hopefully, your child will never accidentally chance upon a gun in your own or someone else's household, but if they do, it is important to know that your child understands how to safely handle this situation.

**Erwin** (age six): Why did that man shoot those kids?

**Ruth** (Erwin's mom): Where did you hear about that?

**Erwin:** On the TV at the store, and I heard my teacher talk about it.

**Ruth:** Oh my. That was a very sad thing that happened today. We don't want anyone to get hurt like that—ever—especially children.

**Erwin:** Did kids get hurt?

**Ruth:** Yes, some children died, and that is a very sad thing. The man who did it died too.

**Erwin:** How did he die?

**Ruth:** He shot himself with his gun.

**Erwin:** I don't want that to happen at my school.

**Ruth:** I don't either. That's a very scary thing to think about. Things like this don't happen very often, and we do everything we can to make sure they don't happen, and to keep you safe. Your school does lots of things to keep you safe, too.

**Erwin:** Like what?

**Ruth:** We have to push a code on the keypad to open the door, so only people who have the code can come in. Your classroom also has a camera that shows who is at the door so that your teachers know that the people coming to your school are not dangerous. I can show it to you when we go to school tomorrow.

**Erwin:** Okay.

**Ruth:** You shouldn't have to worry about something like this happening. I love you so much, and all the grown-ups in your life work hard to make sure you and other children are safe.

*What's happening in this conversation:* We see news of school shootings and other tragedies more frequently than we would like. In fact, we wouldn't like to see them at all. There is no "right" age when you should talk with your child about tragedies of this nature. This is a choice that parents need to make based on their own comfort level, as well as their child's maturity and ability to understand the situation. Regardless, parents should help children avoid exposure to graphic images that might be hard for children to understand or that might cause extreme fear or anxiety. Parents should consider if there is a practical reason to talk with children about a tragedy, for example, if there is something children should know to help keep them safe. Sometimes, parents need to have a conversation with a child about a tragedy because their child heard about a situation from another source, such as the media. Hearing about other children getting hurt or killed may be scary or even terrifying for some children. When you have conversations with your child about tragedies such as these, carefully decide the level of detail to share, focus on what is being done to help prevent things like this from happening in the future, and share with your child what is being done to help keep them and other children safe at home, at school, and in the community.

## Chapter conclusions

Chapter IV includes examples of many different conversations about a number of challenging topics. Each of these topics on its own could fill an entire chapter or even a book if we explored them in depth. Although each topic and example is different from the others, there are similarities that we can see between these conversations that may help guide the conversations you have with your own child. In each conversation, parents take their children's questions and feelings seriously and show their children that they are available to talk with them about any topic at any time and without fear of judgment or punishment. The parents in these conversations do not always know much about the topics children ask about, but they are not afraid to share that with their children, modeling how to find information so that they can learn more together.

As you consider which conversations to introduce to your child and when, think about the benefit of being the first to introduce a topic to your child. Children will eventually be exposed to each topic in this book in some way, whether it is through their teachers and school, on the news and in the media, from friends and peers, by overhearing conversations that were not intended for them, or in other ways. When we choose to introduce a topic to our children, we are able to shape the content of that conversation and help our children learn skills they need to think critically about an issue. In addition, we can help children think about what they might do if they were faced with a particular challenge or how they can support others who face challenges they never face themselves. There are many other topics not included in this chapter that you can discuss as your child gets older, including social media and Internet safety; politics; news and world events; poverty; mental illness (e.g., depression); religion, racism, prejudice, and injustice; homelessness; trauma; strangers; natural disasters; war; and others.

As you have conversations with your child about challenging topics, you might find the following strategies helpful:

1. **Start with conversations that are meaningful and relevant to your child's life.** For example, talk with your child about issues that

are happening in your family or community. Your child already has exposure to these topics to some degree and you can help them make sense of the world around them.

2. **Learn what your child already knows about the topic.** Hearing what your child knows can help you decide where it might be best to start. Understanding what your child is thinking about and what questions they have can also help you ease their fears and clear up misunderstandings or misperceptions.

3. **Share your feelings.** You and your child are likely to have many different feelings about each topic. If the topic is something serious that your child and your family have experienced (e.g., death or loss), share your own feelings with your child and encourage them to share their feelings with you as well, if they are able and ready to do so. This helps your child know that their feelings are okay. If the topic is about something your family has not experienced, talk about how you think people who are in that situation might feel to help your child practice empathy.

4. **Help your child practice skills to address or cope with the issue now or in the future.** Think about the information and skills your child needs to make good choices if a challenging situation arises in the future. Encourage your child to think about what they can do, who they can talk with, and things that happen that might make it hard to make good choices. Reading stories about characters experiencing challenging situations is one way to talk with children about how to make good choices. Role playing with dolls, action figures, puppets, or through imaginary play is another way to help children practice using words and actions that might help them when facing challenges in the future.

5. **Reassure children that they are safe and focus on what you can do together to be a helper for others.** There are many topics that might be confusing to children (e.g., *"Why would a grown-up hurt a child?"*). Some topics may even lead to a child feeling anxious, afraid, or even terrified. Sometimes these fears won't emerge during a conversation, but sometime later after a child has had a chance to reflect. If you suspect your child is feeling afraid of something or if your child shares that they are feeling afraid, assure your child that they are safe.

Talk together about what you can do when you feel afraid. Brainstorm ways to be a helper for others who might be in a challenging situation. Challenging situations can often feel scary because they are out of your control. By focusing on things you and your child can think, say, and do, you can bring a sense of control back to your child.

## Question and answer: Apply what you learned to parenting challenges

**Q:** How can I help my child avoid stressful situations?

**A:** *There is no definite way to help your child avoid stress, but there are things you can do to help minimize the stress your child experiences and to develop skills they need to manage that stress. Stress is the mental or emotional strain that comes with challenging situations. Some stress is a normal part of life. There are actually several types of stress: positive stress, tolerable stress, and toxic stress. Positive stress is the stress that comes with normal everyday living. This might be stress that a child feels meeting someone new, taking a test, or facing a challenge (e.g., trying to tie their own shoes or cross the monkey bars). If we have the coping strategies to manage this everyday stress, it can actually be good for us. Positive stress doesn't last long, and it can be motivating. Positive stress might help us recognize when something is challenging and help us rise to the occasion.*

*In contrast to positive stress, tolerable stress is the stress that has the potential to harm us. Tolerable stress comes with life challenges (e.g., divorce, being bullied, experiencing a natural disaster). This type of stress is more serious than positive stress, but it can still be manageable. What makes it manageable is having supportive, loving relationships in our lives. Children who have secure attachment relationships are better equipped than those who don't to deal with this kind of stress, making it tolerable. It's through relationships with parents and caregivers that children learn coping strategies to manage their stress.*

*When children don't have warm and trusting relationships, stress can become toxic. Toxic stress is what we really need to worry about for children. Toxic stress is long-lasting, chronic stress that children don't have the support to manage. Children who experience toxic stress can face serious long-term impacts on their health and well-being.*

*When your child does experience stress, use those situations as learning opportunities. Help your children practice expressing their emotions in effective ways (e.g., using words to talk about their feelings). Then, practice taking deep breaths, talking to friends or family, stepping away from a situation and trying again later, or other stress management strategies. When children are young, their experiences with positive stress (or even tolerable stress), when you are there to support them, can help them learn valuable skills that they can use when they are older.*

**Q:** It feels impossible to prepare my child for everything they might face in the world. What can I do?

**A:** *As parents, we will never be able to anticipate all the challenges that our children might face in the future, and new challenges will arise involving technology that doesn't even exist yet. Rather than trying to anticipate the challenges they will face, we can instead focus on teaching our children the skills they need to manage the challenges that come their way, including flexibility, critical thinking, skills related to managing emotions and stress, knowing how and when to ask for help, and being compassionate toward themselves and others.*

**Q:** What if my child asks me something that I don't feel comfortable talking about?

**A:** *If your child asks you about something that you don't feel comfortable talking about, let them know that. If you are able to, let them know why.*

- *"This is something I'm not very comfortable talking about."*
- *"I had a really bad experience with that when I was growing up, so it's too hard for me to talk about now."*

*If it is a topic that you would like your child to learn about even though you're not comfortable discussing it, help your child find another trusted adult whom they can ask, or another reliable source:*

- *"Why don't you ask your mom about it? She would be a good person to talk to."*
- *"I found a great book at the library that I think will help explain it better than I can, but I can try to answer questions if you have any after you read it."*

*It's also possible that your child will ask about a topic that you don't think they should know about yet:*

- *"I would rather not talk about this right now. I think this is something that would be better for you to learn about when you are a little older."*
- *Even if you think your child is not ready to discuss a topic, it might be helpful to find out what they already know and if they have any questions so that you can address what is on their mind.*

**Q:** How can I have a conversation with my child about a topic that is too painful for me to even think about?

*A: There may be topics that arise that are challenging for you to talk about with your child because of previous experience, trauma, or closeness to a situation (e.g., a recent death in the family). Let your child know that you would like to talk with them (but only if that is true) and then help them find a trusted family member, friend, or counselor to talk with. You do not need to be the one to introduce every conversation topic to your child, but you may want to make sure they have access to other trusted adults they can talk to if you are not able to address a certain topic, or if they are not comfortable asking you about a topic.*

**Q:** What strategies can I use to answer my child's questions about challenging topics?

*A: As you share conversations with your child about adversity and other challenging topics, your child will likely have questions for you. Some of the questions children ask are easy to answer.*

> *"Can I have a piece of candy?"*

> *"Not now, but you can after dinner."*

*Some of the questions children ask are a little complicated.*

> *"Where do babies come from?"*

> *"Why don't you ask your mom."*

*Sometimes children ask questions that make us laugh.*

> *"Can astronauts poop in space?"*

> *"They have to go somehow. Let's look up how they do it."*

*And sometimes children ask questions that leave us speechless.*

> *"What is the 'F' word?"*

> *"Where did you hear that?!"*

*Then there's the relentless "Why? Why? Why?"*

*Sometimes we feel prepared for our children's questions and sometimes we don't. Through their questions, our children give us a glimpse of their inner thoughts. They let us know what they are thinking about, how they are interpreting what they see and hear, and what is interesting to or confusing for them. The way we respond to our children's questions tells them something, too. By answering our children's questions openly and honestly, we can communicate to our children that we are available to have conversations with them about anything that comes to mind, even if we don't have the answer to one of their questions ("I don't know. Let's look it up together on the Internet to find out.").*

*When your child asks a question, try the following:*

*Stop yourself from gut reactions like, "Who told you that?" or "Where did you hear that?" Questioning your child before having a conversation may cause them to feel embarrassed, ashamed, or afraid to continue the conversation. Instead, think about where your child is coming from. They are likely repeating something they heard somewhere (e.g., on television, in a book, or from someone else). If they are coming to you with a question, celebrate the fact that your child believes you are someone who can help them understand something, that they want to learn from you, and that they feel safe asking you about something new, interesting, confusing, or unknown.*

*Answer your child's question in the best way that you can, with the information you have, and in a way that makes you feel comfortable. This may be easier to do with some questions than others. For example, you may feel comfortable talking with your child about any question they have about money, but not any question they ask about illegal drug use. If you're not sure how much you want to share with your child, it's okay to take time to think about it (e.g., "Let me think about it for a few minutes" or "How about we talk about this tomorrow after I have a little time to think about it?"). For any explanations you provide your child on a topic, simplify your explanation so that it is in words that your child can understand. Be sure to clarify words you use that they don't know.*

*If you don't have an answer, let your child know that, and then problem-solve together about how to find the answer or learn more (e.g., "How do stars float in the sky?" "They don't really float. Well, actually they . . . hmm . . . I'm not really sure how to answer that question. Let's look it up." Or "I don't know. How do you think we could find the answer to that question? Is there anyone else you think we could ask?").*

*Ask your child if your answer helped, and then ask if they have any other questions (e.g., "Did that answer your question? Do you have other questions that you want to talk about?").*

*Follow up by asking about where they learned about the topic. Now that you have demonstrated to your child that it's okay for them to have brought this question to you, they are likely feeling safe about talking with you about this (or other topics) again.*

**Padme** (age five): What does shit mean?

**Sneha** (Padme's mom): (To self: "Thank goodness my child is asking me and not a friend at school!") Shit means poop, but it's a grown-up word. It's considered a "bad word," and sometimes older kids or grown-ups say things like "Oh shit!" when they are upset or angry or because they think it's cool.

**Padme:** Oh shit! Like that.

**Sneha:** Yes. Just like that. It's not a word for kids to use, though. It's definitely not okay to say that at school, and it's not okay at home either. Where did you hear that word? Did you hear someone say it at school or on TV?

**Padme:** Gina's brother said it to her.

**Sneha:** I see. Did Gina know that it was a bad word?

**Padme:** Yes. She told her mom on him, and he had to go to his room.

**Sneha:** Her mom probably told her brother that it's not a word for kids, just like we talked about.

*In response to your children's questions and through conversations, let them know what to expect from you if they find themselves in a challenging situation. No matter how disappointed you would be if you learned that your child was taking or selling drugs, became pregnant as a teenager, or committed a crime, you would likely be more upset if they hid this fact from you and neglected to seek your help and advice when they needed support. Letting your child know at a young age that you will be there for them no matter what the circumstance may make it easier for them to come to you later on.*

**Q:** How much should I tell my child about my own past and experiences? If we have friends or family members who have been involved in questionable behaviors or challenging situations, should I talk to my child about that?

**A:** *This is a personal decision that parents and family member will need to answer for themselves. It's up to you to decide what to share with your child and how much to share based on your experiences, your comfort level, and what you think it is helpful for your child to know. For example, sharing stories with your child about times you struggled or were successful making friends might help your child feel closer to you and provide them with strategies they can use in their own lives. Sharing stories about more sensitive topics like drug use or sexual activity may be more appropriate with older children rather than younger children, so long as poor decisions or risky behaviors are not glorified (e.g., "I miss being able to smoke whenever I wanted."). Let your child know why you made the choices you did and what you hope they will do if faced with those same choices.*

## Extend the conversation through read-alouds

Reading books together about characters who experience challenges can provide opportunities for you to talk with your child about what they can think, say, or do in many different situations. These stories can also help you and your child develop an appreciation for the many different challenges that can have an impact on other children's lives. Talk with your child about how the characters in the book tackled their challenges, how those challenges made them feel, how they overcame their challenges (or what they did if they couldn't), what your child can do if faced with those same challenges, and what they can do to help others.

## Books about having challenges with others

*A Bad Case of Stripes* by David Shannon

*The Berenstain Bears and the Double Dare* by Stan and Jan Berenstain

*A Big Guy Took My Ball!* by Mo Willems

*Chrysanthemum* by Kevin Henkes

*Crow Boy* by Taro Yashima

*Forgive and Let Go! A Book About Forgiveness* by Cheri Meiners

*Llama Llama and the Bully Goat* by Anne Dewdney

*One* by Kathryn Otoshi

*I Just Forgot* by Mercer Mayer

*Lily's Purple Plastic Purse* by Kevin Henkes

*My Friend and I* by Lisa Jahn-Clough

*Stand Tall, Molly Lou Melon* by Patty Lovell, illustrated by David Catrow

*We All Need Forgiveness* by Mercer Mayer

*Words are Not for Hurting* by Elizabeth Verdick, illustrated by Marieka Heinlen

*The Invisible Boy* by Trudy Ludwig, illustrated by Patrice Barton

*The Name Jar* by Yangsook Choi

## Books about death

*The Dead Bird* by Margaret Wise Brown, illustrated by Remy Charlip

*Everett Anderson's Goodbye* by Lucille Clifton, illustrated by Ann Grifalconi

*The Fall of Freddie the Leaf: A Story of Life for All Ages* by Leo Buscaglia

*I'll Always Love You* by Hans Wilhelm

*I Miss You: A First Look at Death* by Pat Thomas, illustrated by Leslie Harker

*Jim's Dog Muffins* by Miriam Cohen, illustrated by Ronald Himler

*Lifetimes: The Beautiful Way to Explain Death to Children* by Bryan Mellonie with Robert Ingpen

*Love Never Stops: A Memory Book for Children* by Emilio Parga

*Nana Upstairs & Nana Downstairs* by Tomie de Paola

*The Saddest Time* by Norma Simon, illustrated by Jacqueline Rogers

*Samantha Jane's Missing Smile: A Story About Coping with the Loss of a Parent* by Julie Kaplow and Donna Pincus, illustrated by Beth Spiegel

*The Tenth Good Thing About Barney* by Judith Viorst, illustrated by Erik Belvad

*When a Pet Dies* by Mr. Rogers

*When Dinosaurs Die: A Guide to Understanding Death* by Laurie Krasny

*You Hold Me and I'll Hold You* by Jo Caron, illustrated by Annie Annon

### Books about suicide

*Luna's Red Hat* by Emmi Smid

*Why Would Someone Want to Die?* by Rebecca Schmidt, illustrated by Cynthia Brundage

### Books about keeping our bodies healthy and safe

*Do You Have a Secret?* by Jennifer Moore-Mallinos, illustrated by Marta Fabrega

*I Said No! A Kid-to-Kid Guide to Keeping Private Parts Private* by Kimberly King and Zack King, illustrated by Sue Rama

*A Terrible Thing Happened* by Margaret Holmes and Sasha Mudlaff, illustrated by Cary Pillo

*Your Body Belongs to You* by Cornelia Maude Spellman, illustrated by Teri Weidner

*Be Careful and Stay Safe* by Cheri Meiners

*Just Going to the Dentist* by Mercer Mayer

*Little Pea* by Amy Krouse Rosenthal, illustrated by Jen Corace

*My Trip to the Hospital* by Mercer Mayer

*What's So Yummy? All About Eating Well and Feeling Good* by Robie H. Harris, illustrated by Nadine Bernard Westcott

### Books about pregnancy

*It's Not the Stork: A Book about Girls, Boys, Babies, Bodies, Families, and Friends* by Robie H. Harris, illustrated by Michael Emberley

*It's Perfectly Normal: Changing Bodies, Growing Up, Sex, and Sexual Health* by Robie H. Harris, illustrated by Michael Emberley

*It's So Amazing! A Book About Eggs, Sperm, Birth, Babies, and Families* by Robie H. Harris, illustrated by Michael Emberley

## Books about diverse life experiences

*Abuela's Weave* by Omar S. Castañeda

*The Can Man* by Laura E. Williams, illustrated by Craig Orback

*Clothesline Clues to Jobs People Do* by Kathryn Heling and Deborah Hembrook, illustrated by Andy Robert Davies

*The Colour of Home* by Mary Hoffman

*Four Feet, Two Sandals* by Karen Williams, illustrated by Khadra Mohammed

*Fly Away Home* by Eve Bunting, illustrated by Ronald Himler

*Hero Dad* by Melinda Hardin, illustrated by Bryan Langdo

*Hero Mom* by Melinda Hardin, illustrated by Bryan Langdo

*H is for Honor: A Military Family Alphabet* by Devin Scillian, illustrated by Victor Juhasz

*Lily and the Paper Man* by Rebecca Upjohn, illustrated by Renné Benoit

*The Journey* by Francesca Sanna

*Maddi's Fridge* by Lois Brandt, illustrated by Vin Vogel

*Mama's Nightingale: A Story of Immigration and Separation* by Edwidge Danticat, illustrated by Leslie Staub

*My Name is Sangoel* by Karen Lynn Williams, illustrated by Khadra Mohammed

*Night Catch* by Brenda Ehrmantraut, illustrated by Vicki Wehrman

*The Night Dad Went to Jail* by Melissa Higgins, illustrated by Wednesday Kirwan

*The Ox-Cart Man* by Donald Hall, illustrated by Barbara Cooney

*The Poppy Lady: Moina Belle Michael and Her Tribute to Veterans* by Barbara Walsh, illustrated by Layne Johnson

*A Shelter in Our Car* by Monica Gunning, illustrated by Elaine Pedlar

*Shoebox Sam* by Mary Brigid Barrett, illustrated by Frank Morrison

*Those Shoes* by Maribeth Boelts, illustrated by Noah Z. Jones

*Uncle Willie and The Soup Kitchen* by Dyanne Disalvo-Ryan

*Visiting Day* by Jacqueline Woodson, illustrated by James Ransome

*The Wall* by Eve Bunting, illustrated Ronald Himler

## Books about family change

*Babies Come from Airports* by Erin Dealey

*Dinosaurs Divorce: A Guide for Changing Families* by Laurie Krasny Brown
and Marc Brown

*Families Change* by Julie Nelson, illustrated by Mary Gallagher

*I Don't Want to Talk About It* by Jeanie Franz Ransom, illustrated by Kathryn Kunz Finney

*Julius, The Baby of the World* by Kevin Henkes

*Just Me and My Little Brother* by Mercer Mayer

*Little Miss, Big Sis* by Amy Krouse Rosenthal, illustrated by Peter
H. Reynolds

*Mama and Daddy Bear's Divorce* by Cornelia Maude Spelman, illustrated
by Kathy Parkinson

*My Family's Changing* by Pat Thomas

*Peter's Chair* by Ezra Jack Keats

*The New Baby* by Mercer Mayer

*Waiting for Baby* by Rachel Fuller

*Was It the Chocolate Pudding? A Story for Little Kids About Divorce* by Sandra
Levins and Bryan Langdo

*We Are Moving* by Mercer Mayer

*When My Parents Forgot How to Be Friends* by Jennifer Moore-Mallinos,
illustrated by Marta Fabrega

### Read-aloud and discussion questions

- How are the lives of the characters in the book like yours? How are they different from yours?
- What challenges did the characters face?
- How do you think those challenges made them feel?
- Have you ever had those feelings? What made you feel that way?
- What helped the characters face their challenges?
- What would you do if you were in this situation?
- Who would you talk to if you were in this situation?
- Who could you ask for help if this situation (or something else) happened to you?
- What would you do to help a friend in this situation?
- Was there anything confusing or surprising about the story we read? What was it?
- Do you have any questions about the story we read?

## Extend the conversation through family activities

*Read the newspaper together.* Whether you read a paper copy or online version, take time to talk with your child about what is happening in the news as you feel it is appropriate. There may be news stories that you prefer not to share with your child (that's okay!), but reading the news may also give you ideas for topics related to your community that you wouldn't have thought to talk about. Reading a newspaper gives you more control to pick and choose what stories you want to share with your child and in what way than listening to the radio or watching television together.

*Look up news from the year your child was born.* Visit the library or search online for news from the year your child was born. Talk about what was happening then and how it was different from or similar to what is happening in the world now. Look up news from the year you were born as well! Your child might find it interesting to hear what the world was like when you were growing up. Talk about how the world has changed (e.g., what technology exists now that didn't before) and how it has stayed the same.

*Share stories with your child about times when you had to make tough decisions.* Tell your child about times when you were faced with peer pressure or when you saw instances of bullying. What did you do when you were younger? What do you wish you would have done? It's okay to tell children about times when you made good choices, as well as times when you made choices you wish you hadn't. Both of these are good learning opportunities that can be used to help children brainstorm what they would do if faced with that same situation.

*Make a family stress-less list.* Talk with your child about how it feels when someone is stressed and the types of challenges that might make someone feel stressed in daily life, as well as when more serious things happen. Share with your child that taking care of yourself (e.g., eating healthy food, exercising, getting enough sleep) is one way to help your body deal with stress, and that there are other ways too. Brainstorm a list of things that can be helpful when you are stressed. Include things that are helpful for adults as well as children (e.g. listening to music, talking with a friend).

*Family choice night.* Choose a night to be "family choice night" once a week, once a month, or as often as your family schedule allows. On that night, let one member of the family choose something special for everyone to do together—go out to eat at a favorite restaurant, eat a favorite meal together at home, play a game, take a family walk—whatever that family member wants that is reasonable for the amount of time you have and the family budget. Alternate who gets to choose the activity for family choice night so that everyone has a turn and knows when their turn will be. Talk about the importance of having family choice night—a night when you set aside other distractions (e.g., electronic devices) to be together and do something that is special to each member of the family. Making time for activities like these shows each family member (children and adults) that they are valued and that making time to do the things they like is a family priority.

## V

# You can be a helper:
## *Promoting compassion*

ONE DAY WHEN MY DAUGHTER was about 3½, we were walking together toward our car talking about her day at preschool. Out of the corner of my eye, I noticed a man making his way toward us from across the street. His clothes were torn and unkempt. His hair was wild, and his beard was littered with debris. I tightened my hold on my daughter's hand, quickened my step, and avoided eye contact as I hurried by, giving all the signs I could that I would not engage. I breathed a sigh of relief as he passed without so much as a glance.

As we reached the car, my daughter asked:

"Mom, did you see that man?"

"Yes."

"His leg was hurt."

"How do you know that?"

"He walked funny and had a cane. I hope he is okay."

The tension I felt making a beeline for the car melted away in that moment. With her words, my daughter taught me an important lesson about empathy. In my haste to protect my daughter from a perceived threat, I put my own sense of empathy on hold. Although I convinced myself that this man might be a threat to our safety (he wasn't), the real threat was that he made me feel uncomfortable. In exchange for saving myself that discomfort, I gave up an opportunity to be the parent I want to be—the kind of parent who models empathy and kindness, even when it is uncomfortable to do so. Even if all I had to offer was a connection through eye contact or a smile, I could have made another choice— the choice my daughter made to consider the feelings of another human being.

A few weeks later, my daughter overheard a man asking people walking by to buy him a sandwich because he was hungry. She stopped and opened her lunch bag. I had seen this man with his bloodshot eyes before. On other days, I had chosen to walk around him. Standing with my daughter that day, I made a different choice—the choice to be the model that I want to be. My daughter held out her applesauce and spoon, and I said, "My daughter heard you say you were hungry and wanted to share her lunch with you."

Much to my surprise, the man got down on his knees, looked my daughter in the eyes, and gently said, "Thank you. You did the right thing today by sharing. Your mama taught you right. I'm not going to take your lunch because you're a growing girl and you need it. I'm already grown. I'm big and I need a big sandwich, but don't you worry about me. Someone is going to share a sandwich with me soon. Just know that you did the right thing."

He stood up, gave me a big grin, and gave my daughter a big thumbs up. I apologized for not having money with me to buy him a sandwich. He smiled back. "Don't worry about that. Just keep teaching your daughter what you're teaching her."

I will never forget the lesson in empathy and kindness I learned that day both from my daughter and from our new friend, "Mr. C." Sometimes as parents, we step out of our own comfort zones for our children. This was one of those times for me, and I am grateful that I did.

There are many opportunities to take action and to model compassion for our children. Some opportunities arise unexpectedly. Other opportunities can be planned. In order to take advantage of these moments, we have to be open to them, look for them, and plan ahead so that we can be ready to act when they arise. Up to this point, the conversations in this book have focused on building children's awareness of themselves and others, as well as learning about challenges that they or others may face. Children who have a secure and trusting relationship with their parents, a strong sense of self-awareness, and the skills they need to tackle challenges are those best equipped to feel comfortable enough to reach beyond themselves to help others. The intent of this final chapter is to encourage parents and children to have conversations that extend compassion to others by focusing on other people's feelings, making friends, and finding ways to make a difference.

There are many ways to make a difference in your home and community. Parents can help children learn to see themselves as helpers by encouraging them to think about other people's feelings, engaging in the community, and finding their own voice. Being a helper might mean stepping outside of your comfort zone, but it doesn't have to, depending on the type of involvement you, your family, and your child are seeking. Everyone can be a helper.

## WE SHOULD BE KIND TO EVERYONE, STARTING WITH OUR OWN FAMILY

Children learn how to interact with others from the relationships they know. The relationships parents have with their children show them how to treat others and teach them how they can or should expect to be treated. Parents can point out to children the way their actions affect other people's feelings, beginning with the people in their family.

### Key messages for children:

- Our home should be a comfortable and safe place for everyone in our family.
- The feelings of all our family members are important.
- We should always strive to treat others kindly, inside and outside of our family.

**Roisin** (Ethan's mom)**:** You won't believe what Ethan said today.

**Tovah** (neighbor)**:** What?

**Roisin:** When he was getting out of the bath, he said—

**Ethan** (age four)**:** Mom. Don't tell.

**Roisin:** Oh, sorry, Ethan! It was just so cute. It's just Tovah, she won't tell anyone else.

**Ethan:** I don't want you to tell.

**Roisin:** Okay. I won't tell.

**(Later when Ethan and Roisin were alone together)**

**Roisin:** I should have asked you earlier before I started telling a story about you.

**Ethan:** I didn't want you to tell.

**Roisin:** I know. I realized that when I was talking to Tovah. I didn't think about that it might be something you wanted to keep private. Next time I'll ask you first before I tell stories about you, to make sure it's okay with you. Parents just love talking about their kids because we think you're so great, but I never mean to embarrass you.

*What's happening in this conversation:* When Roisin started telling a story about her son, Ethan, Ethan asked his mom not to share. Roisin paused and took time to think about Ethan's feelings in that moment. She realized he might feel embarrassed by her talking about him—even though the story was one that she thought was cute and knew her neighbor would enjoy. Like many parents, Roisin continually reminds Ethan that he needs to think about other people's feelings. This is an example of one way she shows him that she is thinking about his feelings and taking them seriously.

**Carmen** (age two): Uh-oh!

**Andrea** (Carmen's mom): Uh-oh? What happened?

**Carmen:** Uh-oh! Milk!

**Andrea:** Oh, I see. It looks like you spilled your milk on the ground.

**Carmen:** Uh-oh! Big mess!

**Andrea:** Uh-oh is right! That is a big mess! Let's clean it up together. Come over here with me to get a kitchen towel.

**Carmen:** Tow!

**Andrea:** That's right, a towel. Here's one for you and one for me. We can clean up the mess together.

**Carmen:** Keen! Keen!

**Andrea:** Clean! Clean! When someone makes a mess, we can help each other clean up.

**Carmen:** Keen up!

**Andrea:** Clean up! I'm helping you clean up your milk, just like you helped me pick up all that pasta I spilled on the floor yesterday.

**Carmen:** Pasa! Big mess pasa!

*What's happening in this conversation:* When her daughter, Carmen, spills milk on the floor, Andrea leads her to find a towel and models how to clean up her spilled milk. Rather than insisting that Carmen clean it on her own ("It's your mess. You take care of it!"), she helps her daughter and they clean together, modeling helping behaviors. She encourages Carmen to do the same when other family members need help, such as when she herself spilled pasta on the floor the day before. In taking this approach, Andrea encourages her daughter to engage in helping behaviors and fostering compassion. Teaching children to help others in little ways (everyone pitching in to clean up a mess, rather than insisting everyone clean up their own mess) sends the message that it's okay (and encouraged!) to help others when we see someone in need. A child who is taught that they need to clean up their own mess may be less likely to ask for help when they need it ("No one will help, even if I ask") and less likely to engage in helping behaviors when asked ("That's your problem to take care of. Not mine.").

**Ron** (Iris's dad): You know what I love most about your mom?

**Iris** (age five): What?

**Ron:** Every morning when she leaves for work, she makes extra coffee so that there will be some ready for me when I wake up. She does lots of little things like that every day to show me she loves me. She does lots of things like that for you, too. I want to try and think of more things I can do to show her that I love her too.

**Iris:** You could pick her some flowers.

**Ron:** She does love flowers. Do you want to go with me and get some for her today?

**Iris:** Yes! Orange ones. That's mom's favorite color.

*What's happening in this conversation:* As a parent, the way you interact with your partner or spouse as well as other relatives or friends serves as a model for your child. In this conversation, Ron points out to his daughter things that his wife (her mom) does that he appreciates. In doing so, he shows Iris what it means to be in a positive relationship and explains what he values in a relationship and why. He also models how to treat others and show appreciation for them. Without having this conversation, Iris might still notice the positive exchanges between her parents, but she might not spend much time thinking about them. Parents can draw attention to what they value in relationships by pointing out the way people in your family demonstrate kindness and compassion toward one another.

**Riley** (Jayden's mom): How was your time with grandpa?

**Jayden** (age four): Bad!

**Riley:** What happened?

**Jayden:** He made me hold his hand, and I didn't want to!

**Riley:** This was the first time grandpa walked with you to the library. He probably didn't know that you know how to stay with him without running in the street.

**Jayden:** I don't like it. I don't want to hold hands. I can do it by myself!

**Riley:** I understand that. We can talk to grandpa about what our family rules are for tomorrow and let him know that we let you walk by yourself except when you cross the street.

**Jayden:** Humph.

**Riley:** I know you didn't like having to hold hands, but it's important to think about grandpa's feelings, too. He loves you so much and wanted to make sure you stayed safe.

**Jayden:** I am safe!

*What's happening in this conversation:* When Jayden feels upset about her grandpa insisting that she hold his hand while walking to the library, her mom, Riley, encouraged her to think about her grandpa's feelings. Sometimes grandparents or other family members have different rules or ways of interacting with children. Although there may be some rules that Riley does not want her parents enforcing with Jayden, she tries to consider their feelings and their desire to be helpful, and encourages Jayden to do the same.

## THINKING ABOUT OTHER PEOPLE'S FEELINGS CAN HELP US GET ALONG

From young ages, most children show signs that they are thinking about other people's feelings. At around 6 months, children look for cues from their parents about how they are feeling and use those cues to decide how to respond in new situations. At around 18 to 24 months, children become aware that others have thoughts and feelings that might be different from their own. Just because children are aware that other people have feelings doesn't mean that they are actively thinking about those feelings. Thinking about other people's feelings is a skill like any other that needs to be practiced and developed. Children need to be taught to think about other people's feelings, and then to think about how they can adjust their actions and words to support those feelings as well as their own.

### Key messages for children:

- Everyone has feelings.
- Feelings can help us connect with others, no matter how similar or different we may be.
- Thinking about other people's feelings can help us look at situations from another person's perspective and help us get along better with others.

**Rebecca** (Sawyer's mom): You have been sitting there so quietly looking out the window. I wonder how you're feeling.

**Sawyer** (age two): (continues looking out the window)

*What's happening in this conversation:* Asking your child how they are feeling (or wondering out loud about their feelings, as Rebecca did in this example) communicates to your child that you care about how they feel, and lets them know that their feelings matter to you. Not only that, using these words encourages children to do the same with others in their lives. The thinking or wondering you do out loud can help shape your child's inner voice—the words they say to themselves. Saying things like, "I wonder how you're feeling," can help foster this same thought in your child. It may also serve as a reminder to you to pause and consider your child's and others' feelings more often as you go through your day.

**Zane** (age four): That boy is crying.

**Ty'Shawn** (Zane's dad): You see a boy crying? How do you think he's feeling?

**Zane:** Sad.

**Ty'Shawn:** He looks sad to me, too. I wonder what happened.

**Zane:** His mom said no cookie.

**Ty'Shawn:** Oh, you saw him asking for a cookie?

**Zane:** Yeah.

**Ty'Shawn:** How do you think you would feel if you couldn't have a cookie you wanted?

**Zane:** Mad!

**Ty'Shawn:** You'd feel mad? What do you think you would do?

**Zane:** I would do this! (crosses his arms and stomps his feet on the ground)

**Ty'Shawn:** That's what you would do if you couldn't have a cookie? I wonder how his mom's feeling. It looks like she might be having a hard time trying to help him calm down.

**Zane:** He's crying a lot.

**Ty'Shawn:** Yes, he's still crying.

*What's happening in this conversation:* While at the park, Zane notices another boy crying. His dad, Ty'Shawn, asks Zane how he thinks the other boy is feeling and how he would feel if he were in that situation. Asking questions like *"How is he feeling?"* or making comments like *"I wonder how she is feeling,"* encourages children to stop and think about the feelings another person is having. Instead of focusing on feelings, Ty'Shawn could have said, "That boy looks like he's in trouble," or "That boy is bad. He's misbehaving." Either of these statements would have required Ty'Shawn's to judge the situation or label the child. Focusing instead on the feelings the boy and his mother were having encouraged Zane to look at the situation with empathy.

**Ned** (age seven): There's going to be a new boy in our class tomorrow.

**Mallory** (Ned's mom): His first day is tomorrow?

**Ned:** Yep.

**Mallory:** Wow. I wonder what it would feel like to start a new school in the middle of the year. How do you think he might feel?

**Ned:** Scared.

**Mallory:** Maybe. Are there other feelings he might have? Excited maybe?

**Ned:** I wouldn't be excited.

**Mallory:** You wouldn't be excited, but other people might be. It could be exciting to make new friends, but it could also be pretty scary starting in a new school if you don't know anyone. Is your class doing anything to help him feel welcome?

**Ned:** I don't know.

**Mallory:** I wonder if there's anything you could do to help him feel included.

**Ned:** I know! I could ask him to sit with me at lunch.

**Mallory:** That would be a really nice thing to do, and hey, you might even make a new friend!

**Ned:** Yeah!

**Mallory:** And if not, that's okay too. You don't have to be friends with everyone, but it's nice to help him feel included while he settles in.

**Ned:** Maybe he'll want to play soccer with us outside, too.

**Mallory:** Sure. You could ask if he likes to play soccer.

**Ned:** I'll ask him!

**Mallory:** I can't wait to hear how it goes.

*What's happening in this conversation:* When Ned tells his mom, Mallory, that there will be a new kid in his class, Mallory encourages Ned to think about how the new boy might feel about starting a new school in the middle of the year. She also encourages Ned to think about things he could do to help the new kid feel included. Conversations like these help children not only to think about other people's feelings, but also to consider how to be proactive and think about what they can do to positively impact other people's feelings with their own words and actions.

**Calvin** (age five): I win! I win! I win, I win, I win!

**Marco** (Calvin's dad): You did win. Great job.

**Calvin:** I win! I win! I win and you lose! You lose, you lose, you lose!

**Marco:** Okay, okay. I'm glad you're excited about winning. That was a tough game, and you played really well. But stop for a minute and look at everyone else. How do you feel when you lose a game?

**Calvin:** I hate losing, but I didn't lose.

**Marco:** I know you won, but everyone else at the table lost. How do you think they are feeling?

**Calvin:** Sad.

**Marietta** (Calvin's grandmother): I'm not sad, I don't mind.

**Marco:** Well, grandma doesn't mind, but think about the other people at the table who might feel sad or disappointed about losing. It's okay to feel excited about winning, but you also want to be a good winner. How about thanking everyone for playing with you? You could shake hands and say, "good game" or "thank you for playing."

**Calvin:** Thank you for playing. (shakes hands with dad) Thank you for playing. (shakes hands with grandma) Thank you for playing. (shakes hands with sister)

**Marco:** That's a nice way to help other people feel good after a game. And it makes it easier for us to be good losers. Instead of pouting, then I can say, "Good game! Thanks for playing with me, too!" If you keep singing about winning and other people losing, you might hurt their feelings, and then they might not want to play with you anymore.

**Calvin:** I didn't know that.

**Marco:** That's okay. You're still learning, and you won! But maybe no more singing about it.

**Calvin:** Okay.

*What's happening in this conversation:* Many young children don't like to lose, but love to win. Learning to be a good sport both when winning and when losing takes practice and attention to other people's feelings. Some children struggle with losing so much that they refuse to play games if they even think they might lose. Parents can play a role in helping children learn to stop and think about their own and other people's feelings when playing games whether they win or lose, as Marco did in this situation. With practice, children can learn to feel comfortable with losing and to be a kind winner.

> **Nyla** (age six): What does that man's sign say?
> **Leon** (Nyla's dad): It says, "Homeless. Anything helps."
> **Nyla:** He doesn't have a home?
> **Leon:** That's what his sign said. I wonder how he's feeling standing out there like that.
> **Nyla:** I would be sad if I didn't have a home.
> **Leon:** I would be sad too. I bet it's very hard to stand on a street corner like that and ask for help from people. It might be a little embarrassing or even demeaning.

*What's happening in this conversation:* Sometimes it's hard to know what to say when children ask us about someone they see in the community. One way to answer a child's questions is to focus on the feelings of that individual. No matter how that individual might look similar to or different from your child or your family, taking a moment to consider that person's feelings can help your child see a connection between themselves and the other person in a way that promotes compassion, rather than judgment.

> **Pamela** (age four): Can I have my bunny back?
> **Lance** (age four): I'm playing with it.
> **Pamela:** But I was playing with it first. (grabs stuffed bunny)
> **Lance:** (pulls bunny back, starting a tug-of-war)
> **Pamela:** (hits Lance)
> **Lance:** (cries)
> **Audrey** (Pamela's and Lance's mom): What happened?
> **Pamela:** He took my bunny from me!
> **Lance:** She hit me!
> **Audrey:** May I have the bunny for a minute? Thank you. Pamela, stop and look at your brother's face. How do you think he's feeling? See that he's crying and crossing his arms?
> **Pamela:** Yes, Lance is sad?

**Lance:** Humph.

**Audrey:** How are you feeling, Lance?

**Lance:** I want the bunny! (continues crying)

**Audrey:** Lance, I want you to look at Pamela's face. What do you see? How do you think she's feeling?

**Lance:** Mad.

**Pamela:** Nuh-uh. I'm not mad. I'm really, really mad! I want the bunny!

**Audrey:** It looks to me like you both have hurt feelings. What do you think we should do?

**Pamela:** I want my bunny back.

**Audrey:** Having the bunny might help you feel better. How do you think it would make Lance feel?

**Lance:** That wouldn't be fair!

**Pamela:** Mad.

**Audrey:** Okay. Can you think of an idea that would help both of you feel better?

**Lance:** We could take turns.

**Pamela:** Can I go first?

**Lance:** Only if you promise to let me have a turn, too. You can't keep it!

**Audrey:** I can help with that. We could set a timer so that Pamela could play with the bunny for three minutes, and then it will be Lance's turn. How does that sound?

**Pamela:** Okay.

**Lance:** Okay.

*What's happening in this conversation:* For a parent, it can be tempting to step in and serve as a judge when children have a disagreement (e.g., *"Everyone stop doing what you're doing and go to your rooms,"* or *"I saw you take that from her. Give it back. Say sorry and give him a hug."*). When we respond in this way, however, we don't give children a chance to think about one another's feelings and practice problem solving. In order for parents to help children learn skills to navigate conflicts on their own, they need to give children practice in stopping and thinking about the other person's feelings as well as their own feelings, and coming up with solutions. In this conversation, Audrey asks, *"What happened?"* giving her children a chance to share. She then asks questions to help them think about one another's feelings and what they can do next. If children are emotionally charged, a conversation like this may not be possible until they have had a chance to express their feelings and then calm down.

There are many opportunities each day to help children think about other people's feelings. Parents can ask questions that encourage children to stop and think about how other people feel, and model this approach in their own lives (*"How is she feeling?" "How do you think he is feeling?" "What happened that made them feel that way?"*). If these questions and phrases are regular parts of your conversations at home, in the community, and while reading books or during screen time, children will begin to stop and think about others' feelings on their own as part of their natural thought processes.

## HAVING GOOD MANNERS IS ONE WAY TO SHOW KINDNESS AND COMPASSION

One way that children are taught to think about other people's feelings is through learning about manners. As parents, we often worry about how our children behave and treat others, including family, friends, and strangers, especially when out in public. It's not uncommon to hear parents remind their children:

> "Don't forget to say 'please' and 'thank you!'"
> "Cover your mouth when you cough."
> "Wait until someone is done talking—don't interrupt them."
> "It's not polite to spit out your food at the table."

Every family has their own set of rules about manners, and these rules vary. In some families, burping loudly at the dinner table might be a sign of contentment after a good meal. In other families, this might be seen as a rude or even an obscene gesture. And for other families, a good burp might be hilarious, but only when guests are not present. Teaching children about being kind and having good manners is not just about our own family's rules about what is and isn't polite, but also how our rules are similar to and different from other people's rules. Having good manners is one of the ways we practice being compassionate at home, as well as at school and in the community.

### Key messages for children:

- Our family has rules about how to behave and treat other people in a kind way. We call these rules manners.
- Other people's rules about manners might be different from ours, and that's okay.
- It is important to do our best to remember to use good manners no matter where we are—at home, at school, or in the community.

**Conan** (age four): I want the pink one.

**Eddie** (Conan's dad): (in a whisper) Don't forget to say, "May I have the pink one, please?"

**Conan:** May I have the pink one, please?

**Darcy:** Sure. Here you go. One pink doughnut.

**Conan:** Thank you!

**Darcy:** You are welcome. Thank you for being so polite! We don't see very many children in here who use such good manners.

**Eddie:** May I have a chocolate doughnut please?

**Darcy:** Absolutely.

**Eddie:** (to Conan) You did a really nice job showing your good manners! The lady at the counter even noticed.

*What's happening in this conversation:* Just like any other skill, using good manners is something children learn from seeing others use good manners and from being taught what is polite to say and do in different situations. In this conversation, Eddie reminds his son, Conan, how to ask politely for what he wants. He does so in a discreet way by whispering quietly to Conan to avoid putting him on the spot or embarrassing him. When it's his turn to order, Eddie uses the same polite words he asked his son to use so that he can be a good role model.

**Benjamin** (age three): Mom! I'm hungry!

**Drea** (Benjamin's mom): What was that, Ben?

**Benjamin:** I'm hungry! Hungry! Hungry!

**Drea:** If you would like a snack, you could say: "Mom, will you make me a snack, please?"

**Benjamin:** Mom, will you make me a snack, please?

**Drea:** Sure. That's a much kinder way to ask than yelling, "I'm hungry!"

*What's happening in this conversation:* Opportunities to practice good manners can happen anytime. Family members tend to be more forgiving than non-family members when it comes to our own children's words and behaviors, so we don't always take the time to encourage our children to use the same words with us that we want them to use with strangers. Doing so, however, helps children get the practice they need to remember their manners no matter where they are or who they are with.

**Mari** (Danesh's mom): Let me hold that door for you.

**Karidee** (woman carrying groceries): Thank you!

**Danesh** (age five): Let's go, mom!

**Mari:** Just a minute. I was holding the door for that woman because she had a big bag of groceries in her arms. I think it would have been hard for her to open the door by herself, so I wanted to be a helper.

**Danesh:** I like helping too.

**Mari:** Do you want to help me hold the door now? I see someone else coming this way.

**Danesh:** Okay! I can hold it by myself.

**Raymond:** Thank you, young man.

**Mari:** That was a nice way to be a helper!

**Danesh:** I helped.

**Mari:** Yes, you did.

*What's happening in this conversation:* When you act as a role model for your child, it isn't enough to just show how to act. Your child may or may not notice what you did and they may not understand why. Without having a conversation, Danesh might have continued to feel frustrated with his mom for slowing him down. Instead, she told him why she had stopped to hold the door. Once Danesh understood what his mom was doing, Danesh wanted to be a helper, too, and his mom gave him the chance to do so. Talking about what you are doing and why can help children recognize moments when you stop to think about other people's feelings during the day, and may encourage them to do the same.

**Laticia** (age six): (walks into a neighbor's house with her shoes on)

**Melinda** (Laticia's mom): (in a whisper) Look, Laticia.

**Laticia:** What?

**Melinda:** See that pile of shoes by the door?

**Laticia:** Yeah.

**Melinda:** Our neighbors might have a rule about no shoes in the house.

**Laticia:** Oh. (sits down and starts taking her shoes off)

**Maureen** (neighbor): Oh, no. Please don't worry about that. You're our guests. You can do whatever you feel most comfortable doing—taking your shoes off or leaving your shoes on.

**Laticia:** (stops what she is doing and looks up at her mom)

**Melinda:** It looks like taking shoes off is your family rule. We're happy to take our shoes off, too! (sits down next to Laticia and takes her shoes off)

**Laticia:** (finishes taking her shoes off)

*What's happening in this conversation:* When Melinda and her daughter, Laticia, visit a neighbor's house, they notice a pile of shoes by the front door. Even though they keep their shoes on in their own home, they choose to take their shoes off to respect their neighbor's house rules. Following their visit, Melinda might extend the conversation with Laticia by talking about the fact that it is good manners to follow another family's rules when visiting their home, and also good manners to relax your rules for guests (if appropriate in your family culture), just as Maureen had done by letting them know they could leave their shoes on if they were more comfortable that way.

Talking with children about having good manners is one way that we encourage children to apply understanding, empathy, and compassion when they are interacting with others. Helping children learn about the social rules and manners that are important in our own family, as well as being aware of the fact that these rules might be different for other families, can help them become more mindful about their actions.

## THERE ARE THINGS YOU CAN DO TO BE A GOOD FRIEND

Having good friends and social support is one of the strongest predictors of resilience for children and adults (Torres, Southwick, & Mayes, 2011). In order to have good friends, children need to learn, practice, and develop social skills.

From a very young age, most children are interested in other children. Early friendships start with children playing side by side, noticing one another, but not really playing together. This is called parallel play. As children get older, they are more interested in cooperative play.

Even from early ages, however, children have different comfort levels making new friends. Some children are very comfortable with new people in new situations. Other children are not. Some children feel comfortable having many different friends. Other children prefer a small group of close friends. This is true for adults, too.

Parents play an important role in helping children learn and practice the social skills they need to be a good friend while also helping them feel comfortable in social settings. Children's early friendships are typically short-lived, but they are still important chances for children to learn what it means to be a good friend. Parents can help children practice social skills during these early friendships by prompting them with suggestions for words and actions when help is needed, and then by stepping back and letting children practice these skills on their own. The skills children learn through their early friendships can help them build relationships on their own in the future.

### Key messages for children:

- Friends are special people in our lives.
- There are certain qualities that make a good friend.
- You can learn and practice skills that help you be a good friend.
- Some people are more comfortable making friends than others.
- Some people like to have a few friends. Some people like to have lots of friends. Both are okay.

**Reya** (age two): Baby inna sand.

**Elisabeth** (Reya's mom): Do you see that boy sitting in the sandbox? He doesn't look like a baby to me. He looks like a big boy!

**Reya:** Baby inna sand.

**Elisabeth:** Do you want to say hi?

**Reya:** Hi!

**Aidan** (age three): Hi.

**Elisabeth:** My daughter wants to say hi to you. (to Reya) Can you tell him your name?

**Reya:** Ya-ya.

**Aidan:** Ya-ya? Your name is Ya-ya?

**Reya:** Ya-ya.

**Elisabeth:** That's how she says, "Reya." What's your name?

**Aidan:** Aidan.

**Elisabeth:** How old are you, Aidan?

**Aidan:** Three (holds up three fingers).

**Elisabeth:** Three! Wow! Reya is only—Reya, can you tell Aidan how old you are?

**Reya:** Two! Ya-ya two!

**Elisabeth:** Reya is two. Reya, do you want to ask Aidan, "Can I play with you?"

**Reya:** Play wis you?

**Aidan:** Okay.

*What's happening in this conversation:* In this conversation, Elisabeth sees that her daughter, Reya, is interested in talking with a boy in the sandbox. Elisabeth gets the conversation started by helping Reya introduce herself to Aidan. She also tries to show Reya how to hold a conversation by asking Aidan questions. She decides then to step back, and asks questions that allow Reya to be involved in the interaction, rather than doing all the talking herself. Some days when they visit the park, Elisabeth plays a very hands-on role guiding Reya when she interacts with other children. Other days, she sits back and lets Reya navigate social situations on her own unless Reya looks to her for help. Using a combination of these strategies is important for Reya to learn positive words and behaviors with support, as well as for her to have the chance to try these skills on her own.

Even as children get older, it's still important to make sure they have support in social situations. Rather than telling a child to "go make friends" and leaving them to fend for themselves, think about what your child needs. Telling a child to "go make friends and play" while at the park, public library, or swimming pool and sitting to the side may be all that some children need, but it might not be enough for others. Some children have personalities that make it easy for them to walk up to another child and start a conversation on their own. Other children need a lot of encouragement and coaching. When children are young, parents have an opportunity to help them develop skills to meet new people, make friends, and to be a good friend.

**Judah** (age three): Clinton is my best friend.

**Alex** (Judah's mom): That's nice to hear. What does it mean to have a best friend? What does a best friend do?

**Judah:** He's nice to me. We play trucks together.

**Alex:** It sounds like you're saying that best friends are people who are nice to each other and like to do the same things?

**Judah:** Uh-huh. Clinton likes trucks, like me.

**Alex:** Are there things you do to be a good friend to Clinton?

**Judah:** I share my trucks with him.

**Alex:** I bet Clinton likes it when you share your trucks.

**Judah:** That's why I'm his best friend!

*What's happening in this conversation:* When Judah shares with his mom that he has a best friend, she helps him think about what it means to be a good friend. Even at this early age, Judah is able to identify things that he likes about Clinton. Judah's understanding of what it means to be a friend will probably change over time. Helping him put words to what he believes about friendship will encourage him to think about the friends he has now and those he chooses in the future.

**Quinn** (Regan's dad): Tomorrow is your first day of preschool. How are you feeling about that?

**Regan** (age four): (shrugs)

**Quinn:** You're not sure?

**Regan:** (shakes her head)

**Quinn:** Do you want me to guess?

**Regan:** Okay!

**Quinn:** Okay. I'll say a feeling and if you are feeling that way, touch your nose.

**Regan:** (giggles)

**Quinn:** Angry.

**Regan:** (shakes her head and giggles)

**Quinn:** Happy.

**Regan:** (touches her nose)

**Quinn:** Sad.

**Regan:** (shakes her head)

**Quinn:** Scared.

**Regan:** (touches her nose) A little bit happy. A little bit scared.

**Quinn:** What are you feeling scared about?

**Regan:** Friends.

**Quinn:** Are you scared that you won't know anyone?

**Regan:** I don't know.

**Quinn:** Do you want to talk about making new friends?

**Regan:** Okay.

**Quinn:** There are lots of ways to make friends. You could tell someone your name and ask if they want to play with you. Do you think you could try that?

**Regan:** Maybe. But what if they say no?

**Quinn:** They might, but then you could ask someone else. Your teacher will help you get to know other kids, too. It might take a while before you make a friend, but that's okay. Making good friends takes time. Can you think of other things you could do?

**Regan:** Read a book together?

**Quinn:** Sure! You could try that. Anything else you can think of?

**Regan:** I don't know.

**Quinn:** We could also try to set up play dates with other kids in your class so that you could get to know them after school. Would you like to do that?

**Regan:** Maybe.

*What's happening in this conversation:* The night before her first day of preschool, Regan is feeling scared that she might not have any friends. Her dad offers a few suggestions for things that she could try, and also asks Regan if she has ideas. He reassures her that it takes time to make good friends, and thinks about other ways that he could support her, such as through setting up play dates with children in her class.

**Lou** (Lisa's dad)**:** How was school today?

**Lisa** (age six)**:** I had a bad day.

**Lou:** Oh no! What happened?

**Lisa:** Alexis wouldn't play with me at recess.

**Lou:** Did you ask if you could play with her?

**Lisa:** I asked her, but she just wanted to play zombie girls with Gabby, and I didn't want to. I wanted her to play tag with me.

**Lou:** How did that make you feel?

**Lisa:** Sad.

**Lou:** Do you think she would have let you join in playing zombie girls?

**Lisa:** I didn't want to. I wanted her to play tag with me, not with Gabby.

**Lou:** Oh, I see. It sounds like you were feeling left out. Is that how you were feeling?

**Lisa:** (nods)

**(Lou and Lisa hug a while)**

**Lou:** What do you think you could do at recess tomorrow?

**Lisa:** I don't know.

**Lou:** Are you going to try to play with Alexis again?

**Lisa:** I want to, but she won't play with me.

**Lou:** Have you tried joining in her game?

**Lisa:** No.

**Lou:** Do you think if you played zombie girls with her a while that she might then play tag with you?

**Lisa:** Maybe. I guess I could play zombie girls for a little while and then ask if they will play tag with me.

**Lou:** That sounds like a good plan.

*What's happening in this conversation:* When Lisa's dad, Lou, asks her about her day at school, she tells him about a situation with a friend that upset her at recess. She wants to play *her* game with Alexis, but Alexis wants to play another game. Lou validates Lisa's feelings by letting her know that it's okay to feel sad about being left out. He also asks her about her plans for tackling the challenge the next day, and listens and supports her ideas. As children get older, they may experience both successes as well as challenges in their social interactions. Helping children celebrate the successes they have and problem-solve about the challenges gives them an opportunity to learn how to navigate new experiences with your guidance.

**Felix** (Sophie's dad)**:** I have a parent meeting at your school tonight.

**Sophie** (age seven)**:** Can I come too?

**Felix:** No, you're going to stay home with grandma. It's just for parents so we can learn about all the things you are doing in your classroom. You know what?

**Sophie:** What?

**Felix:** I'm a little nervous about it.

**Sophie:** Why, dad?

**Felix:** I don't really like big groups and I'm not very good at meeting new people. I don't know any of the other parents in your class.

**Sophie:** Ian's mom is nice. You should talk to her. Ian sits at my table.

**Felix:** Thanks for the tip. I'll introduce myself if I'm feeling brave. How about if I say, "My name's Felix. You probably already know my daughter because she's the loudest one in the whole class."

**Sophie:** Dad . . .

**Felix:** I'm just kidding. I'll just say, "Hi, I'm Felix. Sophie is my daughter. Nice to meet you."

**Sophie:** That's better.

*What's happening in this conversation:* In this conversation, Felix shares his own feelings about meeting new people with his daughter, Sophie. Sophie enjoys meeting new people and looks forward to social events, but her father often feels anxious about these types of situations. By having this conversation, he is teaching her about his own personality and letting her know that different people may have different feelings about meeting new people. By talking out loud about what he is going to say, he gives Sophie ideas for words that she can use when she meets new people in the future.

There are many other ways adults can model social skills for children. For example, introduce yourself to other parents or families at the park or grocery store when you are with your child. Share with your child what that experience is like for you. If it's uncomfortable, let your child know: *"I feel nervous meeting new people, but today I decided to be brave and make a new friend,"* or *"I really like meeting new people, but not everyone feels that way. How do you feel when you meet someone new?"* When your child has the opportunity to meet someone new, suggest words they can use, such as: *"My name is . . . What's your name? Do you want to play together?"* Parents can also help children practice recognizing social cues. *"It looks like she really wants to play with you. I noticed her watching you and smiling when you were in the sandbox."* or *"I don't think he wants that shovel. He keeps trying to push it away when you give it to him. Why don't you set it down?"* In addition, parents can point out their child's social cues to others. *"I don't think he wants a hug right now. Maybe a high five or a fist bump instead?"* Showing your child that you are thinking about their feelings and helping them recognize others' teaches children to treat others the way they want to be treated (rather than treating them how we think they want to be treated, which is not always accurate).

In addition to needing support and help from adults as they make new friends, children also need space to practice and try social interactions on their own so that they can gain confidence in their skills. Having the opportunity to make mistakes and practice correcting those mistakes is another part of learning how to make friends and how to be a good friend. As hard as it can be, it's important for parents to step back at times and let their child manage situations on their own more and more often. Shift back and forth between providing your child with real-time support so that they learn what to do, and stepping back to provide your child with the chance to navigate social situations on their own. As children get older, they don't necessarily want their parents hovering over them and offering advice on what to say or do. With an older child, you will likely spend less time providing real-time guidance and instead spend more time problem solving with your child before and after challenging social situations arise.

## MAKING AMENDS MEANS MORE THAN SAYING SORRY

Imagine your child as a teenager coming to you and saying: *"Can we talk? You know last night when I got mad and yelled at you? I shouldn't have done that. I'm really sorry, dad. I was so upset when you wouldn't let me take the car that I just lost it. I really wanted to see my friends, but I shouldn't have screamed. Next time, I'll try to keep my cool so that we can talk it out instead of fighting."* Having a teenager who is comfortable saying sorry and making amends in this way does not happen overnight. Children and adults alike need practice and support to have these types of conversations. Helping children feel comfortable saying sorry (and to accept apologies from others) takes time, patience, and our own willingness to model these skills as a parent.

### Key messages for children:

- It is important to make amends when we hurt someone, even if it is an accident.
- Making amends means more than saying, "I'm sorry." We should think about the other person's feelings, ask if they are okay, and ask what we can do to help them feel better.

• Sometimes people need time before they are ready to accept an apology, so we should give them space, but remember to come back and follow up.

**Felicity** (Erin's mom): Ouch! That looked like it hurt! You just bonked Donald on the head with your shovel.

**Erin** (age 22 months): (laughs)

**Felicity:** Oh, it's not funny to hurt someone. Look at his face. How is he feeling?

**Erin:** Sad. Dona sad.

**Felicity:** Yes, Donald looks sad. Uh-oh, now he's starting to cry.

**Karla** (Donald's mom): I think he's fine. He was just a little startled.

**Felicity:** When you hurt someone, it's important to say sorry and make sure they are okay. Can you say, "sorry?"

**Erin:** Sorry.

**Felicity:** Now you can ask: "Can I help you feel better?"

**Erin:** Feel better?

**Donald:** (stops crying and continues playing in the sand)

**Karla:** It looks like he's okay now. Thank you for saying sorry.

*What's happening in this conversation:* When Erin hits Donald with a plastic shovel in the sandbox, her mom, Felicity, helps draw Erin's attention to Donald's feelings. She asks Erin to look at his face and think about how he is feeling. She also teaches her daughter that making amends means more than saying "sorry" and helps her ask Donald what she can do to help him feel better. With continued practice, Erin will eventually learn to say these words on her own without her mom's help.

**Isaac** (age six): Ouch. Stop it! MOM! DUNCAN IS HURTING ME!

**Duncan** (age four): NO I'M NOT!

**Allie** (Isaac's and Duncan's mom): What's going on in here?

**Isaac:** Duncan is pulling my hair.

**Duncan:** No I'm not. I was just getting my backpack.

**Allie:** Oh, ouch. It looks like your backpack zipper is caught on your brother's hair.

**Isaac:** See. I told you. You did that on purpose!

**Duncan:** I did not!

**Allie:** There. It's untangled now.

**Isaac:** You hurt me.

**Allie:** I don't think your brother meant to pull your hair on purpose.

**Duncan:** I didn't.

**Allie:** Even if you didn't do it on purpose, you still might have hurt your brother. Look at his face. How do you think he is feeling? Can you make sure he is okay?

**Duncan:** I'm sorry, Isaac. Are you okay?

**Isaac:** No.

**Duncan:** Is there anything I can do to help you feel better?

**Isaac:** No. I'm fine.

*What's happening in this conversation:* When one of her sons hurts her other son accidentally, Allie encourages him to consider his brother's feelings. Asking children to say "sorry" is a common response when one child hurts another. When a child hurts or wrongs another child or adult, whether it is physically or emotionally, asking that child to just say "sorry," should not be where the conversation ends. When a child says, "sorry!" and then turns back to playing, they may not be thinking about the other person's feelings. When an apology is in order, help your child stop and consider the other person's feelings (e.g., *"How do you think that made her feel? How would you feel if that happened to you?"*). Follow up by involving your child in problem solving about the solution (e.g., *"What could you do to make up?" "What do you think you could do to help your friend feel better?"*).

**Annabelle** (age eight): (holding hands with Luisa while running) Come on! Faster! Faster!

**Luisa** (age four): (trips, falls, and starts crying)

**Al** (Luisa's dad): What happened? Are you okay? Oh, I see your knee is all bloody. Let's go inside and clean it up.

**Annabelle:** I'm sorry, Luisa. Are you okay?

**Luisa:** (continues crying)

**Annabelle:** I'm sorry, Luisa.

**Luisa:** (continues crying)

**Al:** Thanks, Annabelle. I'm sure it wasn't your fault. You didn't do it on purpose. I'm going to take Luisa inside and clean her up.

**Luisa:** My knee! Annabelle was running too fast!

**Al:** Oh, is that how you fell? You girls were running together?

**Luisa:** Uh-huh.

**Al:** There we go. All cleaned up now. Let's put a bandage on. There. Does that feel any better?

**Luisa:** Uh-huh. (sniffs)

**Al:** You know what, I think Annabelle felt really badly about what happened. Shall we go let her know that you are okay? She was really worried about you.

**Luisa:** Okay, daddy.

**Al:** Hi, Annabelle.

**Annabelle:** I'm sorry, Luisa. Are you okay?

**Luisa:** I'm okay, Annabelle.

**Al:** It wasn't your fault, Annabelle. It sounds like you two just had an accident while running together.

**Annabelle:** Do you forgive me, Luisa?

**Luisa:** Okay.

*What's happening in this conversation:* Making amends involves not only learning to apologize, but also learning to accept an apology and forgive another person. Being able to accept an apology involves thinking about the other person's feelings, too. This can be especially hard to do when we are hurt or feel as if we have been wronged. In early childhood, apologies can happen frequently. Sometimes a quick apology might even go unnoticed by a child. In order to help children take these moments seriously, parents can help their children go beyond saying sorry, to asking the other person if they are okay and what they can do to help them feel better, to forgiving the other person and letting them know when an apology has been accepted. In this conversation, Annabelle was left feeling worried that she had hurt Luisa. Resolving the situation involved helping Luisa manage her feelings and her sore knee, as well as letting Annabelle know that everything was okay and they had made amends.

**Troy** (Ashley's dad): Can we talk about something?

**Ashley** (age five): What?

**Troy:** I'm sorry for yelling this morning. I lost my temper and I should not have yelled. I was really upset when it was time to leave for school and you weren't dressed.

**Ashley:** I couldn't find the dress that I wanted.

**Troy:** I know you couldn't, but we didn't have time to keep looking.

**Ashley:** I don't like it when you yell at me.

**Troy:** I don't like it either. I felt really badly about it afterward. Next time, I am going to take a deep breath and use my calm voice instead. Is there anything I can do to help you feel better?

**Ashley:** (hugs Troy)

**Troy:** I like hugs. Do you forgive me?

**Ashley:** Okay.

**Troy:** I also want to talk about what you said to me. When you said, 'I hate you!' that really hurt my feelings.

**Ashley:** I'm sorry, dad.

**Troy:** Thank you for saying sorry. That does help me feel better. I don't think you really meant it, but it hurt my feelings a lot.

**Ashley:** Is there anything I can do to help you feel better?

**Troy:** How about another hug? (hugs Ashley) I think we also need to talk about a new plan for tomorrow so that what happened today doesn't happen again. We need to work together to make tomorrow morning better. What do you think we could do?

**Ashley:** (shrugs)

**Troy:** How about if you choose your clothes tonight so that you'll be ready for tomorrow morning? That might help.

**Ashley:** Okay. I know what I want to wear already.

**Troy:** That's great!

*What's happening in this conversation:* After a rough morning together, Troy apologizes to his daughter, Ashley, for getting upset with her and for yelling—something he didn't feel good about. Although it was hard for him to do, he realized that if Ashley had been the one to yell, he would have wanted her to apologize and think about what she could do differently next time. He modeled the words and behaviors that he would want her to use and offered a genuine apology to let her know that he was sorry for his actions. He also let her know that she had hurt his feelings. Following her dad's lead, Ashley apologized to Troy as well, something she might not have done without him doing so first.

When a child offers an apology, it is important for parents to acknowledge and accept the apology in a way that allows the child to feel like they have made amends or are at least working toward making amends. What if when

Ashley apologized, Troy had said, "I don't care that you're sorry. Sorry is not good enough." This response might have left Ashley feeling badly for having apologized. It certainly would not encourage her to apologize again in the future. When Troy thanked Ashley for her apology, he let her know that the apology helped. An apology may not solve an issue, but parents can let children know that they appreciate their child's positive intent while also helping them identify what else they can do to make amends.

**Isabelle** (Arturo's mom): I need to apologize to your dad.

**Arturo** (age six): Why, mom?

**Isabelle:** This morning I was running late for work. Your dad tried to help me get ready, but tripped and spilled milk all over the shirt I was wearing. I had to go change and yelled at him to get out of my way. Then I ran out the door to work without apologizing.

**Arturo:** That's not very nice.

**Isabelle:** You're right. It's not. I shouldn't have done that. I was feeling stressed, but that's no excuse. I should have been kinder to your dad. He was trying to help. That's why I need to let him know that I'm sorry. What do you think I should tell him?

**Arturo:** You should say, "I'm sorry."

**Isabelle:** Okay. Anything else?

**Arturo:** "I love you"?

**Isabelle:** That's a good idea, too.

**Arturo:** And you should ask if there's anything you can do to help him feel better.

**Isabelle:** Okay, I got it! I'm ready.

*What's happening in this conversation:* Earlier that morning, Arturo had watched the situation that his mother described in their conversation. He had seen his mother leave the house in a rush and his father shaking his head after her. Usually the interactions that he saw between his parents were positive and caring, but from time to time, things like this happened. In their conversation, Isabelle admits to her son, Arturo, that she did not feel good about her words and actions that morning. She points out to him what she did that was not kind (yelling at her husband to get out of the way). She also lets Arturo know why it happened (she was stressed and running late), but also does not justify or defend the behavior. She then shares with him that she feels badly and makes a plan to apologize to her husband. Conversations like this one let children know that even adults make mistakes. By having this conversation with Arturo, Isabelle serves as a role model demonstrating how to recognize and admit a mistake and how to make amends. She also gives him the opportunity to see the situation resolve in a positive way.

## THERE ARE NO BAD KIDS, BUT SOME KIDS HAVE MORE CHALLENGES THAN OTHERS

When a child struggles with social skills (e.g., hitting and pushing instead of using words to communicate), it can be easy to label them as a problem child—a "bad" or "mean" kid. Children notice when others are not following rules or are behaving in a way that is unkind. They start to avoid these children and may even say things like, "I don't like you," or "You're a meanie." Sometimes it may even be your child who is labeled in this way. All children have moments when they struggle with expressing themselves or when they use their bodies instead of their words to communicate. Sometimes these actions can be destructive or hurtful to themselves or to others. Whether it is your child or another child who is acting as the "bad kid," we can respond with compassion and show our children how to do the same. By taking a step back and thinking about how the other child was feeling and what skills they need help practicing (rather than focusing on what they did wrong), we can reframe the idea of a "problem child." In doing so, we teach our own children to take someone else's perspective, positively reframe a situation, and be a good friend and role model.

### Key messages for children:

- Everybody has to learn and practice how to be kind.
- Sometimes people do things that are unkind because they are still learning. That does not mean they are bad people.
- When we see someone do something that is not kind, we should think about their feelings and our own.
- Sometimes you might do things that are unkind because you are still learning.
- When we are kind, we can show others how to be kind, too.

**Laurel** (age four): I hate Amelie. She's mean.

**Shannon** (Laurel's mom): Why do you say that? Did something happen at school today?

**Laurel:** Amelie pushed me. She always pushes me, and I don't like it!

**Shannon:** I don't like being pushed, either. What did you do when she pushed you?

**Laurel:** I said, "STOP IT!"

**Shannon:** And then what happened?

**Laurel:** The teacher made her go to the back of the line.

**Shannon:** Does Amelie push other people, too?

**Laurel:** She pushes all the time. She gets upset if we have to wait too long. She pushes everyone. That's why she's always in trouble.

**Shannon:** It's not okay for her to push other people, and I'm sorry that happened to you. It sounds like Amelie is still learning how to control her body. It's hard to be a good friend when—

**Laurel:** She's not my friend.

**Shannon:** I wouldn't want to be someone's friend who pushed me, either. But it might be helpful to know that it takes some kids more practice than others to learn how to control their bodies and to be a good friend at school. Maybe there are things your teacher and you and your class can do to help her learn to be a nicer friend.

**Laurel:** I don't push her.

**Shannon:** That's a good start. Maybe you could invite her to stand next to you in line and see if she acts more kindly when she feels invited.

**Laurel:** She was nice to me yesterday when we played together in the sandbox.

**Shannon:** That's good to hear! Maybe when she feels like she's being included, she has an easier time controlling her body.

*What's happening in this conversation:* When Laurel came home from preschool saying that she hated Amelie, her mom, Shannon, could have reacted strongly to the conversation by telling her that Amelie was a bad kid or a bad influence and that she should just stay away from her. Instead, she tried to help her daughter consider Amelie's point of view and problem-solve about what might help her change her behaviors (e.g., changing how she was feeling standing in line, from upset to included). An important note is that Shannon

Adrienne came home from kindergarten distraught after a classmate, Henry, told her that he was going to stab her with his pencil. She told her teacher, who reassured her she was safe and moved her to the other side of the classroom.

Her mom, Izzy, asked Adrienne if anything else had been done to help the other child. Adrienne replied: "I don't think so."

This bothered Izzy. As a parent, she wanted her daughter and the other children in the class not only to feel safe, but to be safe. Physically moving her helped Adrienne feel better in the moment, but it wasn't a long-term solution for her or for Henry.

The next day, Adrienne shared that Henry was sent to the principal's office for hitting another child. Adrienne told Izzy that he has to go to the principal's office every day for "hitting and pushing and stuff." She was glad he did because it made the classroom quieter when he was gone.

Izzy was concerned about what Adrienne was learning from this situation. The message she shared with her mom was that when someone shows problem behaviors, you should isolate them. Henry was probably hearing this message, too—that he was a problem and no one wanted to be near him. Izzy called the kindergarten teacher with her concerns, but Mrs. Harris couldn't share any details about Henry, in order to protect his and his family's privacy. It's possible that a plan was in place to help Henry practice using words and develop the social skills he needed to be a good friend and student in the classroom, but maybe not. Adrienne continued coming home with the message that Henry was "mean" and a "problem" at school.

No parent wants their child to be in an unsafe situation. A child like Henry is probably not invited on many play dates or to many birthday parties. Instead, children like Henry are at risk of being isolated by others. The problem with isolating children like Henry is that he is missing out on opportunities he needs to learn the skills he is missing—skills to express his own feelings in appropriate ways, skills to recognize other children's feelings, and skills to be a good friend. What other skills might be helpful to Henry?

Unfortunately, Henry cannot learn these skills on his own. He needs support from his teacher to model for him what to do to have successful interactions with other children in the class. He needs supportive feedback from her along the

continued

way, to let him know when he's doing well and when he's off track. He needs the children in the class to understand that "Henry is learning to be a good friend—just like all of us," and to feel like part of a team helping one another. And Henry needs to hear these same messages from his family at home. Changing patterns of behavior takes constant practice across the different contexts of children's lives. It's not an easy process, and supporting children like Henry will take his entire community.

In this scenario, we don't know much about Henry. Knowing more about his family life might help shed light on the kind of support he needs at home and at school. Consider the following young children, all of whom find themselves in the principal's office with Henry on a regular basis:

Henry: Henry's dad is in jail, his mom left, and he is being raised by his grandparents, who are also raising three of his teenage cousins. His grandparents love him very much, but don't have much energy to spend time with him, so he spends most of his time at home playing video games.

Paris. Paris is generally upbeat, but her parents are going through a divorce, and this has affected her at school. She cries a lot at her desk, which is distracting to the other children, so she is sent to the principal's office to cry there instead. On the playground, some of the children have teased her for crying, and she punched one of them.

Ragev: Ragev has special needs that make it difficult for him to express himself through words. He often hits other children when he feels excited and wants to play with them. His intent is not malicious, but hitting is not allowed in his classroom, so he's sent to the principal's office until he calms down.

Each of these children needs help learning skills and needs support from the community around them. Too often, children who demonstrate challenging behaviors are isolated rather than embraced and not supported in the way they need.

- What conversations can you have with your child to help them approach all children with understanding and compassion (without condoning negative/hurtful behavior)?

- What could you and your child do to be a role model and helper more often for other children in your neighborhood, school, and community?

acknowledged Laurel's feelings as well. She validated that it was justified to feel angry about being pushed and that it was okay to not want to be friends with someone who did not act kindly.

**Yael** (age five)**:** Harry said I was a meanie. I'm not a meanie!

**Ry** (Yael's dad)**:** That doesn't sound like a nice thing to say. Sometimes people say things that are unkind when they are upset. Did something happen that upset Harry?

**Yael:** I knocked over his blocks.

**Ry:** Oh. How do you think he felt when you knocked over his blocks?

**Yael:** He was mad.

**Ry:** I can understand that. I would have been mad too. Why did you knock over his blocks?

**Yael:** He had all the big blocks and wouldn't give me any.

**Ry:** I see. So you felt upset that he had all the big blocks and wouldn't share, so you pushed over his blocks.

**Yael:** Uh-huh.

**Ry:** And then he felt mad and called you a meanie. Is that what happened?

**Yael:** Yes! And I didn't like it.

**Ry:** I wouldn't like it either, but I think there are two people's feelings we need to think about. First, it sounds like you did something that made Harry feel upset. Pushing over his blocks was not a kind thing to do. What do you think you could have done instead of knocking over his blocks?

**Yael:** I could have waited.

**Ry:** Yes. You could have waited and asked him for a turn when he was done. Or you could have asked your teacher if there were other big blocks around.

**Yael:** There were no other big blocks.

**Ry:** Then you could have waited.

**Yael:** Sorry.

**Ry:** I think Harry is the one that you should apologize to. Is there anything you can think of that might help make up with him?

**Yael:** He likes cars. I could draw him a car picture!

**Ry:** That sounds like a nice idea. The other thing you could do is let him know that you didn't like it when he called you a meanie. You can apologize for knocking down his blocks, but also let him know that you didn't like it when he called you a name.

**Yael:** Okay, dad. I'm going to draw a car picture now.

**Ry:** Sounds like a good plan.

*What's happening in this conversation:* Yael was upset that another child had called her a "meanie" at school. Her dad asked her to explain what happened leading up to this name calling, noting that sometimes people do unkind things when they are upset. Yael then shared that she had actually done something (knocking over blocks) that had made Harry upset, leading him to call her a name. Importantly, Yael's father drew her attention to both her feelings and Harry's and helped her make a plan to address both sets of feelings.

**Jessie** (Mendel's mom): I can't believe he said that. What an idiot!

**Mendel** (age six): Who's an idiot, mom?

**Jessie:** Oh, I shouldn't have said that. That's not a nice word, actually. I was talking about someone at work who said something that made me feel frustrated.

**Mendel:** What did they say?

**Jessie:** He thought we should do a project one way, but I don't think his idea is going to work, so I wanted to do it a different way.

**Mendel:** Maybe you could talk about it.

**Jessie:** I think that's a good idea. I just needed a little time to cool down first. I shouldn't have called him a name—he's not a bad person. He's doing what he thinks is best. He just doesn't have all the information he needs, so I might be able to help by talking about it.

**Mendel:** You should definitely use your words. That's what you always say to me.

**Jessie:** Thanks for the idea, kiddo.

**Mendel:** You're welcome.

*What's happening in this conversation:* There are many things parents can say (or avoid saying) to model compassion toward others whom we might see as "the problem child" in our own lives. Even as adults, it can be easy to call others names without thinking about it. When someone cuts in front of us in line at the grocery store, swerves in front of us while driving, or says something we disagree with on the news, we may have the impulse to call that person a name or mutter obscenities about them. When this happens in front of your child, stop yourself and practice positive reframing:

> "I get upset when people cut in front of me in line, but maybe she didn't realize I was standing there first."
> "I don't like what that man on TV just said. Even if I don't agree with him, though, it's not nice for me to call him a name."

Modeling positive reframing is another way to help your child develop these skills. Help your child approach others with positive intent–the assumption that others are doing the best that they can. It's okay to be realistic about this, too by sharing with your child that even though people should strive to be their best, not everyone is thinking about that all the time. There are people who hurt other people on purpose, but people with these kinds of intentions are not as common as people who are doing their best to be kind.

## PRIVILEGE IMPACTS OUR LIVES IN DIFFERENT WAYS

**Privilege** is a complicated topic that plays out in our society in many ways. Privilege refers to the special rights or advantages that a particular group of people has that are not available to another group. Privilege can relate to money, race, religion, sexual orientation, and any other characteristic that defines an individual or a group. No one should feel bad about who they are or where they come from. Children do not have a choice about whether they are born or adopted into a family that is wealthy, impoverished, or somewhere in between; black, brown, or white; in a First, Second, or Third World country; in a dangerous and abusive environment; or a safe and loving one. Children do not choose their families or where they start out in life. Everyone faces challenges, but some people are born with challenges that are greater than those others face.

Recognizing privilege and helping children understand the role that privilege plays in their lives is part of understanding their position and power in the world (or lack thereof), as well as fostering compassion for others when they are in more or less fortunate positions. Understanding privilege is also part of building awareness that where people start out in life is not anyone's "fault," and that where you start can impact the opportunities you have and how far you are likely to go. Helping children learn about privilege can help ensure that all children have the support, understanding, and opportunities they need to thrive.

### Key messages for children:

- No one should feel bad about who they are or where they come from.
- Different groups of people have different privileges that impact their lives.
- Learning about privilege can help us make sure all people have access to the same kinds of opportunities.

**Hailey** (age five): Can I do it?

**Leslie** (Hailey's mom): You want to help me swipe my debit card?

**Hailey:** Yes!

**Leslie:** Sure. Go ahead. Turn the stripe the other way.

**Hailey:** I did it. It worked!

**Leslie:** You did it. Do you know what you did?

**Hailey:** I swiped your card?

**Leslie:** Yes! But you used that swipe to pay for our groceries. This card has information that connects to my bank account. When we buy groceries, we use the card to pay for them with money from the bank. Do you know where that money comes from?

**Hailey:** The bank?

**Leslie:** Well, it's in the bank, but it comes from me going to work. When I go to work, I get paid money to do my job. Then I put that money in the bank and use it to buy our groceries and pay our bills. When I pay for groceries, some of that money will pay the people who work at the supermarket. Then that lady who helped us earns money, and she can use it to pay her bills or buy groceries for her family!

*What's happening in this conversation:* During a trip to the grocery store, Hailey asks her mom if she can swipe her debit card for her. Leslie agrees and uses the opportunity to teach her daughter about the transaction. There are many moments that arise on any given day when we can use what's happening in our lives to teach children about how money is used in our society. From depositing a paycheck, to putting gas in the car, to paying bills, to filing for unemployment benefits, each of these moments can be a learning opportunity to explain to children about the relationship between our lives and money.

Conversations about money come up in many different ways in children's lives, from why and how we use money to comparisons between themselves and others regarding resources and lifestyle (e.g., "Genesis got a new bike for her birthday. How come I can't have one?"). Socioeconomic differences are among the ways that privilege can be discussed and acknowledged. Whether your family has a little or a lot of money, help your child learn about the value of money in our society, as well as how money is earned, spent, and saved. In addition, help your child learn that issues related to poverty and wealth (and everything in between) are complex and much more than just about whether or not someone has a job or how hard someone works.

**Corbin** (Eloise's dad): You know what I don't like about Santa Claus?

**Eloise** (age seven): He's a creepy man who comes down your chimney?

**Corbin:** No, that's what you don't like about Santa Claus. (laughs) You never liked Santa Claus, not even when you were little.

**Eloise:** Why?

**Corbin:** I don't know. Why do you think you didn't like him?

**Eloise:** He scared me! I didn't want a strange man to come in our house.

**Corbin:** That's why we started telling you he wasn't real from the time you were little.

**Eloise:** How come you don't like Santa Claus?

**Corbin:** The story about Santa Claus says that good children get presents, not bad children.

**Eloise:** I'm always good!

**Corbin:** Well, you're good most of the time, but sometimes you make mistakes like everyone else does. (laughs) Who really buys presents?

**Eloise:** Parents.

**Corbin:** Yep. Parents, grandparents, and other people who take care of kids. What if a family doesn't have very much money and can't buy presents for their kids?

**Eloise:** Then they don't get very many presents?

**Corbin:** So what if those kids think they are bad because Santa didn't bring them anything, but really their family didn't have much money to buy them presents or couldn't buy them presents that were as fancy as their friends' presents? That's why I don't like the story about Santa Claus— it's not really fair to kids and families who don't have a lot of money.

**Eloise:** Oh. I never thought about that.

*What's happening in this conversation:* In this conversation, Corbin shares with his daughter, Eloise, something that doesn't sit well with him regarding a holiday their family celebrates. Even though he grew up celebrating Christmas and Santa Claus and enjoys these traditions with his own family, he points out to his daughter aspects of this holiday tradition that he feels may unfairly exclude families living in poverty. Pointing out traditions or rules that may exclude one group or another can help children learn to start recognizing privilege in the world around them.

**Jackson** (Violet's dad): Did you know that people in different jobs make different amounts of money?

**Violet** (age eight): No.

**Jackson:** It's true.

**Violet:** Like what?

**Jackson:** People in certain jobs make a lot more money than people in other jobs—like a doctor. Do you think anyone could walk in to the hospital and be a doctor?

**Violet:** No.

**Jackson:** No, you're right. Doctors have to go to school for a very long time, and medical school is very expensive, so it takes very hard work, lots of learning, and lots of money to become a doctor. Doctors usually get paid a lot of money to do their jobs.

**Violet:** I want to be a doctor!

**Jackson:** If you want to be a doctor when you get older, you will have to study hard and apply to medical school. Doctors work very hard at their jobs, but other people work hard at their jobs too. The man who picked up our trash this morning was working really hard!

**Violet:** Does he make lots of money?

**Jackson:** Not really. He may not have had to go to college to get his job.

**Violet:** So people who go to college make more money?

**Jackson:** Sometimes that's true, but not always. But you know what's not fair is that even though we talk about being able to do and be anything you want, that's not always true. So even if someone wanted to be a doctor, they might not have a chance. If your parents didn't go to college, they might not know how to help you get ready for college or be able to afford the opportunities you might need.

**Violet:** Oh, but mom went to college so she can help me, right?

*What's happening in this conversation:* Jackson begins having a conversation about privilege with his daughter, Violet, by talking about different jobs people have and how these jobs might be valued in different ways. He might extend the conversation by talking with her about the opportunities that he had and didn't have in his own life, and how those opportunities as well as the choices he made led him to his own career as a tradesman.

In your discussions with your child about money (poverty and wealth), careers, and other related topics, help your child understand how complex this topic can be. The idea that money relates to hard work is true to a certain degree, but there are many other factors that play into money as well, including where you started, opportunities that were available to you and your family, whether or not you had role models, type of family support, and more. Not everyone has an equal chance of attaining any level of socioeconomic status. There are "rags to riches" examples, but these tend to be the exception rather than the norm.

**Caroline** (Anthony's mom): Do you know what privilege means?

**Anthony** (age six): No.

**Caroline:** Privilege is when a person or a group has special rights and advantages that other people don't have. Does that make sense?

**Anthony:** Not really.

**Caroline:** Let me see if I can think of some examples. There are things that some people worry about every day that other people never have to worry about.

**Anthony:** Like what?

**Caroline:** Let's see . . . people who are white in our country don't usually have to worry about other people discriminating against them because of the color of their skin. Milo says that whenever he goes into a store, the people who work there follow him around because they think he is going to steal something.

**Anthony:** Milo doesn't steal things!

**Caroline:** I know he doesn't, but because he's black, some people are suspicious of him.

**Anthony:** Why?

**Caroline:** That's a good question. Sometimes people are biased or prejudiced without realizing it. So people who are white are privileged in that way. They don't usually have to worry about being followed around in the store, or people thinking they will do something wrong without even knowing them. Let me see if I can think of another example. Oh—did you know that in some jobs, women get paid less than men do?

**Anthony:** That's not fair!

**Caroline:** No, it's not fair, but it's true. So that's another kind of privilege related to being a man.

**Anthony:** I'm going to be a man.

**Caroline:** That's true, so knowing about this, you might be able to help change those rules. Do you want to hear more examples?

**Anthony:** Okay.

**Caroline:** For a long time, people who were gay or lesbian weren't able to get married, so they missed out on lots of rights that other married people had.

**Anthony:** But everyone can get married now.

**Caroline:** That's true. Sometimes things change. So privilege is not having to worry about the things that other people have to worry about because of who you are.

**Anthony:** We're pretty lucky, huh mom?

**Caroline:** Yeah. We're really lucky. And that's why we need to think about the privileges we have and how we can use them to help other people who don't have those same privileges.

*What's happening in this conversation:* This conversation between Caroline and her son Anthony is packed full of examples of the various ways that privilege might appear in our society. You might not have one conversation with your child that tackles so many issues related to privilege all at once, but instead spread out talking about these and other examples over time through many short conversations.

**Luann** (Nina's mom): I noticed something interesting about the dolls they have here.

**Nina** (age six): What, mom?

**Luann:** Take a look around and see if you notice anything they have in common.

**Nina:** They all have pink boxes?

**Luann:** Well, that's true. Anything else?

**Nina:** I don't know.

**Luann:** How many dolls do you see that have black or brown skin?

**Nina:** That one has brown skin.

**Luann:** Okay, that's one. Any others?

**Nina:** No.

**Luann:** How many do you see that have white skin?

**Nina:** One, two, three, four, five, six, seven, eight, lots of them.

**Luann:** What about dolls that are Asian or other races?

**Nina:** That one looks Asian.

**Luann:** Okay. Do you see any dolls that might have disabilities?

**Nina:** No.

**Luann:** What about dolls with different kinds of bodies?

**Nina:** Most of them look the same. Those ones have really big heads.

**Luann:** But do you see different types of bodies that look like real people's bodies?

**Nina:** Not really.

**Luann:** Me neither. You have light-colored skin like most of these dolls do, so it's easy for you to find dolls that look like you.

**Nina:** Like this one! She has brown hair and brown eyes just like me.

**Luann:** Yes! You found her quickly. What about kids who have darker skin or who have disabilities? What do you think it feels like to come to a store like this and look for a doll that looks like you?

**Nina:** I don't know. They could make more dolls with different colored skin or that look different.

**Luann:** They could. Some companies are doing that now, but not very many. I wonder how it feels to girls or boys who come to the toy store and don't see any toys that look like them on the shelves.

**Nina:** Sad?

**Luann:** Maybe. It might make them feel like they don't matter, and I wouldn't want any child feeling that way.

*What's happening in this conversation:* While looking at dolls in the store, Luann notices that there is very little diversity in the way the dolls on the shelf look. There are a few dolls that are nonwhite, but not many. Having access to rows of dolls representing the dominant culture makes it easier for children from that culture to find dolls that they identify with. It also makes it more likely that a child's collection of dolls will lack diversity, so that their play will represent a segregation of sorts. This same conversation might look different between a parent and child who are struggling to find dolls (or other toys) that resemble their child:

> **Tracy** (age six): I really want to find a doll that looks like me.
> **Paulina** (Tracy's mom): I know you do, honey, but it's hard. This one has black skin.
> **Tracy:** But it doesn't look like me.
> **Paulina:** No, you're right. It doesn't. Can you find any others?
> **Tracy:** This one is sort of brown looking because it's supposed to be tan, but that's not really like me, either.
> **Paulina:** I think it's really frustrating that there aren't more dolls that have beautiful brown skin like yours. Let's go home and look online.
> **Tracy:** But it's not fair.
> **Paulina:** You're right. It's not fair.

Parents can use conversations like this one as starting points to talk with children about how people from different groups are left out in other ways, too—not just in the way they are or are not represented by dolls. Certain groups are included or left out of advertising campaigns. Certain groups have historically been paid less than others. Certain groups live in certain parts of town or have access to certain schools, but not to others.

When parents and children see examples like these in society, they can think about how and if they would like to respond. For example, changing the nature of what is offered in a store might require that families speak up about wanting access to dolls that represent the actual community that families are a part of, or supporting stores or companies that represent many different forms of diversity in their products.

> **Sid** (Bart's dad): I heard the most amazing story today from a woman at work.
> **Bart** (age seven): Tell me!
> **Sid:** Well, she came to the United States a few years ago from Syria with her three children. They lived in a refugee camp for two years before

they were able to come to the United States. While they were there, they didn't have much, but she tried to teach her kids to read every day so that they would keep learning. Their family has been through a lot. What do you think about inviting them to join our family for Thanksgiving?

**Bart:** Okay! Will her kids come too?

**Sid:** I hope so. It's their first Thanksgiving in the United States, so I wanted to be welcoming, and we could get to know them better.

**Bart:** They can play in my room with me!

*What's happening in this conversation:* Every individual and family has a story. Taking time to listen to other people's stories and learn about the experiences they have had in life, including the ups and downs, what has helped them along the way, and what has been challenging can help build understanding, empathy, and ultimately, compassion. In this conversation, Sid shared with his son a story he heard from a coworker about her family's life—a life that was very different from their own family's experience. Learning the stories of other individuals and families can help children see beyond stereotypes and consider how privilege has played out in the lives of people they know. Sid can extend this conversation with his son by reading books together about the lives of others from many different backgrounds throughout history, and talking about how each family's experience is similar to and different from their own.

Helping children understand privilege doesn't happen through one conversation. It happens through many different conversations about the role of money in our lives, the role of race, gender, religion, sexual orientation, and any other qualities that define who we are as individuals or groups. Getting to know individuals for who they are and hearing personal stories about successes and challenges can help children build an understanding of the world that allows them to consider privilege without feeling defensive about their own privileges or lack of privileges. Having conversations with children about privilege can be an opportunity to teach children that some people and some groups have more challenges than others, and to encourage them to think about ways we can shape the world to ensure that all children have equal opportunities.

## WE CAN EACH MAKE A DIFFERENCE IN OUR OWN WAY

This final topic focuses on conversations that let children know there are many ways to make a difference. As we have discussed throughout this book, children have their own personalities and their own special qualities that make them who they are. There are many ways to be kind and compassionate, and parents can play a role in helping children find ways that best fit who they are. Some children are comfortable speaking up loudly when they see an injustice; others prefer to ask an adult for help; and still others prefer to quietly reach out and let a friend know they care. Some children express themselves with words, others with actions, and still others through creative endeavors, such as art or music. Have conversations with your child about the fact that there are many ways to be a helper and many ways to be a compassionate kid.

### Key messages for children:

- Everyone can make a difference in big or small ways.
- There are things we can do to be a helper at home and in our community.
- We are all part of the world that we live in, and we can all help make it a better place.

**Rod** (Karolina's dad): Do you want to help me take the recycling out?

**Karolina** (age four): Okay.

**Rod:** Do you know why we have two different bins?

**Karolina:** Because we have lots of garbage?

**Rod:** One is for garbage, but one is for recycling.

**Karolina:** What's recycling?

**Rod:** Recycling is when we take things that we have used and turn them into things we can use again. So when we recycle these plastic bottles, they can be turned into new bottles that other people can use. We have a picture on the refrigerator of all the types of things that can be recycled. Let's go look at it.

**Karolina:** Whoa. That's a lot of things.

**Rod:** It sure is. It's our job to make sure we put these things in the recycle bin so that they can be used again. Otherwise, things get sent to the landfill, and the pile of garbage that we create will get bigger and bigger. Which of these things can we recycle?

**Karolina:** This one and this one!

**Rod:** Yes! Anything else?

**Karolina:** This one too!

**Rod:** You're getting the hang of it!

**Karolina:** Can this be my job every day?

**Rod:** Sure, if you want to! I can always use the help, and it's more fun to do this together than by myself.

*What's happening in this conversation:* There are many ways to make a difference in the community. One way is to help take care of the environment. In this conversation, Rod teaches his daughter, Karolina, what it means to recycle and involves her in sorting the recycling in their home. After discovering how much they enjoyed working on this project together, they might think about other ways they can spend time together while improving their community, from recycling to taking care of their yard or mowing a neighbor's lawn and anything else they can think of to do together.

**Lola** (Quincy's mom): We see you in here a lot. I'm Lola.

**Fran** (cashier at a local market): It's nice to meet you. I'm Fran. And who is this little one?

**Lola:** Do you want to tell her your name?

**Quincy** (age two): Quincy!

**Fran:** Quincy! How old are you?

**Quincy:** Two!

**Fran:** Two! Wow. What a big girl. How long have you lived in the neighborhood?

**Lola:** About two years now. We moved here about the time Quincy was born.

**Fran:** I thought I'd been seeing you for a while. It's nice to know your names!

**Lola:** You too, Fran. See you next time!

**(after leaving the market)**

**Lola:** Usually I just walk in and out of the market to buy what we need, but today I decided to introduce us. I like knowing people in our community. Now we can say hi to Fran when we come in!

**Quincy:** Fran! Fran!

**Lola:** I'm glad we did it. We should introduce ourselves to other people, too. I just never really thought about it before.

*What's happening in this conversation:* When she's on her own, Lola typically prefers to walk in and out of local stores without talking to anyone. After giving it some thought, she realized that she would like her daughter, Quincy, to have a community around her. Feeling brave, she introduced herself to Fran, a cashier at a local market whom she sees frequently. In doing so, she modeled to Quincy how to meet someone new. This conversation won't end here. Now that Lola and Quincy have met Fran, they will likely have ongoing conversations the next time they visit the same market.

**Edith** (age four): What are you making?

**Sara** (Edith's mom): I'm making some cards.

**Edith:** Can I help?

**Sara:** Sure! Here are some different blank cards and paper you could use to cut out shapes and decorate them.

**Edith:** May I have the glue?

**Sara:** Here you go. I was going to send a card to grandma. Do you want to send a card to anyone?

**Edith:** Could I send one to Inge?

**Sara:** Absolutely! I bet she will love it. People don't send cards very often, but it's a nice way to let people know you are thinking about them.

**Edith:** I want to tell her about my new puppy. Can I send one to Desiree too?

**Sara:** Sure. Anyone you want.

*What's happening in this conversation:* In this conversation, Sara involves her daughter in one of her hobbies, card making. When Edith joins in, Sara encourages her to think about people she could send cards to, pointing out that sending a card is one way to let people know you are thinking about them. Sara can extend this conversation by brainstorming together other ways they can let Edith's grandma and other special people in their lives know that they are loved and appreciated.

**Gordon** (Poppy's uncle): Let's do something today to make our neighborhood a little nicer.

**Poppy** (age five): Okay!

**Gordon:** Do you have any ideas of something we could do?

**Poppy:** Maybe we could give free Popsicles to everyone?

**Gordon:** Free Popsicles for everyone in the neighborhood? That's a nice idea, but I think we only have two Popsicles left.

**Poppy:** We could give one to Mrs. Onaga.

**Gordon:** Do you think she likes Popsicles?

**Poppy:** I saw her eating one yesterday.

**Gordon:** I guess so then. I was thinking about getting a garbage bag and picking up trash in our neighborhood. Do you want to help me do that? We could pick up trash on the way to Mrs. Onaga's house to deliver a Popsicle.

**Poppy:** Can I have a Popsicle too? There are two.

**Gordon:** Sure.

*What's happening in this conversation:* Gordon invites his niece, Poppy, to join him doing something to improve their neighborhood. Gordon incorporates Poppy's idea of taking a Popsicle to an elderly neighbor with his own idea of cleaning up litter along the sidewalk. This combination of activities may be one that they participate in frequently, or one of many that they choose as they explore different ways that they can make a difference.

**Elijah** (Kenji's dad): Do you see that woman across the street?

**Kenji** (age six): Yeah.

**Elijah:** She's been there for about five minutes looking around like she's confused. Let's go over and see if she needs help.

**Kenji:** Those people can help her.

**Elijah:** Maybe, but no one else seems to be helping. Come on!

**(They cross the street together.)**

**Elijah:** Excuse me. Do you need help?

**Chanda:** Oh thank you, yes. Do you know how I can get to East Rock Coffee?

**Elijah:** Yes. Cross Whitney and then keep going until you get to Orange Street. Turn left on Orange, and it will be on your right in about two blocks.

**Kenji:** They have really good hot chocolate!

**Chanda:** Thank you so much.

**Elijah:** You're welcome. (turns back to Kenji) I'm glad we stopped to help!

**Kenji:** Me too. I like being a helper.

**Elijah:** I know you do. Sometimes when other people are around, it's easy to do nothing because we might think that someone else will help instead. No matter how many other people are around, we should always be ready to help.

**Kenji:** Okay, dad.

*What's happening in this conversation:* When Elijah sees a woman looking lost, he points this out to his son, Elijah. The two of them cross the street to ask if she needs help. Modeling helping behaviors and explaining what you are doing and why can help children learn to look for opportunities to be a helper when similar situations arise in the future. In addition, parents can point out to children the importance of being a helper, even when others are around who could step in. Studies have shown that children (and adults) are less likely to offer their help when others are around (Plötner, Over, Carpenter, & Tomasello, 2015). This is sometimes called the bystander effect. Talking with children about the bystander effect may help them do something positive when they see someone who needs help.

**Kaia** (Jascha's mom): The boy in that show you were watching was really mean to the other kids. I didn't like the way he was acting, but I was also disappointed in the other kids. When he acted mean, no one did anything about it.

**Jascha** (age seven): They were scared of him. I wouldn't do anything either if there was a boy like that at my school.

**Kaia:** I think they were scared too, but even if you're scared, if you see someone hurting someone else, there are lots of different ways to be a helper.

**Jascha:** Like what?

**Kaia:** You could ask a grown-up for help, or tell a teacher about what you see. If that grown-up doesn't believe you, tell another. You could also let the person know who was picked on that you saw and didn't think it was fair or okay, even if you didn't feel brave enough to speak up at the time. Letting someone know that you care could make a difference for them. Can you think of any other ways to help?

**Jascha:** You could ask a friend for help.

**Kaia:** Sure you could. Friends can be helpers too. You can also ask the person who is getting picked on or hurt if there's anything you can do to help them. They might have ideas too. The important thing is to not stand by and do nothing if you see something wrong. You don't have to be the one to stand up in front of everyone else, but you should do something.

**Jascha:** Okay, mom.

**Kaia:** I'm proud of you, kiddo. I know you're a good helper for your friends.

**Jascha:** Thanks, mom.

*What's happening in this conversation:* After watching a show together that depicted a boy picking on other children, Kaia talks with her son, Jascha, about the importance of standing up for others. They talk about the many different ways that children can be helpers.

## Chapter conclusions

The conversations in this final chapter focused on helping children practice and develop compassion at home and extending these skills to the world around them. There are many stories about people who have made a difference that come from individuals or groups that have experienced hardship as they strive to overcome those hardships. For your child, this might be what inspires them to action, but it doesn't have to be. Everyone has the potential to make a difference in their own way. Some children and adults feel comfortable raising their voices in a loud way, while others prefer a quieter approach. Making a difference might mean speaking up or taking action when you see an injustice, doing something to take care of the environment, letting someone know that you care about them, or playing an active role in your community in other ways. By exposing your child to many different role models in real life and in stories, you can show your child examples of the many ways people can make a difference. Learning about others through stories can help children learn about what is possible and give them opportunities to practice thinking about other people's feelings and learn words and actions they can use as they reach beyond themselves.

Teaching your child compassion is also an opportunity for you to grow as well, as you strive to be the role model you would like your child to have. As you continue to have conversations with your child aimed at building compassion, consider the following strategies:

1. **Use words that you would like to hear your child use now and in the future.** As you choose the words you say to your child and to

others, imagine how you would feel hearing those same words from your child. Taking a moment to consider how the words you use would sound in your child's voice can help you be intentional with your own word choices and help you choose to think and speak with compassion.

2. **Live each conversation beyond your words.** Do more than have conversations about being compassionate with your child, look for ways to act compassionately at home and in your community. Explain to your child what you are doing and why so that your child hears what you are thinking and brings a compassionate perspective to their own thought process.

3. **Look for role models and examples of compassion in your own community.** Seek out examples of individuals and groups in your community that are working to make your community a better place. Point these activities out to your child and talk to them about the needs and challenges faced by your community as well as what others are doing to be helpers.

4. **Recognize that building compassion takes time.** Just like any set of skills, building compassion takes time and lots of practice. You may feel discouraged at times when you see your own child acting out or struggling to think about someone else's feelings, but this is normal. Developing compassion is a lifelong process that is easier for some people than others, and one that is challenging for everyone.

5. **Learn from your child along the way.** As you and your child find your voices together, take time to listen to and learn from one another. You may be surprised by the insights your child offers. Your child might think about other people's feelings in ways that you may not consider. When you learn something new from your child, let them know that. With all the ways they learn from you, they will love hearing that you learn from them, too!

## Question and answer: Apply what you learned to parenting challenges

**Q:** Should I try to make my child be friends with everyone?

*A: The short answer is no. Just like adults, children will connect with some people more easily than others. Telling children to be friends with everyone will not necessarily lead them to be friends with everyone. Instead, let your child know it's okay not to be friends with everyone, but encourage them to always treat others kindly, whether they are friends or not.*

**Q:** What should I do if my child has a friend I don't want them to have?

**A:** *Your child will likely have friends at some point in their life that you worry may be a bad influence. When children are young, parents often play a role in choosing who children play with outside of school by deciding who is invited to play dates or birthday parties. Some parents even avoid the park on specific days, knowing that certain children will be there that they don't want their child to be around. The trouble with taking this avoidance approach is that when children are young, you have the opportunity to shape their interactions—an opportunity you probably won't have with an older child. When your child plays at the park with another child who is struggling to manage their emotions or behaviors, you have a chance to coach your child through those interactions (and maybe even the other child). Following challenging interactions, you can talk with your child about what you saw, what worked well, what didn't, and what they could try next time. You can also talk with your child about the importance of being kind to everyone, even when others have challenging behaviors.*

*You and your child can also serve as role models of positive interactions for the friend. Your child's friend may have plenty of positive role models in their life, but they may not. The other child will likely continue to be a part of your child's community. Investing time and energy in other children's wellbeing is an investment in creating a compassionate community around your child.*

**Q:** Not everyone has the best intentions in mind. How do I help my child be compassionate toward others while also understanding that there are real dangers and people with negative intentions in the world?

**A:** *As you teach your child to view others through a compassionate lens, you might choose to share with your child that most people have good intentions. In other words, most people are doing their best to be helpful and kind. When we assume that people have good intentions, it's easier to approach them compassionately and to try to understand their perspective. There are times, however, when people don't have good intentions, and it's okay to let children know that, too.*

*"Most people are doing their best to be kind to others, but sometimes there are people who do things to hurt other people on purpose."*

*You might introduce this idea as you talk with your child about safety issues, including not going anywhere with or taking anything from a stranger unless a parent is with them and says it's okay. We can remind children that most people want to help children–not hurt them–but just in case, there are things we can do to make sure we stay safe.*

**Q:** How can I teach my child to speak up for someone else if they see something getting hurt or if they see an injustice? How can I teach my child to speak up for him/herself if they are being hurt or experience an injustice?

*A: First, teaching children that it is okay to express their own feelings and needs can help them develop the confidence to express themselves in other contexts. Second, teaching children to recognize and think about other people's feelings is an important part of helping children identify when someone is being hurt or experiencing an injustice. Talk with your child about what to do if they see someone who is being hurt or treated unfairly. Help your child practice saying words that they can use in those instances (e.g., "Stop! That's not fair." "Are you okay? Can I help you?"). Help your child brainstorm strategies for what they can do in those moments as well (e.g., stepping in and asking if they can help, finding an adult). If your child has practice thinking about and role playing what they can say or do when someone needs help, it will be easier for them to follow through with those words and actions in those moments. A list of children's books that highlight characters who find their own voice as role models, leaders, and advocates is provided at the end of this chapter. Reading books together about different ways people have found to share their voice can provide your child with additional examples.*

**Q:** What if I don't think I'm the role model that I want my child to have?

*A: No matter how you feel about yourself as a role model, you are and will be one of the most important role models in your child's eyes. You are the role model your child wants to have. Being a role model does not mean that you will feel good about who you are or what you do all the time, and that's okay. As a parent, realize that the struggles you have may be struggles your child has some day, too. Learning from you that these struggles are normal and then watching you work on learning and growing as a person will show your child how to do the same. If you talk with your children about what you are working on, why it is challenging, and what you are doing to improve, you may be giving your children tools that they will be able to use in their own lives in the future.*

**Q:** It sounds like helping my child create a more compassionate society means that I have to think about myself, the words I use with my child, and how I show my child that I'm trying my best to be the best parent and person I can be. This seems like a lot of work.

*A: It is. I completely agree, and it's worth it.*

### Extend the conversation through read-alouds

There are many books that include stories focused on friendship, being a helper, and finding your own voice. Use these books to provide your child with role models of fictional characters and real people who have found ways to promote compassion in their own communities and the world. Showing your child examples of how to speak up or lend a helping hand can make those words and skills parts of your child's toolbox of strategies they can use themselves when they see an injustice or an opportunity to make a difference.

### Books about friendship

*Accept and Value Each Person* by Cheri Meiners

*A Color of His Own* by Leo Lionni

*A Letter to Amy* by Ezra Jack Keats

*A Sick Day for Amos McGee* by Philip C. Stead and Erin E. Stead

*Can I Play Too?* by Mo Willems

*Chester's Way* by Kevin Henkes

*Elmore* by Holly Hobbie

*Felicity and Cordelia: A Tale of Two Bunnies* by Lisa Jahn-Clough

*Happy Pig Day!* by Mo Willems

*Hey, Boy* by Benjamin Strouse, illustrated by Jennifer Phelan

*I'm New Here* by Anne Sibley O'Brien

*Join In and Play* by Cheri Meiners

*Making Friends* by Fred Rogers

*My Friend and I* by Lisa Jahn-Clough

*My Friend is Sad* by Mo Willems

*One Green Apple* by Eve Bunting, illustrated by Ted Lewin

*Talk and Work It Out* by Cheri Meiners

*Toot & Puddles: You Are My Sunshine* by Holly Hobbie

*Understand and Care* by Cheri Meiners

*Will I Have a Friend?* By Miriam Cohen and Lillian Hoban

### Books about being a helper

*Extra Yarn* by Mac Barnett, illustrated by Jon Klaasen

*The Giving Tree* by Shel Silverstein

*Helpers in My Community* by Bobbie Kalman

*I Am Helping* by Mercer Mayer

*The Lorax* by Dr. Seuss

*Reach Out and Give* by Cheri Meiners

*Stone Soup* by Heather Forest, illustrated by Susan Gaber

*Miss Rumphius* by Barbara Cooney

*This Tree Counts* by Alison Formento, illustrated by Sarah Snow

*We Planted a Tree* by Diane Muldrow, illustrated by Bob Staake

## Books about being kind and having good manners

*Be Kind* by Pat Zietlow Miller, illustrated by Jen Hill

*Excuse Me! A Little Book of Manners* by Karen Katz

*Have You Filled a Bucket Today?: A Guide to Daily Happiness for Kids* by Carol McCloud, illustrated by David Messing

*I Walk With Vanessa: A Story About a Simple Act of Kindness* by Kerascoët

*Manners* by Aliki

*Please and Thank You* by Jill Ackerman and Michelle Berg

*Richard Scarry's Please and Thank You Book* by Richard Scarry

*Time to Say Please* by Mo Willems

*The Thank You Book* by Mo Willems

## Books about finding your own voice

*A is for Activist* by Innosanto Nagara

*Amazing Grace* by Mary Hoffman and Caroline Binch

*The Artist Who Painted a Blue Horse* by Eric Carle

*The Bracelet* by Yoshiko Uchida and Joanna Yardley

*Child of the Civil Rights Movement* by Paula Young Shelton, illustrated by Raul Colon

*Hidden Figures: The True Story of Four Black Women and the Space Race* by Margot Less Shetterly, illustrated by Laura Freeman

*I Dissent: Ruth Bader Ginsburg Makes Her Mark* by Debbie Levy, illustrated by Elizabeth Baddeley

*I Have a Dream* by Dr. Martin Luther King Jr., illustrated by Kadir Nelson

*I, Too, Am America* by Langston Hughes, illustrated by Bryan Collier

*Little Blue and Little Yellow* by Leo Lionni

*Little Leaders: Bold Women in Black History* by Vashti Harrison

*Malala: A Hero for All* by Shana Corey, illustrated by Elizabeth Sayles

*Of Thee I Sing* by Barack Obama, illustrated by Loren Long

*A Picture Book of Harriet Tubman* by David A. Adler

*Pride: The Story of Harvey Milk and the Rainbow Flag* by Rob Sanders, illustrated by Steven Salerno

*Separate is Never Equal: Sylvia Mendez & Her Family's Fight for Desegregation* by Duncan Tonatiuh

*Shaking Things Up: 14 Young Women Who Changed the World* by Susan Hood

*She Persisted: 13 American Women Who Changed the World* by Chelsea Clinton, illustrated by Alexandra Boiger

*She Persisted Around the World: 13 Women Who Changed History* by Chelsea Clinton, illustrated by Alexandra Boiger

*Sit-In: How Four Friends Stood Up by Sitting Down* by Andrea Davis Pinkney, illustrated by Brian Pinkney

*The Sneetches and Other Stories* by Dr. Seuss

*The Story of Ruby Bridges* by Robert Coles, illustrated by George Ford

*We March* by Shane W. Evans

*The Word Collector* by Peter H. Reynolds

### Read-aloud and discussion questions:

- What do the characters do to be a good friend in the book?
  - What did the characters say or do when they met someone new?
  - How did they feel about making a new friend?
  - What do you like best about having friends? What do you do to be a good friend?
- How are the friends in the book like one another, and how are they different from one another?
- What happens when the characters in the book disagree?
  - How do you think you could tell someone in a kind way that you didn't like something they said or did?
  - How would you like someone to tell you that they didn't like something that you said or did?
- How did the friends in the book make up when something went wrong?
  - How did the characters say they were sorry?
  - Do you think saying sorry helped the other character feel better? What else do you think the character could do?
  - Have you ever had to make up with someone? What was it like?
  - What helps you feel better when someone hurts your feelings?

- How do the characters show that they care about each other?
- Did anything happen in the story that was unfair or unjust?
  - What did the characters do when this happened?
  - What would you do if you saw something unfair happening?
- What did the characters do to be helpers?
- What did the characters do make their community a better place to live?
- What do you think we could do to be a helper in our community?

## Extend the conversation through family activities

*Role-play friendships with puppets, stuffed animals, dolls, or action figures.* Role-play how to be a good friend using toys or homemade puppets. If your child likes battling with action figures, show how action figures can help one another when they are on a team working together (e.g., *"Come on, battle buddy! Let's work together to defeat the monster! Wow. I'm glad you were here to help me. I couldn't have done it by myself!"*). If your child enjoys playing with dolls, act out examples of how good friends act during play (e.g., *"Do you want to play with us? It looks like you're new here!"*). If your child is struggling with or still developing certain social skills, use these imaginary play opportunities to practice.

*Set up play dates with your child and other children in the neighborhood, from school, or community groups.* Involve your child in extending the invitation and choosing activities. Even if your child gets plenty of time interacting with other children at school, one-on-one time with a friend or classmate can help strengthen the relationship and provide an opportunity where you can help support during their interactions.

*Join a parenting group or take a parenting class.* Parenting groups can be a wonderful way to get to know other families with children in your community. Being part of a group can give your child the opportunity to interact with other children and adults outside of your family and connect you with a supportive network of parents. Parenting classes are a great source of information about child development and what to expect at different ages and stages. These classes also offer evidence-based parenting strategies to add to your toolbox. Taking classes with other parents can give you an opportunity to share with and learn from other families in your community and help you realize that you are not alone in your parenting journey.

*Write a letter to a friend.* Talk with your child about the qualities you look for in a friend and what you like best about your friends. Help your child write a letter to one of their friends to tell them what they like about them. Write a letter to one of your own friends as well. Let them know how much you value and appreciate them.

*Introduce yourselves to someone you haven't met before in your community.* Together, bake cookies for a new neighbor, stop by and visit a neighbor you haven't seen for a while, introduce yourself to someone who works at a local market, or greet a new family at the park. Modeling for your child how to interact with neighbors and community members can build your child's comfort within your community and teach them skills to build new relationships themselves.

*Share personal stories with your child about times you apologized to someone, or when someone else apologized to you.* Children love to hear stories about their parents when they were young. They may be especially interested in hearing about a time when you did something wrong and had to apologize. Use stories about your own life to model for your child how you apologized and talk about how an apology helped (or didn't help) the situation.

*Saying sorry brainstorm.* Together with your child, brainstorm all the ways you can think of that people might say they are sorry and help someone else feel better. See how many different ideas you can come up with, and make a list or draw a picture together to show your ideas. As you draw together, ask your child, "Which of these things would help you feel better?" Talk about the fact that different things might help different people feel better. For example, some people might like a hug, but others might not. Having many different ideas to draw from can help your child learn strategies they can use to make amends in the future.

*Take a community trash walk.* Carry a garbage bag and take a walk through your neighborhood. Pick up litter that you see along the way with a pair of trash grabbers or plastic gloves. As you walk together, talk about all the things you like best about your neighborhood (e.g., *"That's my favorite tree. Which one is your favorite tree?"*). Count the number of steps from one neighborhood landmark to another (e.g., *"How many steps from the light post to the mailbox?"*). As you walk, talk about how much nicer your neighborhood looks after picking up the litter that you found along the way. Talk about how your neighborhood is similar to or different from other neighborhoods.

*Identify ways to contribute to and to be a part of your community.* There are many different ways that you and your child can be a part of your community:

- **Donate.** Take items to a food pantry or shelter. Call the organization first to find out what items would be most helpful and involve your child in gathering and delivering them.
- **Volunteer.** Identify nonprofit organizations in your community that will allow you to volunteer as a family, such as community organizations, assisted living facilities, or animal shelters.
- **Create.** Together with your child, make care packages to send to those in need (e.g., immigrant and refugee families, soldiers, children's hospital patients).
- **Participate.** Look for free or low-cost, family-friendly community events that you and your family can be a part of to get to know the people in your community.

*Be a role model of compassion.* Look for ways you can extend each conversation you have with your child through your own actions. As you model compassion, be sure to explain to your child what you are doing and why. For example, when picking up trash around your neighborhood, let your child know: "This is something we can do to make our neighborhood a nicer place! I bet our neighbors will be so surprised when they see how nice our street looks!" Or when holding the door open for a stranger, tell your child: "I noticed he looked tired, so I wanted to help out!" Through your actions, you serve as a role model for your child. By narrating your own actions, you help support the development of your child's inner voice and help shape that voice into one that is compassionate.

# Conclusion

THERE IS NO RIGHT WAY to hold a conversation, no perfect way to parent, and no recipe for creating a compassionate kid. As every parent quickly discovers, our children have their own personalities and agendas. Along our parenting journey, life sends us curveballs we can't anticipate and don't expect. Despite all these unknowns, there are things we can do and conversations we can have to help our child thrive. Through conversations like the examples in this book, we can help our children feel safe as they build their self-awareness, foster their resilience, and develop compassion.

Are all these conversations actually essential? Probably not, but having conversations with your child is. No matter which conversations you choose to have, having back-and-forth conversations with your child is what matters. Conversations can build your relationship with your child, and they can let your child know that you will be there for them, no matter what. Conversations can also be used to teach your child important skills, including how to manage and express emotions, communicate needs, recognize other people's feelings, make friends and be a good friend, navigate life challenges, and approach others with compassion. You may not always know what to say or how to say it, but showing your child that you are doing your best will go a long way toward helping your child be the best they can be.

We all have moments that we feel are parenting successes and others that we feel are parenting fails. It's not each of these moments that matters and defines us as parents, it's all of them together and the collective experience our children remember. Maya Angelou said: "I've learned that people will forget what you said, people will forget what you did, but people will never forget how you made them feel." During your interactions with your child and in your conversations, think about how you want your children to feel. If children feel loved and supported more often than not, that's what they are likely to carry forward with them in the way they approach their own relationships and the world around them. Creating compassionate kids starts with compassionate parenting. Showing your child the compassion you want to see in the world gives them a model of what's possible.

Thank you from the bottom of my heart for sharing these conversations with me, for having these conversations with the children in your life, and for taking steps to create the compassionate society we want for all children—your child and mine.

# References

American Academy of Pediatrics (2012). *Firearm-related injuries affecting the pediatric population.* Retrieved from https://www.aap.org/en-us/advocacy-and-policy/federal-advocacy/Pages/AAPFederal GunViolencePreventionRecommendationstoWhiteHouse.aspx

Anderson, C. A., & Bushman, B. J. (2001). Effects of violent video games on aggressive behavior, aggressive cognition, aggressive affect, physiological arousal, and prosocial behavior: A meta-analytic review of the scientific literature. *Psychological Science, 12*(5), 353–359.

Baker, C. N., Tichovolsky, M. H., Kupersmidt, J. B., Voegler-Lee, M. E., & Arnold, D. H. (2015). Teacher (mis)perceptions of preschoolers' academic Skills: Predictors and associations with longitudinal outcomes. *Journal of Educational Psychology, 107*(3): 805–820. doi:10.1037/edu0000008.

Beckett, M. K., Elliott, M. N., Martino, S., Kanouse, D. E., Corona, R., Klein, D. J., & Schuster, M. A. (2010). Timing of parent and child communication about sexuality relative to children's sexual behaviors. *Pediatrics, 125*(1), 34–42.

Benton, B. H. (2013). Gender, games, and toys: Role communication and socialization through play. *Communication Teacher, 27*(3), 141–145.

Berk, L. E. & Meyers, A. B. (2012). *Infants and children: Prenatal through middle childhood.* Upper Saddle River, NJ: Prentice Hall.

Bernier, A., Beauchamp, M. H., Carlson, S. M., & Lalonde, G. (2015). A secure base from which to regulate: Attachment security in toddlerhood as a predictor of executive functioning at school entry. *Developmental Psychology, 51*(9), 1177–1189.

Bernier, A., Carlson, S. M., & Whipple, N. (2010). From external regulation to self-regulation: Early parenting precursors of young children's executive functioning. *Child development, 81*(1), 326–339.

Bigler, R., Hayes, A. R., & Hamilton, V. (2013). The role of schools in the early socialization of gender differences. In *Encyclopedia on Early Childhood Development: Gender: early socialization,* 14–17. Retrieved from http://www.child-encyclopedia.com/sites/default/files/dossiers-complets/en/gender-early-socialization.pdf#page=6

Boukydis, C. Z., & Burgess, R. L. (1982). Adult physiological response to infant cries: Effects of temperament of infant, parental status, and gender. *Child development,* 1291–1298.

Bowlby, J. (2008). *A secure base: Parent-child attachment and healthy human development.* New York: Basic Books.

Brown, G. L., Craig, A. B., & Halberstadt, A. G. (2015). Parent gender differences in emotion socialization behaviors vary by ethnicity and child gender. *Parenting, 15*(3), 135–157.

Budge, S. L., Adelson, J. L., & Howard, K. A. (2013). Anxiety and depression in transgender individuals: the roles of transition status, loss, social support, and coping. *Journal of consulting and clinical psychology, 81*(3), 545–557.

Carlson, M. J. & Berger, L. M. (2013). What kids get from parents: Packages of parental involvement across complex family forms. *The Social Service Review, 87*(2), 213–249.

Carrell, S. E. & Hoekstra, M. L. (2010). Externalities in the classroom: How children exposed to domestic violence affect everyone's kids. *American Economic Journal: Applied Economics, 2*(1), 211–228.

Caughy, M. O. B., & Owen, M. T. (2015). Cultural socialization and school readiness of African American and Latino preschoolers. *Cultural Diversity and Ethnic Minority Psychology, 21*(3), 391–399.

Chan, S. M., & Chan, K. W. (2013). Adolescents' susceptibility to peer pressure: Relations to parent-adolescent relationship and adolescents' emotional autonomy from parents. *Youth & Society, 45*(2), 286–302.

Chess S., & Thomas A. (1991). Temperament and the Concept of Goodness of Fit. In: Strelau J., Angleitner A. (eds) Explorations in Temperament. Perspectives on Individual Differences. Springer, Boston, MA.

Child Trends Data Bank (2017). *Family structure: Indicators of child and youth well-being.* Retrieved from https://www.childtrends.org/wp-content/uploads/2015/12/59_Family_Structure.pdf

Child Welfare Information Gateway (2015). *Foster care statistics 2015.* Retrieved from https://www.childwelfare.gov/pubs/factsheets/foster/

Cimpian, A. (2010). The impact of generic language about ability on children's achievement motivation. *Developmental Psychology, 46*(5), 1333–1340.

Denham, S. A., Bassett, H. H., & Wyatt, T. (2007). The socialization of emotional competence. *Handbook of socialization: Theory and research,* 614–637.

Deptula, D. P., Henry, D. B., & Schoeny, M. E. (2010). How can parents make a difference? Longitudinal associations with adolescent sexual behavior. *Journal of Family Psychology, 24*(6), 731–739.

Durlak, J. A., Weissberg, R. P., Dymnicki, A. B., Taylor, R. D., & Schellinger, K. B. (2011). The impact of enhancing students' social and emotional learning: A meta-analysis of school-based universal interventions. *Child development, 82*(1), 405–432.

Dweck, C. S. (2015). Carol Dweck revisits the 'growth mindset'. *Education Week, 35*(5), 20–24.

Dweck, C. S. (2006). *Mindset: The new psychology of success.* Random House Incorporated.

Eggum, N. D., Eisenberg, N., Kao, K., Spinrad, T. L., Bolnick, R., Hofer, C., Kupfer, A. S., & Fabricius, W. V. (2011). Emotion understanding, theory of mind, and prosocial orientation: Relations over time in early childhood. *The Journal of Positive Psychology, 6*(1), 4–16.

Frodi, A. M., Lamb, M. E., Leavitt, L. A., & Donovan, W. L. (1978). Fathers' and mothers' responses to infant smiles and cries. *Infant Behavior and Development, 1,* 187–198.

Gershoff, E. T., & Grogan-Kaylor, A. (2016). Spanking and child outcomes: Old controversies and new meta-analyses. *Journal of Family Psychology, 30*(4), 453.

Gilliam, W. S., Maupin, A. N., Reyes, C. R., Accavitti, M., & Shic, F. (2016). *Do early educators' implicit biases regarding sex and race relate to behavior expectations and recommendations of preschool expulsions and suspensions?* (research study brief). New Haven, CT: Yale Child Study Center, Yale University.

Gonzales, A. L., & Hancock, J. T. (2011). Mirror, mirror on my Facebook wall: Effects of exposure to Facebook on self-esteem. *Cyberpsychology, Behavior, and Social Networking, 14*(1–2), 79–83.

Gottman, J. (2011). *Raising an emotionally intelligent child.* New York: Simon & Schuster.

Grogan, S. (2016). *Body image: Understanding body dissatisfaction in men, women and children.* Taylor & Francis.

Groh, A. M., Fearon, R. P., Bakermans-Kranenburg, M. J., Van IJzendoorn, M. H., Steele, R. D., & Roisman, G. I. (2014). The significance of attachment security for children's social competence with peers: A meta-analytic study. *Attachment & Human Development, 16*(2), 103–136.

Hakovirta, M. & Kallio, J. (2016). Children's perceptions of poverty. *Child Indicators Research, 9*(2), 317–334.

Hamm, M. P., Newton, A. S., Chisholm, A., Shulhan, J., Milne, A., Sundar, P., Ennis, H., Scott, H. D., & Hartling, L. (2015). Prevalence and effect of cyberbullying on children and young people: A scoping review of social media studies. *JAMA Pediatrics, 169*(8), 770–777.

Hanson, D. J. 2015. Drug Abuse Resistance Education (D.A.R.E.). *The Encyclopedia of Clinical Psychology.* 1–3.

Hart, B. & Risley, T. R. (2003). The early catastrophe: The 30 million word gap by age 3. *American Educator, 27*(1), 4–9.

Hart, L. M., Damiano, S. R., Cornell, C., & Paxton, S. J. (2015). What parents know and want to learn about healthy eating and body image in preschool children: A triangulated qualitative study with parents and early childhood professionals. *BMC Public Health, 15*(1), 596.

Harvard Center on the Developing Child (2017). *Five numbers to remember about early childhood development.* Retrieved from https://developingchild.harvard.edu/resources/five-numbers-to-remember-about-early-childhood-development/

Heath, P. (2012). *Parenting-child relations: Context, research, and application.* New York: Pearson.

Heron, K. E., Smyth, J. M., Akano, E., & Wonderlich, S. A. (2013). Assessing body image in young children: A preliminary study of racial and developmental differences. *SAGE Open, 3*(1), 2158244013478013

Hollingsworth, H. L. & Winter, M. K. (2013). Teacher beliefs and practices relating to development in preschool: Importance placed on social-emotional behaviours and skills. *Early Child Development and Care, 183*(12), 1758–1781.

Holt, S., Buckley, H., & Whelan, S. (2008). The impact of exposure to domestic violence on children and young people: A review of the literature. *Child Abuse & Neglect, 32*(8), 797–810.

Howell, K. H., Graham-Bermann, S. A., Czyz, E., & Lilly, M. (2010). Assessing resilience in preschool children exposed to intimate partner violence. *Violence and Victims, 25*(2), 150–164.

Huansuriya, T., Siegel, J. T., & Crano, W. D. (2014). Parent–child drug communication: Pathway from parents' ad exposure to youth's marijuana use intention. *Journal of Health Communication, 19*(2), 244-259.

Hughes, D. (2003). Correlates of African American and Latino parents' messages to children about ethnicity and race: A comparative study of racial socialization. *American Journal of Community Psychology, 31*(1–2), 15–33.

Hughes, D., Rodriguez, J., Smith, E. P., Johnson, D. J., Stevenson, H. C., & Spicer, P. (2006). Parents' ethnic-racial socialization practices: A review of research and directions for future study. *Developmental Psychology, 42*(5), 747–770.

Hutchinson, M. K., & Cederbaum, J. A. (2011). Talking to daddy's little girl about sex: Daughters' reports of sexual communication and support from fathers. *Journal of Family Issues, 32*(4), 550–572.

Joseph, M. A., O'Connor, T. G., Briskman, J. A., Maughan, B., & Scott, S. (2014). The formation of secure new attachments by children who were maltreated: An observational study of adolescents in foster care. *Development and Psychopathology, 26*(01), 67–80.

Kim, S. J., & Tinajero, J. (2016). Teaching diversity to bilingual children: Mexican-origin kindergarteners' discussions about children's literature depicting non-traditional gender roles. *Linguistics and Literature Studies, 4,* 171–180.

Kosciw, J. G., Greytak, E. A., Bartkiewicz, M. J., Boesen, M. J., & Palmer, N. A. (2012). *The 2011 National School Climate Survey: The experiences of lesbian, gay, bisexual and transgender youth in our nation's schools.* New York: The Gay, Lesbian, and Straight Education Network.

Kuntsche, S., & Kuntsche, E. (2016). Parent-based interventions for preventing or reducing adolescent substance use—A systematic literature review. *Clinical Psychology Review, 45,* 89-101.

Lambie, J. A. & Lindberg, A. (2016). The role of maternal emotional validation and invalidation on children's emotional awareness. *Merrill-Palmer Quarterly, 62*(2), 129–157.

Lareau, A. (2003). *Unequal childhoods: Class, race, and family life.* Los Angeles: University of California Press.

Leaper, C. (2013). Parents' socialization of gender in children. In *Encyclopedia on Early Childhood Development: Gender: Early Socialization.* (pp. 6–9). Retrieved from: http://www.child-encyclopedia.com/sites/default/files/dossiers-complets/en/gender-early-socialization.pdf#page=6

Lee, J., Moriarty, K. P., Tashjian, D. B., & Patterson, L. A. (2013). Guns and states: Pediatric firearm injury. *Journal of Trauma and Acute Care Surgery, 75*(1), 50–53.

Leff, S. S., Power, T. J., Manz, P. H., Costigan, T. E., & Nabors, L. A. (2001). School-based aggression prevention program for young children: Current status and implications for violence prevention. *School Psychology Review, 30*(3), 344.

Longobardi, E., Spataro, P., Frigerio, A., & Rescorla, L. (2016). Language and social competence in typically developing children and late talkers between 18 and 35 months of age. *Early Child Development and Care, 186*(3), 436–452.

Lowell, A., Renk, K., & Adgate, A. H. (2014). The role of attachment in the relationship between child maltreatment and later emotional and behavioral functioning. *Child Abuse & Neglect, 38*(9), 1436–1449.

Margolin, G., & Vickerman, K. A. (2011). Posttraumatic stress in children and adolescents exposed to family violence: I. Overview and issues. *Professional Psychology: Research & Practice, 1*, 63–73.

Martin, A., & Oliva, J. C. (2001). Teaching children about money: Applications of social learning and cognitive learning developmental theories. *Journal of Family and Consumer Sciences: From Research to Practice, 93*(2), 26–29.

Martin, K. A., & Luke, K. (2010). Gender differences in the ABC's of the birds and the bees: What mothers teach young children about sexuality and reproduction. *Sex Roles, 62*(3–4), 278–291.

Masten, A. S. & Gewirtz, A. H. (2006). Vulnerability and resilience in early child development. In K. McCartney & D. Phillips (Eds.), *Blackwell handbook of early childhood development* (pp. 22–43). Malden, MA: Blackwell Publishing.

McCabe, M. P., Ricciardelli, L. A., Stanford, J., Holt, K., Keegan, S., & Miller, L. (2007). Where is all the pressure coming from? Messages from mothers and teachers about preschool children's appearance, diet and exercise. *European Eating Disorders Review, 15*(3), 221–230.

McDowell, D. J. & Parke, R. D. (2000). Differential knowledge of display rules for positive and negative emotions: Influences from parents, influences on peers. *Social Development, 9*(4), 415–432.

Moretti, M. M. & Peled, M. (2004). Adolescent-parent attachment: Bonds that support healthy development. *Paediatrics & Child Health, 9*(8), 551–555.

Murphy, T. P. & Laible, D. J. (2013). The influence of attachment security on preschool children's empathic concern. *International Journal of Behavioral Development, (37)*5, 436–440.

Murray, J., Farrington, D. P., & Sekol, I. (2012). Children's antisocial behavior, mental health, drug use, and educational performance after parental incarceration: A systematic review and meta-analysis. *Psychological Bulletin, 138*(259), 175–210.

Musher-Eizenman, D. R., Holub, S. C., Miller, A. B., Goldstein, S. E., & Edwards-Leeper, L. (2004). Body size stigmatization in preschool children: The role of control attributions. *Journal of Pediatric Psychology, 29*(8), 613–620.

National Center for Education Statistics (2017). *Children and youth with disabilities.* Retrieved from https://nces.ed.gov/programs/coe/indicator_cgg.asp

National Children's Alliance (2015). National Statistics on Child Abuse. Retrieved from: http://www.nationalchildrensalliance.org/media-room/media-kit/national-statistics-child-abuse

National Institute of Justice (2014). *Recidivism.* Retrieved from https://www.nij.gov/topics/corrections/recidivism/Pages/welcome.aspx

Neumark-Sztainer, D., Paxton, S. J., Hannan, P. J., Haines, J., & Story, M. (2006). Does body satisfaction matter? Five-year longitudinal associations between body satisfaction and health behaviors in adolescent females and males. *Journal of Adolescent Health, 39*(2), 244–251.

Oakley, M., Farr, R. H., & Scherer, D. G. (2016). Same-sex parent socialization: Understanding gay and lesbian parenting practices as cultural socialization. *Journal of GLBT Family Studies, 13*(1), 56–75.

Obeng, C. (2010). Should gun safety be taught in schools? Perspectives of teachers. *Journal of School Health, 80*(8), 394–398.

Oregon Health Authority (2017). Oregon Healthy Teens Survey. 2017 OHT State Report. Retrieved from: http://www.oregon.gov/oha/PH/BIRTHDEATHCERTIFICATES/SURVEYS/OREGONHEALTHYTEENS/Documents/2017/2017_OHT_State_Report.pdf

Panfile, T. M. & Laible, D. J. (2012). Attachment security and child's empathy: The mediating role of emotion regulation. *Merrill-Palmer Quarterly, 58*(1), 1–21.

Park, S. & Schepp, K. G. (2015). A systematic review of research on children of alcoholics: Their inherent resilience and vulnerability. *Journal of Child and Family Studies, 24*(5), 1222–1231.

Patchin, J. W., & Hinduja, S. (2010). Cyberbullying and self-esteem. *Journal of School Health, 80*(12), 614–621.

Plötner, M., Over, H., Carpenter, M., & Tomasello, M. (2015). Young children show the bystander effect in helping situations. *Psychological Science, 26*(4), 499–506.

Powell, B., Hamilton, L., Manago, B., & Cheng, S. (2016). Implications of changing family forms for children. *Annual Review of Sociology, 42*(1), 301–322.

Priest, N., Walton, J., White, F., Kowal, E., Baker, A., & Paradies, Y. (2014). Understanding the complexities of ethnic-racial socialization processes for both minority and majority groups: A 30-year systematic review. *International Journal of Intercultural Relations, 43*, 139–155.

Puhl, R. M. & Latner, J. D. (2007). Stigma, obesity, and the health of the nation's children. *Psychological Bulletin, 133*(4), 557–580.

Reese, E., Bird, A., & Tripp, G. (2007). Children's self-esteem and moral self: Links to parent-child conversations regarding emotion. *Social Development, 16*(3), 460–478.

Renaud, S.-J., Engarhos, P., Schleifer, M., & Talwar, V. (2013). Talking to children about death: Parental use of religious and biological explanations. *Journal of Psychology & Christianity, 32*(3), 180–191.

Romeo, R. R., Leonard, J. A., Robinson, S. T., West, M. R., Mackey, A. P., Rowe, M. L., & Gabrieli, J. D. E. (2018). Beyond the 30-million-word gap: Children's conversational exposure is associated with language-related brain function. *Psychological Science*, 1-11.

Rose, E., Lehrl, S., Ebert, S., & Weinert, S. (2017). Long-term relations between children's language, the home literacy environment, and socioemotional development from ages 3 to 8. *Early Education and Development*, 1–15.

Rubin, K. H., Bukowski, W. M., Parker, J. G., Eisenberg, N., Damon, W., & Lerner, R. M. (2006). Peer interactions, relationships, and groups. In N. Eisenberg (Ed.), *Handbook of child psychology, Vol. 3: Social, emotional, and personality development* (6th Ed.). (pp. 571–645). Hoboken, NJ: John Wiley & Sons, Inc.

Scott, S., Miller, C., Kelly, L., Richman, M., & Park, L. (2016). "See, I'm not racist!": Aversive racism, peer pressure, and blaming adolescents. *Race and Pedagogy Journal: Teaching and Learning for Justice, 2*(1), 3.

Seçer, Z. & Karabulut, N. (2016). Analysis of emotional socialization behaviors of mother-fathers and social skills of preschool children. *Education & Science/Egitim ve Bilim, 41*(185), 147–165.

Sheridan, S. M., Sjuts, T. M., & Coutts, M. J. (2013). Understanding and promoting the development of resilience in families. In: S. Goldstein & R. Brooks (Eds.), *Handbook of resilience in children* (pp. 143–160). New York: Springer.

Simpson, B. V. (2007). *Exploring the influences of educational television and parent-child discussions on improving children's racial attitudes.* Austin, TX: The University of Texas at Austin.

Simpson, E., Duarte, J., & Bishop, B. (2016). When moms say bad words: Family and peer influence on the frequency of swearing. *University of Central Florida Undergraduate Research Journal, 8*(2).

Slaughter, V., & Griffiths, M. (2007). Death understanding and fear of death in young children. *Clinical child psychology and psychiatry, 12*(4), 525–535.

Solish, A., Perry, A., & Minnes, P. (2010). Participation of children with and without disabilities in social, recreational and leisure activities. *Journal of Applied Research in Intellectual Disabilities, 23*(3), 226–236.

Spencer-Cavaliere, N., & Watkinson, E. J. (2010). Inclusion understood from the perspectives of children with disability. *Adapted Physical Activity Quarterly, 27*(4), 275–293.

Stone, N., Ingham, R., & Gibbins, K. (2013). 'Where do babies come from?' Barriers to early sexuality communication between parents and young children. *Sex Education, 13*(2), 228–240.

Testa, R. J., Michaels, M. S., Bliss, W., Rogers, M. L., Balsam, K. F., & Joiner, T. (2017). Suicidal ideation in transgender people: Gender minority stress and interpersonal theory factors. *Journal of Abnormal Psychology, 126*(1), 125–136.

Theixos, H. & Borgwald, K. (2013). Bullying the bully: Why zero-tolerance policies get a failing grade. *Social Influence, 8*(2–3), 149–160.

Thompson, E. H. & Trice-Black, S. (2012). School-based group interventions for children exposed to domestic violence. *Journal of Family Violence, 27*(3), 233–241.

Torres, A., Southwick, S. M., & Mayes, L. C. (2011). Childhood resilience: Adaptation, mastery, and attachment. In S. Southwick et al. (Eds.), *Resilience and mental health: Challenges across the lifespan* (pp. 307–322). Cambridge, UK: Cambridge University Press.

U.S. Department of Health & Human Services (2017). *What is cyberbullying?* Retrieved from https://www.stopbullying.gov/cyberbullying/what-is-it/index.html

Vandewater, E. A., Park, S. E., Huang, X., & Wartella, E. A. (2005). "No - you can't watch that": Parental rules and young children's media use. *American Behavioral Scientist, 48*(5), 608–623.

Völlink, T., Bolman, C. A., Dehue, F., & Jacobs, N. C. (2013). Coping with cyberbullying: Differences between victims, bully-victims and children not involved in bullying. *Journal of Community & Applied Social Psychology, 23*(1), 7–24.

Wallach, L. B. (1993). Helping children cope with violence. *Young Children, 48*(4), 4–11.

Warren, H. K., & Stifter, C. A. (2008). Maternal emotion-related socialization and preschoolers' developing emotion self-awareness. *Social Development, 17*(2), 239–258.

Williams Institute (2017). *Marriage for same-sex couples.* Retrieved from https://williamsinstitute.law.ucla.edu/headlines/marriage-for-same-sex-couples/

Wilson, E. K., Dalberth, B. T., Koo, H. P., & Gard, J. C. (2010). Parents' perspectives on talking to preteen-age children about sex. *Perspectives on Sexual and Reproductive health, 42*(1), 56–63.

Wright, E. R., & Perry, B. L. (2006). Sexual identity distress, social support, and the health of gay, lesbian, and bisexual youth. *Journal of homosexuality, 51*(1), 81–110.

Yale Center for Emotional Intelligence (2015). Emotion Revolution. Retrieved from: http://ei.yale.edu/what-we-do/emotion-revolution-student/

Zentall, S. R., & Morris, B. J. (2010). "Good job, you're so smart": The effects of inconsistency of praise type on young children's motivation. *Journal of experimental child psychology, 107*(2), 155–163.

# Index

# ABOUT THE AUTHOR

Shauna Tominey is an Assistant Professor of Practice and Parenting Education Specialist at Oregon State University. She currently serves as the Principal Investigator for the Oregon Parenting Education Collaborative, an initiative to provide high-quality parenting education. Previously, Dr. Tominey served as the Director of Early Childhood Programming and Teacher Education at the Yale Center for Emotional Intelligence. As a former early childhood teacher and family service professional, Dr. Tominey blends practical experience with research to develop and test programs aimed at promoting social-emotional skills for children and adults.